1101 Water Gardening
Questions and Answers

by

Richard Lee
President
William Tricker, Inc.®

The development of this book was based upon the experience of the author with input from numerous resources. The information contained herein is true and complete to the best of the author's knowledge and is not intended to promote the violation of any laws or statutes. Before building or making a water garden, the safety of small children should be taken into consideration and any applicable local ordinances should be followed.

Some aquatic plants can be or are considered to be extremely invasive or noxious by specific states or countries and are regulated or restricted. Specific types of fish, snails, clams, etc. from the ornamental pond should not be released into a natural pond, stream or lake. Reputable distributors of such aquatic plants or animals should alert you of these situations and may refuse or be unable to provide specific aquatic plants or animals to a state or country due to such restrictions.

Published by: William Tricker, Inc.®
7125 Tanglewood Drive
Independence, Ohio 44131

Printed in the U.S.A.

William Tricker, Inc.® is a registered trademark of William Tricker, Inc., Independence, OH. Dipel® is a registered trademark of Abbott Laboratories.

Tricker's 1101 Water Gardening Questions and Answers

ISBN: 0-9649814-1-6

COVER: The cover shows three tropical water lilies (two day blooming and one night blooming) that is reproduced from the cover of the William Tricker, Inc.® 1934 mail order catalog. These three water lilies as shown were offered as an attractive trio in 1934 for $4.75, delivered.

Table of Contents

Tricker's

1101 Water Gardening Questions and Answers

Preface

Who would have ever guessed that when the water lily pioneer William Tricker (1852-1916) hybridized his first tropical water lily in 1893 that water gardeners all over the world would still be enjoying the fruits of his labor over 100 years later. Since water gardening became William Tricker's passion in the early 1890s, he went on to establish a water lily business that not only introduced his new and unique water lily hybrids but those of the new French water lily hybridizer M. Latour Marliac (1830-1911). In 1897 he wrote the first water gardening book that would introduce the world to water gardening. The stage was set and water gardening would soon become established around the world. After the death of William Tricker in 1916, his founding establishment not only continued to introduce some of the most beautiful and unique water lily hybrids in the world but preserved the water lilies created at the turn of the century for us to still enjoy.

Water gardening has become a mysterious world to many and, at times, appears complicated or overwhelming. Water lily pools have been enjoyed and admired for over 100 years. I sincerely hope that this book continues to support the legacy of the William Tricker company and presents the world of water gardening as William Tricker and his followers would have approved.

Richard Lee
President
William Tricker, Inc.®

I. How to Make a Water Garden Pool

* Location and Design * Pool Liners * Making a Liner Water Garden * Concrete Water Gardens * Preformed Water Gardens*

LOCATION AND DESIGN

1. Where should the water garden pool be placed in the yard?

During the 1920s water gardening gained great popularity and many water gardens became a special feature in planing their landscape (figure 1). Selection of the location for a water garden pool should be given careful consideration. It will often become the focal point of the garden or backyard. The water garden pool can be put within a flower garden or standing alone in the center of the lawn. One of the biggest cautions in selecting a location for a water garden pool is to make sure that the final site receives as much full sunlight during the day if the best results are to be expected in growing water lilies.

2. Can a water garden pool be seen at a distant if on level ground?

Yes. The water garden pool can be seen at a distant on level ground. Tropical water lilies characteristically hold their colorful flowers high, at least 12 inches, into the air. The aquatic marginal flowers and green vegetation can also be seen at a distant.

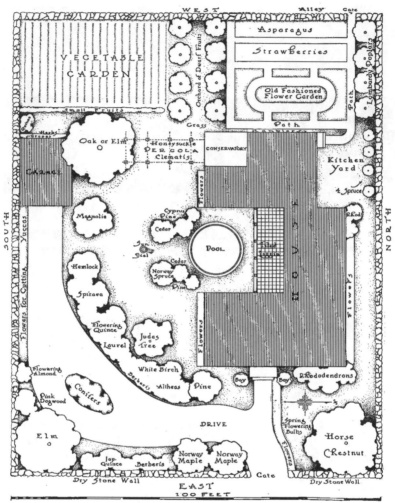

Figure 1. The above plan was designed by J. M. Rose and depicted in the 1920 *Garden Magazine* showing a landscape plan for a "complete place". Note the circular pool is the main focus directly viewed from the house. Privacy is created by the trees and the sight to the sun dial directly in the center as viewed from the house. During the 1920s water gardening was gaining much popularity as a wonderful form of gardening and has always retained a special place in the yard.

3. Should the water garden be visible in the backyard from inside of the home?

Constructing the water garden in a location to be seen from inside the home has many advantages. Many water gardeners find a certain charm when

2

viewing the water garden from a window inside the home. In the summer the display of colors and reflection of water is a very pleasing sight not only viewed from outside, but from the confines of the home. In the winter, many of the aquatic plants that die back will still have remnant stems to hold and catch the snow in northern climates. This winter scene can easily be enjoyed from the comfort of the home. All the busy and timid wildlife attracted to the water garden pool can be watched from a window in the home.

4. How much direct sunlight will be required in selecting a location for a water garden pool?

Most water lilies require at least four to six hours of direct sunlight to flower and grow to achieve their full potential. A water garden pool that receives direct sunlight all day gives the best growing conditions for the water gardener.

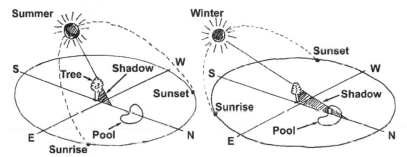

Figure 2. Because shadows change as the season changes, the shadow of a tree or home is important in deciding where to put the water garden pool.

5. If a selected location in the yard for a water garden pool in spring has direct sunlight, is this a good place to put a water garden pool?

Not necessarily. Since the path of the sun changes throughout the year (figure 2), a tree or building structure that was not shadowing the selected spot for a water garden pool in spring may totally be blocking the rays of the sun in the late summer.

6. Is an electrical source necessary by a water garden pool?

No. However, an electrical source is important if you plan to add lighting (underwater or around the pool), a pump for a filter, a water fountain or waterfall.

7. Should a water source be accessible to a water garden pool?

Yes. After filling the water garden pool, normal evaporation of water should be taken into consideration. This will require the periodic addition of water to the water garden pool. It may not be necessary to put in underground water pipes to feed the water garden, however, a hose to occasionally top off the water garden pool should be near.

8. Can the reflections of the surrounding landscape or plants in the water garden pool be predicted?

Yes. Reflections of objects in the water garden pool are extremely important and can be predicted with reasonable accuracy. The object that is desired to be reflected in the surface of the water garden pool (such as a rose bush on the shore) an aquatic plant in the pool such as a large papyrus plant or the tropical water lily flowers, can be predicted when viewing from a particular location near the pool (figure 3). The angle of reflection of the object to the surface of the water will result in the same angle of reflection to the eye. Physicist refer to this as the *"angle of reflection is equal to the angle of incidence"*.

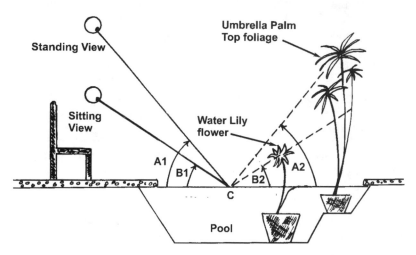

Figure 3. The angle of the reflection will be equal to the angle that is reflected off the surface of the water. The standing view will see a reflection in the pool at point "C" of the Umbrella Palm whereas the sitting view will see the reflection of the flower of the water lily at point "C".

9. What shape is most desirable in designing a water garden pool?

Shapes of the water garden pool vary as much as the personality of people. The shape of a water garden pool is divided into **formal** and **informal** pools. A formal pool characteristically has geometrical shapes, i.e. round, rectangular, square, etc. Informal pools characteristically are irregularly shaped, often fitting into the shape of the surrounding yard or appearing as a natural pond.

10. Should the shape of the pool be influenced by the surrounding landscape?

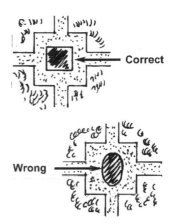

Yes, at least traditionally. Many water gardeners will consider the surrounding landscape (figure 4) when deciding the shape of the water garden pool. In the 1930s, the William Tricker company instructed their customers that *"If the pool is to be in the center of a garden or lawn, either of which is developed along formal lines, it is more fitting to develop some type of square or round pool that would have a pleasing relationship to the lines of the paths and borders about it, thus making the pool incidental to, and part of, the general design. When there is no particular design or arrangement involved, any shape of pool no doubt would be as suitable as another".* It is not unusual to see photographs of these wonderful water gardens still showing their beauty in a design selected so long ago.

Figure 4. The surrounding landscape corresponds with the shape of the pool.

11. Is it a good idea to design and build the water garden to allow runoff rain water to replenish the evaporation of water in the water garden pool?

No. Runoff rain water may be contaminated with herbicides or other chemicals in the surrounding area that may be harmful to plants and fish if allowed to rinse into the water garden pool. Also, runoff surface water from rains can get behind a liner and cause problems by pushing the liner into the water garden pool. To avoid water from reaching behind the liner, runoff water must be redirected away (such as with trenches) from the water garden pool.

12. How deep should the water garden pool be made?

Most of the water garden pools should be made at least 18 to 24 inches deep. The depth of the pond is determined by the size of the planting containers, types of aquatic plants selected and the temperature extremes in the local area. In severe freezing areas, the depth of ice formation should be considered if plants or fish are to winter within the water garden. The water garden pool should be made to ensure that there is water 8 to 12 inches below the depth at which ice is likely to form. In extreme hot climates, on the other hand, a shallow pond will be subjected to abnormally high temperatures and a deeper pond is required. Thus, in certain locations, a shallower pond may be made, but in others a deeper pool may be required.

13. Should the water garden pool have shelves?

Yes, especially if bog or shallow water plants are to be placed into the water garden pool. The bog plants can be placed directly on these custom shelves that will provide the correct planting depths which differ from the water lilies.

14. If the water garden is already completed and there are no shelves, what can be done?

If there are no shelves, the potted water garden bog plants will need to be raised to the correct height. This can be done with bricks, stones, etc. Caution should be used if the lining material is rubber or PVC, since an accidental cut or tear by the bricks or rocks can occur.

POOL LINERS

15. What material can be used to make a water garden pool?

Water garden pools are commonly made by digging holes and lining them with water resistant materials. Many water resistant materials have been used such as **concrete**, **plastic**, **PVC (polyvinyl chloride)**, **rubber** or **fiberglass**. The rubber and PVC liner are the most popular selected materials in making a water garden.

16. Why are "lining materials" necessary after digging a hole in the ground?

Most soils are porous and will not hold water. Ponds can be lined with natural clay but at least a foot or so must be used to prevent leakage and the purchase of clay is not readily available to most individuals. Pests such as ground moles may tunnel through the clay and into the water garden which will drain the water adding future problems.

17. What type of materials are available for making a "LINER" water garden pool?

Selecting the correct lining material for a water garden is very important in bringing years of satisfaction in water gardening. The water gardener would rather enjoy the beauty of the aquatic plants or water displays in the pool and not have to worry about leaks or other problems resulting from a poorly lined water garden pool. Therefore, the water gardener should be aware of the different types of flexible liners offered and select the one that best fits their needs. **Polyvinyl chloride** (PVC) or **rubber liners** (such as **EPDM** or "ethylene propylene diene monomer") are commonly selected to line water garden pools. These liners vary in thickness and cost. The less costly PVC is typically 20 mils (0.020 of an inch thick or 0.020") thick versus 45 mils thick (0.045") for the rubber liner. The PVC normally does not last as long in terms of years and is not as durable as the rubber liner. The rubber liner feels and looks like a rubber bicycle wheel inner tube and the PVC has a plastic-like texture.

18. What is meant by a "fish safe" or "fish grade" liner?

Many liners used with swimming pools and roofs have been found not to be fish safe. Any liner used for a water garden pool should be **fish safe** or **fish grade,** that is, it should be non-toxic or "safe" for fish. Liners that are not fish safe may leak harmful chemicals into the water that will kill fish and other animal or plant life. If the liner is claimed as "fish safe", it can be assumed to be safe for the aquatic plants and animals.

19. Are all rubber lining materials the same?

No. Rubber membranes or lining materials are manufactured differently. Some may be toxic to fish while others may be safe for fish. The lining material used for water gardens must be fish safe and not leach any harmful chemicals into the water.

20. Can a "roofing" rubber membrane be used to line a water garden pool?

Possibly. Only if the roofing rubber membrane is claimed to be fish safe or manufactured for use in a water garden pool should it be considered to be used to line a water garden pool. Many roofing membranes have other chemicals that are used in the manufacturing process that can leach into the water garden pool and may be toxic to fish.

21. How toxic can the rubber roofing membrane be to fish?

The rubber membranes manufactured specifically for roofing can be extremely toxic to fish. The William Tricker company, Independence, Ohio tested many of the available rubber roofing liners in the mid 1980s before being one of the first to introduce a fish safe rubber material to the trade of water gardening. The William Tricker company found that a small four inch by four inch piece of various manufacturers roofing membranes were lethal to fish in a 20 gallon aquarium within a 24 hour period.

22. How does the sunlight effect the lining material in the water garden pool?

Sunlight can be very harmful to lining materials and cause them to crack. The cracks will cause the liner to leak and defeat the purpose using a liner.

23. How does the sunlight damage the lining material in the water garden pool?

The production of **ozone** by the ultraviolet rays (220-290 nm) of sunlight is the major destructive force that damages the liner. Ozone is a different form (the chemist term for it is an **allotrope**) of molecular oxygen (O_3) and is produced by ultraviolet light or a silent electrical charge on oxygen (O_2). Small amounts of ozone can be smelled after a severe thunderstorm from the lightning. Most of us are familiar with old tires that show many fine cracks but may be unaware that these cracks were probably caused from ozone.

24. What makes the rubber liners for water gardens resistant to ozone?

The resistance is due to the chemical bonding characteristics of the carbon molecules. The chemist knows that oxygen and ozone react with the double carbon bond found in natural rubber, especially at elevated temperatures and stretched conditions. The rubber lining material, such as in EPDM, eliminates the double carbon bonding by chemical reactions and thus achieves a rubber material resistant to the harmful effects of ozone.

25. Does ozone effect concrete water garden pools similar to the rubber liners?

No. The ozone destructive quality is in breaking the carbon bonds found in rubber membranes. Concrete does not have any double carbon bonds.

26. Does ozone effect PVC liners similar to the rubber liners for water gardens?

No. Ozone attacks the double carbon bonds. The PVC liner does not have the special double carbon bonds that are found in the synthetic rubber materials.

27. How does the PVC material resist weathering?

The PVC has special additives that are heat resistant and ultraviolet stabilizers.

28. Why is the rubber liner superior to the PVC liner used in lining water garden pools?

The rubber liner has superior weathering properties over PVC. A main difference is the fact that the PVC has plasticizers which are not found in the rubber liners. The plasticizer effects the flexibility and dimensional stability of the PVC material. The rubber membrane has a superior elasticity over the PVC in either extreme cold or hot weather.

29. Why is it important to have a liner of superior elasticity for the water garden pool?

The weight of water is tremendous in a water garden pool. Since one gallon of water weighs approximately eight pounds, an average 10 foot by 15 foot water garden will contain 18,000 pounds of water. Once the water garden is filled for the first time, the tremendous weight of the water will press the liner down upon the soil. Stretching of the liner may occur in certain areas as the soil beneath the liner settles and compacts. If the liner does not have the ability to stretch or stretches poorly, a tear may develop. In addition, a sharp object such as a rock may cut the liner in this weakened stretched area. Thus, a lining material that is able to stretch considerably will prevent the possibility of a future cut or tear.

30. How does the flexibility or stretching of rubber liners compare to PVC liners?

The rubber liner is superior to the PVC liner in flexibility. It is easier to stretch the flexible rubber liner than the PVC and attempts to stretch the PVC results in tears. For example, it has been reported that rubber membranes, respective of different types, have been found to stretch over 125 percent for 30 minutes and return to the original shape. Whereas the PVC, respective of the different types, has been found to break or tear when stretched at approximately 25 percent within several minutes.

31. If the rubber liners are so superior in the water garden pool, what can cause it to leak?

The rubber lining material can be stretched a considerable amount without damage but it can still be punctured or cut causing a leak.

32. What can cut or puncture the rubber liner when it is in the water garden pool?

A sharp object that comes into contact with the liner can cut or puncture it. If any sharp rocks or tree roots were pressed into the liner from the tremendous weight of the water as the ground settled may cut or puncture the liner. Repair patches are available if this occurs.

33. Besides cost, what reason would a new water gardener choose a PVC liner over the superior rubber liner?

If a new water gardener is unsure of the endeavor of entering the water garden field, a lesser investment option can be made by purchasing a flexible PVC liner. All is not lost if the new water gardener becomes attracted to water gardening and wishes to continue. The old PVC liner can be left in place and covered with the superior rubber liner when replacement is required. More importantly, a different water garden size and plan can now be implemented with the gained experience to justify the use of a newly purchased liner. One very common comment made from water gardeners is that they wished they had made the water garden larger.

34. How do you estimate the size of the liner required?

Liners typically come in squares or rectangles. Thus, with any shape desired draw a square or rectangle around this shape. Measure the length and width of the rectangle or square indicated. Add twice the depth of the pool plus one foot for overlap to each measurement of length and width. For example, a 5 foot by 10 foot by 2 foot deep water garden requires a liner:

> **WIDTH:** 5 foot + 4 foot (twice the depth) + 1 foot (overlap) = 10 feet
>
> **LENGTH:** 10 foot + 4 foot (twice the depth) + 1 foot (overlap) = 15 feet

Therefore, in the above example a liner 10 feet by 15 feet is required.

35. What dimensions should the shelves be made in a water garden pool?

The shelve should be approximately 9 to 12 inches wide and 6 to 8 inches below the top rim (figure 5). These will then accommodate the potted marginal aquatic plants allowing a few inches of water over the crown.

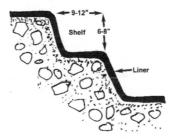

Figure 5. Shelves are very important in the water garden pool.

MAKING A LINER WATER GARDEN

36. How can the shape of an informal water garden pool be shown on the ground before digging?

By using a rope or garden hose (figure 6) the perimeter of the water garden pool can be made by placing the hose on the ground. By this technique the outline of the proposed water garden can be visualized before digging.

Figure 6.   A hose or rope can be used to show the desired shape before digging.

37.   After digging the water garden hole, what can be done with the excess soil?

The soil removed from digging a water garden will appear more than what would be expected. This is because the soil is no longer compacted and contains a great deal of air spaces. Professionals that are experienced with digging holes are aware of the ratio of soil volume removed which is about three or four to one. This excess soil can be spread around plants or used in the garden. In addition, the excess soil can be used as a foundation to make a spectacular waterfall or cascade that will flow into the water garden pool. Many water gardeners use the trimmed excess lining material to cover the foundation of soil in making the waterfall or cascade.

38. Can ledges or shelves be made in making a pool with a liner?

Yes. By digging a shelf or ledge that the liner will cover is a good idea. The shelf should be approximately 9 to 12 inches wide and 8 inches deep. This ledge will hold the marginal aquatic plants (figure 7).

12

39. Should the shelves go around the entire perimeter of the water garden pool or be made only in select locations?

It is a good idea to have shelves go around the entire perimeter (figure 7). The water gardener will be choosing a variety of aquatic marginal plants that will be placed in different locations on this shelf that can not be totally predicted at the time of construction. As growth increases and blooms appear, the marginal plants can be relocated to different and better locations on the surrounding shelf.

Figure 7. Shelves are very important in a water garden pool.

40. If the ground is not level, how can the top of the water garden pool be made level?

It is very important that the top of the water garden pool is level. The use of a string level or a wooden board (figure 8) with a carpenter's level placed across the pond can be used to make sure the pond is level. If the ground slopes this must be taken into consideration.

Figure 8. It is very important to make sure the pool is level.

41. If the ground slopes too much and one side of the finished dug water garden is lower than the other what can be done?

A sloping land gives opportunity for a waterfall at the end that is higher than the surface of the water garden pool. This can be built with rocks and have an flowing waterfall. If a waterfall is not desired, a cliff of rocks can be made or create a rock garden.

42. Is the liner placed directly upon the soil in the dug hole?

No. A method of protecting the liner with the considerable amount of weight of water is necessary before laying it into the dug hole. Rocks or roots remaining in the soil may puncture the lining material after the water is added. Different methods are acceptable to protect the liner. An inch of sand, an old rug or old newspapers can be used to line the hole to protect the liner.

43. After the liner is placed into the hole, should the excess be trimmed?

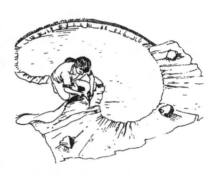

No. The liner should be trimmed **AFTER** the water has been added (figure 9). The water will pull the liner down into the hole. Once the water garden pool is filled then the liner material can be trimmed. If the liner is trimmed before adding water it may be pulled into the hole from the weight of the water and be too short.

Figure 9. The liner is trimmed only AFTER the pool is filled.

44. Can coping be added around the perimeter of the liner water garden pool?

Yes. Rocks or bricks can be added to the perimeter to give it an attractive look (figure 10).

45. Can any type of rocks be used around the perimeter?

No. Limestone rocks should not be used since they will leach alkali into the water garden (increasing the pH) and may be harmful to plants and fish.

Figure 10. A coping of rocks adds a beautiful natural look.

46. What type of rocks can be used around the perimeter of the water garden pool?

Inert rocks such as sandstone, slate or river washed rock should be used around the perimeter of the water garden pool.

47. Can bricks be cemented around the perimeter of the liner water garden pool?

Yes. This technique adds a beautiful pond that appears as if the pond is made entirely of brick. A recessed outer shelf to place a few rows of bricks can be dug before the liner is added. After the liner is in place, a layer of cement and bricks can then be placed on this outer shelf. The liner is folded behind these bricks. Once the water is added the level should be above the lower bricks and give the appearance of a brick water garden pool.

48. Can the coping be laid on the ground around the perimeter of the water garden pool?

Yes, but it is better to have made a separate shallow shelf around the perimeter to set the rocks or coping material on and have the liner fold behind. The water level will then come into contact with the coping and hide the liner. By folding the liner in back of the coping will prevent leaking or seepage of water into the ground (figure 11).

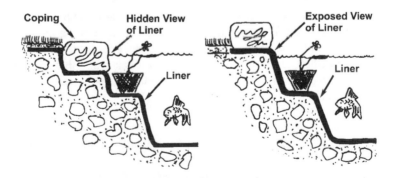

Figure 11. A separate shelf for coping will hide the liner once the pool is filled. The liner should be positioned behind the coping to retain water.

15

49. Can an overflow drain or bottom drain be put into a flexible liner pool?

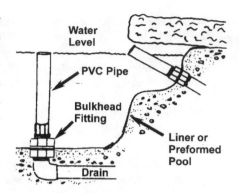

Yes. By cutting a circular hole in the liner and attaching a **bulkhead** fitting will allow a **bottom** or **overflow drain** to be installed (figure 12). A bottom drain will provide a means to completely empty the pool and an overfill drain will regulate the height of the water surface. If the bulkhead fitting is installed on the bottom of the pool it will function

Figure 12. Bulkhead fittings can be installed into flexible liner or preformed pools.

as both an overfill and a bottom drain. On the other hand, an overfill drain can be assembled to the side of the water garden pool and will function only as an overfill drain.

51. Is a bottom drain necessary in the liner water garden pool?

No. A bottom drain provides an easy method of emptying the entire contents of the water garden pool without the need of a siphon or pumps.

52. Is an overflow drain necessary in a liner pond?

No, but it is a good idea to include one in the pool. The overflow drain will regulate the height or top of the water. During heavy rains the pond will fill with water and the overfill drain will maintain a constant depth. If an overfill drain is not included in areas where rain occurs regularly, the pond will continually be filled to the top and may hide a brick ledge that gives the appearance of a concrete pond and worst, it will constantly spill into the surrounding area.

53. Why would the entire water garden pool require being drained?

If debris builds up over time on the bottom of the water garden pool such as fallen leaves, spilled soil from the plants, excrements from fish, etc. the pool may need to be drained and cleaned.

16

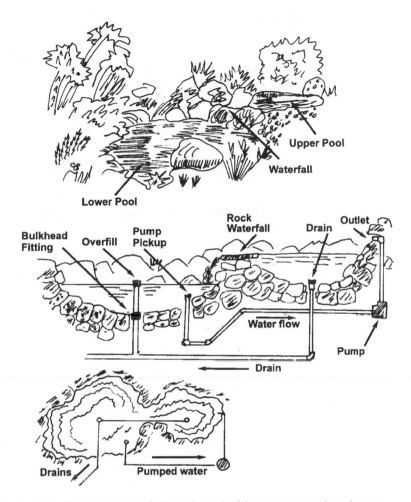

Figure 13. Top shows an informal pool with a upper pool and water fall into a lower pool. The middle drawing shows a cross section of the overfills and drains. The bottom shows a top view of the pools.

54. How can the water garden pool be emptied if it does not have a bottom drain?

If there is no bottom drain, a water garden pump or a tube siphon can be used to empty the water in the pool.

55. How can a siphon be set up to empty the water garden pool if a water pump is not available?

A common siphon method used by water gardeners for decades is to place a garden hose into the water garden pool that is attached to a faucet in the basement. The water is turned on to fill the garden hose. Once water comes out of the hose, it is immediately submerged into the pool to prevent air from entering and breaking the siphon. The water is shut off and the hose is disconnected from the basement faucet which results in a siphon. The hose in the basement can be placed near a drain and the pool is emptied. This method makes sure that the draining water does not flood the surrounding area around the pool.

56. After filling the newly lined water garden pool with water can the plants or fish be immediately introduced?

No, not if the water contains **chlorine** or **chloramines**. Chlorine can be toxic to fish and plants. A commercially prepared **dechlorinator** can be added to remove the chlorine. Dechlorinators are chemicals that remove the chlorine. If the water garden pool sets for 24 hours most of the chlorine will dissipate out of the water without dechlorinators. Some cities add ammonia to the public water supply due to the concern of the Environmental Protection Agency (EPA) indicating that synthetic cancer causing chemicals are formed in the chlorination process which are far more dangerous than the previously added chlorine. These formed chemicals are called **trihalomethanes** (THM's). If both chlorine and ammonia is being added to the public water supply the ammonia chemically reacts with the chlorine and forms **chloramines** which are toxic to plants and fish. In this situation the chloramines have to be removed by a chemical agent and will not dissipate out of the water as free chlorine does.

CONCRETE WATER GARDENS

57. Since the rubber liner for water gardens is extremely durable, why are water gardens still being made of concrete?

The concrete water garden is a permanent feature and, if installed properly, will last over a hundred years as evident from the ones built during the turn of the 19th century. There are many advantages in making a concrete water

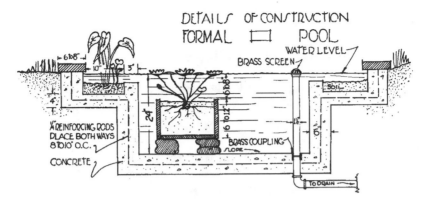

Figure 14. Cross section of a cement formal pool.

garden over the rubber liner. The concern of cutting or damaging the liner is eliminated with a concrete water garden. Cleaning is easier by being allowed to scrape the bottom with a shovel and walking on the concrete without the fear of tearing or cutting as with a liner. Stone statues and additional brick ledges are better supported on a concrete base in the center. Additional brick partitions that cross the center of the pool can be made. Drains can be made permanent and rigid. And last, but very important, the concrete water garden is historic. It is like living in and owning a beautiful century old home. Many liner ponds will attempt to "look" like a concrete water garden pool, but to have the "real" thing has no comparison to many.

58. Is there a special concrete mixture that is used in making a concrete water garden pool?

No. A classical method of getting good results is obtained from a mixture of one part Portland cement, two parts sharp sand and three parts half-inch gravel or crushed stone. This mixture has been recommended by the William Tricker company since the 1930s. Many of these concrete water garden pools are still in existence today and grow wonderful aquatic plants.

59. Is "Portland" cement a special cement for water garden pools?

No. Portland cement got its name from the Isle of Portland which is located near England where it was first developed. It is made by burning limestone (calcium carbonate) and clay and adding gypsum (calcium sulfate). This mixture is then ground into the familiar looking power which we call "cement" or Portland cement.

60. Is there lime in Portland cement?

Yes. In the process of making Portland cement the limestone is heated and the limestone ($CaCO_3$) produces lime (CaO) and carbon dioxide which can be represented by the chemical reaction:

$$CaCO_3 \text{ ---Heat---> } CaO + CO_2$$

61. Is there only one type of Portland cement?

No. There are many brand names used in the manufacturing of Portland cement. In the United States the **American Society for Testing and Materials** (ASTM) has set up standards to identify the different types based upon various physical and chemical requirements for specific purposes. These have resulted in indicating the different "types" of Portland cement by Roman numerals, for example "Type I", "Type II", "Type III" etc.

62. What types of Portland cement should be used in making a water garden pool?

Type I Portland cement is the general purpose cement and used most commonly in all kinds of masonry projects. Type II has been selected by many professionals since it releases less heat than Type I and is suitable for mass concrete projects such as water garden pools. Type II is replacing Type I in some locations. Recommendation by local concrete companies is advisable for specific areas due to the variety of climatic conditions across the county that may require specific types.

63. What should the supporting forms be made of in making a concrete water garden pool?

The forms can be made of wood boards, plywood or metal sheeting.

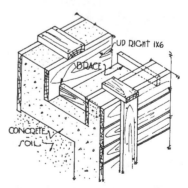

Figure 15. Wood boards as brace in making a shelf in a cement pool.

20

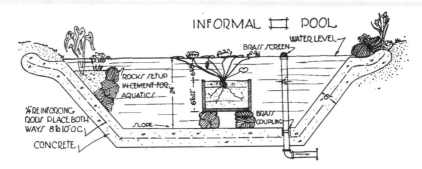

Figure 16.   Cross section of an informal cement pool.

64. How thick should the sides and bottom be in making a concrete water garden pool?

For a long lasting concrete water garden it is recommended that the bottom should be eight inches thick and the sides six inches thick.

65. Should the wood forms or sheet metal be prepared before adding concrete?

Yes. The wood forms should be wet with water and the metal sheeting can be oiled.

66.   Are reinforcing rods or welded wire fabric necessary in the concrete of the water garden pools?

Yes It is recommended to put in 1/4 inch reinforcing rods which are placed eight to ten inches on center or use a 6 inch by 6 inch welded wire fabric. This will add strength to the structure and prevent future cracking.

67. Is it a good idea to let the concrete dry rapidly in the sun?

No, cement in concrete must "cure". Curing is a term referring to the chemical combination of water and cement.

68. What is meant by the "curing of concrete"?

Curing of the concrete is the actual chemical hardening of the cement and water known as **hydration**. This chemical reaction needs water continuously or must be kept moist since actual "crystals" which take time to develop are forming in the concrete. Thus, like all crystals, concrete must cure slowly.

69. How can the curing of the concrete in the water garden pool be made?

Concrete is cured by preventing the mixed water in the cement from evaporating resulting in slow curing. This can be done by covering the concrete with a plastic film or using a **curing compound**. The curing compounds that can be purchased are applied to the surface of the concrete to prevent fast curing.

70. When should curing begin after pouring the concrete?

As soon as the concrete has set and is hard enough not to be damaged by adding water curing should begin.

71. How long should curing of the concrete be done?

The curing should be done for at least three to seven days. After this time the concrete will continue to cure for years on its own.

72. What temperature should it be to pour the concrete?

Concrete curing occurs between 40 and 90 degrees Fahrenheit. The reaction will occur rapidly at first giving off heat and then continues for years afterwards. Thus, it is best to stay within these temperature limits when first pouring concrete.

73. Can a concrete water garden pool be made in temperatures below 40 degrees?

Yes, but additional methods using chemical additives and a possible different Type Portland cements are used. If the water becomes frozen (below 32 degrees Fahrenheit) in uncured concrete it will expand and damage the final concrete. It is best to avoid working with concrete in freezing weather unless done by a professional mason.

74. Should an overflow and bottom drain be put into the concrete water garden pool?

Yes, if possible. It is most appropriate to put in an overflow and bottom drain in a concrete water garden pool. A single pipe installed from the floor of the water garden pool can perform both the functions of drain and overflow. The drain will extend up from the bottom to the desired height, usually a few inches from the top of the margin, and be made to be removed. These type of

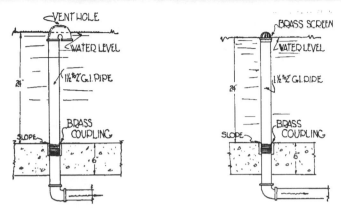

Figure 17. Left: overfill drain with vent hole. Right: brass screen over the overflow drain.

drains were once made of 1 1/2 inch galvanized pipe with a brass sieve. Today these can be replaced with PVC (Polyvinyl chloride) pipe or "plastic pipe". Excess water will flow into the drain pipe and if the water garden pool needs to be empty it can be removed (figure 17).

75. Why should a concrete water garden have a bottom or overflow drain?

Similar to the liner constructed pool, there are reasons to drain the entire water garden pool. Debris such as leaves, soil, wastes, etc. may build up over time and the water garden pool will need to be drained completely for cleaning. Also, if the concrete cracks, requires painting or needs repair, the water garden pool will need to be drained. In addition to draining the entire pool, an overfill drain will keep a constant level of water in the garden pool during heavy rain spells. The overfill drain will maintain the beauty of the margin of water level that is viewed along the sides of the concrete.

76. Can coping stones be added to the top of the concrete water garden pool?

Yes. In making the recommended thickness of six inches of concrete on the sides of the water garden pool the top will support various types of coping stones or bricks. It is recommended that the coping should be above the water line and not be within the water level. This will avoid any leaks from cracks that develop in the joints of the coping over the years which causes the water to drop to an unexpected level. An 8 inch brick coping will fit nicely on top of the six inch concrete wall (figure 18).

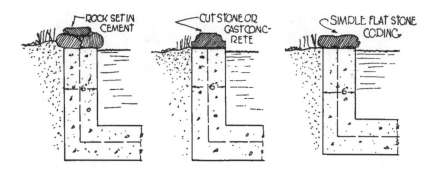

Figure 18. Coping adds a special touch to the beauty of the water garden pool.

77. What type of cement is used with bricks or rocks?

A **mortar** should be used to cement the bricks or rocks. Mortar is a masonry cement which is a mixture of Portland cement and lime (Calcium oxide) mixed with sand. There is no crushed stone or gravel as found in concrete.

78. Is there only one type of mortar?

No. There are five different "types" of mortar identified from the derivation of every other letter of the word **MASONWORK**, more specifically Types M, S, N, O and K. The most commonly used is Type M and Type N. The mortars differ basically on the proportions of lime, Portland cement and sand. Type M is commonly used in construction requiring extra strength and frost resistance. For ordinary uses Type N is often selected. It is best to get the recommendations by the local supplier of the type of mortar to be used in a specific climatic area.

79. After the concrete or mortar has hardened can plants and fish be added?

No. The concrete or mortar has **lime** (CaO) when mixed with water produces **calcium hydroxide** ($Ca(OH)_2$), a process known to chemist as **slaking**, which becomes a strong alkali. Lime (calcium oxide) stands among the alkali or bases as sulfuric acid does among the acids in strength. The lime will drastically increase the pH of the pond and is extremely toxic to plant and animal life.

80. How can concrete or mortar in the newly made water garden pool have the alkali removed or neutralized?

Once the concrete has hardened, the concrete or mortar needs to be neutralized. This can be done by filling and draining with water. The surface of the concrete is washed using a stiff brush or broom with a dilute vinegar solution (one quart vinegar to ten quarts of water) or a dilute acid solution to neutralize the alkaline material. After washing the surface the pool should be rinsed and filled again and allowed to stand for three to four days. It is then drained and refilled. The pH of the pool water can then be checked to see if the alkali has been removed. If the pH is higher than a pH of eight then repeat the entire procedure with vinegar. Once the pH is lower than eight or within the neutral range and stabilizes, the fish and plants can now be introduced.

81. Are slopping sides recommended in a concrete pond?

Straight or perpendicular sides are prone to crack from ice formation. Ice formation will create a tremendous force as it expands when it freezes on the sides of a perpendicular sided water garden. For this reason sloping sides, approximately 20 degrees, are recommended in concrete ponds. Perpendicular sided concrete ponds can survive extreme cold weather if properly mixed concrete and correct placing of reinforcing rods are used and the pond is drained in the winter.

82. Can a 1/2 inch crack be repaired in a concrete water garden pool?

Yes. A crack of about 1/2 inch can be repaired with a special commercial concrete compound. These are known as **hydraulic cements** which will can also be used to repair active leaks. They will set up within minutes and are very strong.

83. If the concrete water garden pool is leaking and small cracks can be seen, what can be done?

A special adhesive concrete paste can be used to seal small cracks. The concrete paste is purchased as a powder. It is made into a paste solution with the addition of water and painted over the concrete surface that contains the cracks. A concrete adhesion additive, usually in liquid form, is also used to better "stick" this paste solution to the old concrete and strengthens the repair. These liquid additives are known as **binders**.

84. If no cracks are seen and the concrete water garden pool leaks what can be done?

If a crack is suspected, the entire concrete water garden pool should be covered with the special concrete adhesive. This should eliminate any leaks.

85. After using concrete repair products on the water garden pond, does it need to be neutralized before adding plants or fish?

Yes. The concrete repair products are made of similar alkali producing substances as concrete. The same procedure should be used as in new concrete ponds to neutralize the alkali produced by the concrete repairing compounds before adding plants or fish.

86. What can be done if no cracks are found, the entire surface of the concrete has been sealed, and the concrete water garden still leaks?

The concrete water garden repair pool products, if properly applied, should repair most leaks. However, many water gardeners prefer to use a rubber pond liner to line the entire concrete pool which immediately solves any type of leaking problem. This method will require no curing as with concrete repair products.

Figure 19. A wonderful water garden pool designed to admire as one passes along a gravel path in the garden. Photograph by Robert Sawyer, Wm. Tricker, Inc.® circa 1930.

PREFORMED WATER GARDENS

87. What is a "preformed" water garden pool?

This is a water garden pool that is made of plastic or fiberglass that is "preformed" or cast into the final shape of the water garden pool.

88. How is the preformed pool installed?

The preformed pool is simple to install. Once the area is selected an outline of the preformed pool in an upright position is made on the ground using a rope or garden hose. The shape is dug to the correct depth with an addition inch for applying a layer of sand. The bottom should be level. Once the preformed pool is in place it should be checked with a level. This can be done using a board with a carpenter's level placed across the preformed pool. If it is not level more sand can be added in specific locations.

89. Can an overfill drain be made in a preformed pool?

Yes. The use of a bulkhead fitting to attach overfill drains is easy to install once a hole is drilled through the preformed pool. If a drain is not used then the method of using a siphon described for draining a liner pond can be used to completely drain the pool.

90. Why is a preformed pool selected over a PVC or Rubber lined pool?

Many consider the preformed pool easier to install than a PVC or Rubber lined pool and somewhat more durable for cleaning.

91. Why would a PVC or Rubber lined pool be selected over the preformed pool?

The PVC or Rubber lined pool can be made to any shape or design. The preformed pool, on the other hand, is limited to the actual purchased shape and depth. Most preformed pools do not exceed sizes over 10 feet long and many water gardeners desire larger sizes which can be achieved with PVC or rubber lined pool material.

II. Water Garden Pumps and Waterfalls

*Water Garden Pumps * Waterfalls * Water Fountain Displays *

Water Garden Pumps

92. What is a "water garden pump" that is used in the water garden pool?

A "water garden pump" is an electrical motor device that draws in water and expels the same water out under force. Most of the water garden pumps weigh only a few pounds. They have a water proof electrical cord and are equipped with an intake for water and an output for the expelling of water.

93. How are the water garden pumps used in the water garden pool?

The water garden pumps are used to make fountains, waterfalls, streams or filtration units.

94. Besides cost, how do the variety of water garden pumps differ?

Water garden pumps differ mainly by the amount of water they pump in gallons per hour and the height they will pump at certain distances from the pump.

95. Before purchasing a water pump how can the "gallons per hour" be visualized?

By taking a common 1 gallon milk jug and regulating the flow of water from a garden hose a visualization of the approximate gallons per hour by the claimed water garden pump can be derived as follows:

Approx. Seconds	Gallons per hour
30	120
21	170
12	300
7	500
3	1200
1	3000

Thus, if the 1 gallon milk jug takes approximately 12 seconds to fill, this would represent a water garden pump of 300 gallons per hour. If the hose is adjusted to fill the milk jug in 30 seconds, this would represent a water garden pump of 120 gallons per hour, and so on.

96. Are the water garden pumps with the electrical cord placed directly into the water?

Yes. The water garden pumps are designed to operate under the water. They are simply placed under the water and plugged into an electrical outlet outside of the pool that is protected by a **ground fault interrupter** (GFI).

97. What is a "ground fault interrupter" or GFI?

Water and electricity do not mix. The use of a **ground fault interrupter (GFI)** should always be used around water. The GFI is a special circuit breaker that in the event of a small amount of electrical short which may cause electrocution will stop the flow of electricity. Any electrical device around the water garden should have a GFI.

98. If the home has standard circuit breakers should a ground fault interrupter (GFI) still be used?

Yes. The ground fault interrupter (GFI) is a special circuit breaker that is activated in areas that are dangerous with a potential shock hazard due to electrical short. It is more sensitive than the standard circuit beakers found in homes. Many cities have ordinances that protect their residents in the home by requiring GFI's in bathrooms and kitchens where water and electricity are in close proximity. Some homes may have GFI's within the main circuits, but a qualified electrician should be consulted when in doubt to make sure it is operating with the electrical plug for the water garden devices.

99. Do water garden pumps have to be under the water to operate?

No. Some pumps have the ability to operate only when they are **submerged** under water and others, known as **non-submersible pumps**, are designed to pump while outside of the water. Another type of pump can operate either under the water or out of the water.

100. Can a pump that is claimed to be only "submergible" in water be used out of the water?

No. The specific water garden pumps are identified as submersible, non-submergible or both and must be used as recommended by the manufacturer.

101. What happens if a submergible pump is used outside of the water garden pool on the ground?

If a submergible pump (any pump designed for use ONLY under the water) is operated out of the water, the pump may overheat and result in damage. If the pump is designed for use only in the water it should never be operated out of the water.

102. Why would someone select a water garden pump that is non-submersible?

Some water gardeners prefer to operate their pumps in a location that is easily accessible such as outside of the water garden pool. Cleaning and other maintenance of a non-submersible pump is easier by not having to recover from the bottom of the pool. In addition, the non-submersible pump can be used as a utility pump in other needs around the home, such as pumping out a flooded basement, that may not require to be submerged in water.

103. Is it easier to install a submersible pump than a non-submersible pump in the water garden pool?

Yes, in most instances. The submersible pump is simply dropped into the water garden pool with attached accessories and plugged in. The non-submersible pump often requires more plumbing and a protective access box.

104. If the water garden pump cord is not long enough to reach out in the pond what can be done?

It is possible that the water garden pump cord can be spliced and additional wire can be attached with special underwater connectors. It is highly recommended that a qualified electrician will make this connection. This type of connection is commonly performed by pumps operated in deep wells. Most aquatic pumps have long cords and do not need to be spliced.

105. When removing the water garden pump from the bottom of the pool, is it correct to lift it by the electrical cord if it is not plugged in?

No. The electrical cord should never be used to lift the water garden pump from the bottom of the pool. This will possibly damage the electrical water tight connection and cause the pump to fail when placed back in the water garden. It is best to reach into the water garden pool and lift the unplugged pump by the main body. Some heavier pumps have handles for this purpose.

106. How does the water garden pump keep debris from clogging inside?

Most pumps are equipped with a small screen to prevent clogs as the water enters. Depending upon the size of the pump, it may be prone to clogging with debris in the water garden pool. Some of the large pumps can pass solids up to a 1/2 inch in size, while others may become hindered by clogging of smaller particles.

107. What is the best method to keep the water garden pump from clogging?

To prevent major clogs the use of a **mechanical pump filter** attached to the water garden pump will "filter" or clean the water as it flows through. This type of filter is commonly made of a plastic box with a sponge-like material for filtering. This sponge-like material can remove smaller particles from the water than the attached screen. The periodic cleaning of the filter is still necessary.

31

Waterfalls

108. How is a waterfall made in the water garden pool?

It is very simple to make a waterfall. A water garden pump with an attached 1/2 inch rubber hose is placed into the water garden pool. The hose can be placed at the top of a set of rocks that are impervious to water in the design of a waterfall. Once the pump is turned on, the water will flow over the rocks making a waterfall that recycles the water continually. Preformed waterfalls can be purchased that are ready-made to look like a natural waterfall in place of making rocks impervious to water.

109. Where should the pump be placed in the water garden pool to make the waterfall?

To get the greatest amount of water over the waterfall, the pump should be placed as near to the waterfall as possible. The greater the distance the slower the flow of water through the hose. Different water garden pumps have different specifications as to how many gallons are pumped over a particular distance. This information is given by the manufacturers of the pumps.

110. Can the waterfall be located by the water lilies in the pool?

No. The water lilies and other aquatic plants do not want the surface of the water to be disturbed. The waterfall should be at a secluded end of the water garden pool without aquatic vegetation.

111. How close to the planted water lily can a water fountain or waterfall be made in the water garden pool?

The desired distance a water lily can be placed from a waterfall or fountain depends upon the strength or flow of water through each display. The water should be placid or not moving in the area of the water lily for best growth. If ripples in the water are evident, the water lily may be stunted in growth or die.

112. Will the cementing of rocks in a waterfall prevent leaks?

No. The rocks and cement will expand and contract at different rates and eventually will develope cracks large enough to allow water to seep through.

113. How can you keep the water from seeping into the ground over a waterfall made of rocks?

A permanent method of keeping the water as it flows over the rocks from seeping into the ground can be made with a liner material. The liner material is placed behind the rocks and overlapped into the water garden. The liner will now function as an excellent water barrier. Cement can be used to hold the rocks in place.

114. How can the sound of a waterfall be increase without making a high fall of water?

Similar to a guitar or other instruments, the reverberations of the sound of water can be enhanced by designing a "sound-chamber" behind the falling water (figure 20). This can be done by increasing the overhang of the rock before it falls upon the surface of the pool. Using this technique the musical murmur of the water can be increased.

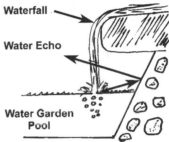

Figure 20. The sound of a waterfall can be enhanced by designing the rock overhang.

115. What size of pump is recommended to create a waterfall as a veil or curtain of water?

A veil or curtain of water over a waterfall depends upon the gallons per hour that the pump can produce and the width of the veil. It has been estimated that a 300 gallon per hour pump will produce a veil or sheet of water one foot wide.

116. What size of pump is recommended to create a rushing or splashing waterfall that does not peal back and flow along the inside wall?

To create a rushing or splashing waterfall that is one inch wide, a pump of at least 100 gallons per hour is required. Thus, a two inch width will require at least a 200 gallon per hour pump.

33

Water Fountain Display

117. How is a water fountain display made?

After selecting a pump and a fountain head with a particular spray pattern, they are simply attached together. Submerging the water garden pump into the pool and turning on the pump will make an attractive display.

118. Does the water fountain spray effect the growth of water lilies similar to a waterfall?

Yes. The water fountain must be in a secluded area of the water garden pool away from water lilies and other aquatic plants. The disturbance of the surface of the water or constant spray of water on the aquatic plants will hinder growth and eventually cause the death of the plants.

III. General Questions on Water Gardening

* Botany of Water Lilies * Potting Aquatics * Fertilizing *

Botany of Water Lilies

119. Geologically, how far back is there evidence of water lilies?

Tropical water lily pollen has been found in the geological formation of ponds and marsh areas over 160 million years ago. This is a time known to geologists as the Mesozoic era where the Earth was portrayed as very warm with extensive lowlands and continental seas.

120. Since the water lilies are old geologically speaking, does that mean that the current flower structure is also very primitive?

Yes. Looking at a flower on a water lily, lotus (*Nelumbo*) or magnolia (*Magnolia*) is like seeing into the past. The botanical structure of the water lily flower is considered primitive based upon the morphological fact that the **petals, sepals** with base, collectively known as the **perianth**, is without sharp separations and is in a spiral arrangement. In looking down into the open

35

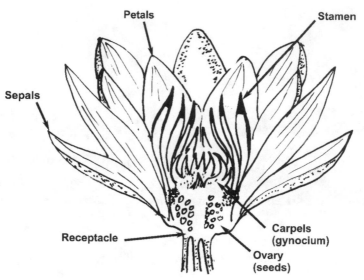

Figure 21. Cross Section of a typical water lily flower showing the botanical parts.

flower of this type one notes a symmetry of the perianth parts which can be cut into two equal parts similar to cutting a pie into equal parts from any selected point. Thus, the water lily flower is an ancient flower.

121. Are the botanical names given to the parts of the water lily flower different than other flowers?

No. There are a multitude of different flower structures in the plant world that have unusually designed parts. The water lily flower is not structurally different than describing a "typical" flower (figure 21). There are four or five **sepals** surrounding the **petals**. The **stamen** consists of the **anther** containing the developing pollen and is found on top of the **filament**. The **carpels** (gynoecium) is where the pollen will land on the **stigma** and grow down through the **style** to the **ovary** where the seeds will develop.

122. What relationship did the ancient Egyptians have with water lilies?

The ancient Egyptians have been well known to have used water lilies in their social and religious lives. They are depicted from their writings on tombs as adorning themselves with water lilies. They buried their dead with the petals and wreaths of the water lilies.

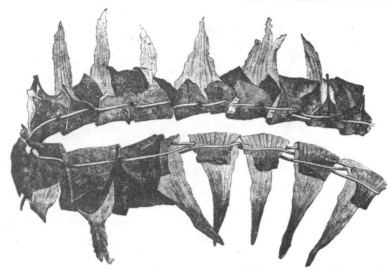

Figure 22. The discovery of the Funeral Wreath from the tomb of Ramses II (1000-1200 B.C.) as depicted in *Nature* page 110, May 31, 1883 showing petals of the tropical water lily *Nymphaea caerulea* stitched together with the leaves of the scared *Mimusops.*

123. How old are the ancient Egyptian tombs found with water lily wreaths and petals?

The tombs of the ancient Egyptians are found with water lily plant remnants as long as 4000 years ago. The water lily wreaths found in some tombs were so very well preserved as to reveal how the wreaths were assembled. The use of flowers in the funeral decorations were especially prominent in the XIX and XXI dynasties. The custom was to lay the water lily wreaths and semicircles of flowers on the breast of the enwrapped corpse until the sacrophagus was quite packed with these floral attributes.

124. Were the water lilies found in ancient Egyptian tombs preserved?

Yes. The ancient Egyptians not only knew how to preserve their celebrated kings and important people to last over 35 centuries with mummification but were able to preserve the water lilies and other flora found within the same ancient tombs (figure 22). The colors of the petals of the water lilies were remarkably preserved with morphological detail.

125. If the water lilies were well preserved in the ancient Egyptian tombs, could they be identified by name?

Yes, the water lilies found in the Egyptian tombs were the two commonly species found growing in Egypt. The water lily known as "the blue lotus of the Nile or Egypt" or *Nymphaea caerulea* was commonly found in the tombs. This is a blue flowered day blooming tropical water lily. Also the petals of the white flowering night blooming tropical water lily "Egyptian lotus" *Nymphaea lotus* was also found buried with the mummies.

126. Where only the petals of the water lily flower used in the ancient Egyptian tombs or was the entire flower preserved?

Both the water lily petals and entire flowers were found preserved in Egyptian tombs. The petals were made into intricate wreaths delicately woven with a local sacred tree leaves of the species *Mimusops*. The entire preserved water lily flower with stems of 18 to 20 inches were also fastened between the bands of papyrus threads encircling the mummy.

127. Did the ancient Egyptians have water garden pools?

Yes.   Amenophis IV of Egypt (c. 1375 B.C.) had a water garden pond sunk in his garden nearly three-quarters of a mile long and over one hundred yards wide. He also designed his bedroom to represent a water garden, the walls and floor decorated with paintings of water lilies and ornamental fish.

128. How does the botanist classify the water lilies among the various plants?

The botanist classifies the water lilies within a large group of plants that produce flowers known as **angiosperms**. The angiosperms characteristically produce seeds and are called "seed producing plants". The water lilies are further subdivided into an aquatic group known as a family called the *Nymphaeaceae* which includes other aquatic plants besides the water lilies. And finally, all the water lilies are placed into the genus known as *Nymphaea*.

129. What does the word *"Nymphaea"* mean?

It is derived from the word *"Nympha"* which in Greek and Roman mythology means a nature-goddess.

130. Are the spatterdocks, yellow pond lilies or cow lilies, in the same genus as the water lilies?

No, at least not after 1805. In 1753 Carolus Linnaeus or Carl Linne' (1707-1778) who was born in Southern Sweden first classified the water lilies and yellow pond lilies under the same genus *Nymphaea*. In 1805 Salisbury first separated them into two parts of the genus. The water lilies were called *Castalia* and the spatterdocks were *Nymphaea*. James E. Smith purchased the collection and library of Linnaeus after his death and in 1807 disregarded Salisbury's work and classified the water lilies and spatterdock as *Nymphaea* and *Nuphur* respectively. Today, this is widely accepted.

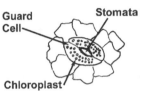

131. Will a water garden pool have more or less evaporation of water if it is covered with water lilies?

Less evaporation. The water garden pool will reduce the evaporation of the water if it is covered with water lilies. **Transpiration** is the term given to plants that refer to the loss of water vapor into the air from the leaves of plants which mainly occurs through openings in the leaf known as **stomatas** (figure 23). A stomata is a lens-shaped pore surrounded by a pair of cells called **guard cells**. They are found

Figure 23. Microscopic stomata (stoma, singular) are openings made by two bean-shaped cells known as "guard cells" located in the epidermis of the leaf which allow gases to enter and exit into and out of the leaf. They are located on the top of the leaf.

on the top of the water lily leaf and allow the exchange of oxygen, carbon dioxide and water to pass from the internal leaf to the outside. They function mainly in providing gas exchange for **photosynthesis** and regulating the amount of moisture the plant retains. The guard cells have the ability to close the stomata and prevent too much water vapor escaping into the air. Therefore, the leaf prevents direct evaporation of water from the water garden pool with minimal diffusion of water vapor from the stomata. In addition to regulating water evaporation, the water lily leaf restricts the movement of air across the water surface which would increase evaporation.

132. Was the location of the stomatas on the top of the water lily leaf recently discovered by botanist?

No. The fact that land plants have stomata mainly on the bottom of the leaf, whereas the stomata of the water lilies are on the top intrigued botanists many years ago and were addressed in old textbooks. The accompanying figure 24 shows an actual plate of the stomata in an 1859 text which also wrote of the unusual location of the stomata on top of the water lily leaf.

133. Is the "transpiration" greater in water lilies than the aquatic shallow water or floating plants?

The water lilies have greater "transpiration" rates than the shallow water plants (i.e. water plantain) or floating plants (i.e. water hyacinth). Interestingly, terrestrial plants, such as trees, have greater transpiration rates than any of the aquatic plants.

Figure 24. The actual representation of the stomata from *Vegetable and Animal Physiology* by H. Goadby 1859 and was labeled "Cuticle-White Lily"

134. Is the inside of a stem of a water lily solid?

No. Cutting the cross section of the different variety of water lily stems will reveal many different morphological types. The stems are made of a series of long air channels which are characteristic of different varieties. By taking the stem of a water lily and holding like a straw and blowing into the water will produce bubbles.

135. Do the longitudinal channels in the cross-section of the different types of water lily stems all look the same?

No. The studying of the cross-section of a water lily **petioles** (stems of water lily pads) and **peduncles** (stems that hold the flowers) have been of interest since the 1870s and much has been recorded. For example, most tropical and hardy day blooming water lilies characteristically have four nearly equal large canals running through the stem of the water lily pad. Whereas, most night blooming water lilies typically have two greatly predominant canals with two smaller ones. The specific differences among the varieties of water lilies are used by commercial aquatic companies in controlled detailed identification of types beyond flower characteristics.

136. What does the microscopic structure of the leaf of a water lily look like?

The microscopic structure (figure 25) of the water lily leaf is very interesting when compared to the leaves of their terrestrial cousins the land plants. The cellular cross-section of the water lily leaf as seen under a

40

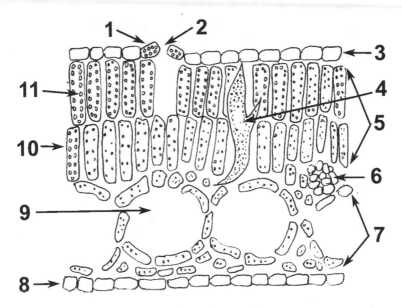

Figure 25. Microscopic cross-section of a water lily leaf. Differing from land plants note the stomata located on top of the leaf and the presence of sclereid cells (Idioblasts) whereas most land pants have stomata concentrated on the bottom and absence of sclereid cells in the leaves. 1. Guard Cells 2. Stomata 3. Upper Epidermis 4. Idioblasts (sclendic) 5. Mesophyll 6. Vein 7. Palisade Mesophyll 8. Lower Epidermis 9. Intercellular Spaces 10. Columnar Cell 11. Chloroplast.

microscope shows similar structures to the land plants. A series of rectangular cells below the **upper epidermis cells** known as the **palisade mesophyll cells** contain **chloroplasts** that stream around the cell reaching the top of the plant to catch sunlight for photosynthesis. Below the palisade cells is the loosely arranged **spongy mesophyll cells.** These cells allow large intercellular spaces for exchanging of gases. One outstanding difference to land plants is the location of the **stomata** which is surrounded by two **guard cells** and is found on "top" of the leaf. The stomata of the land plants are mainly on the "bottom" of the plant. Another unusual feature of the leaf of the water lily is the presence of **sclereid cells** which functions in support and protection. These cells are typically found in plant stems and hard seed shells of plants but they are commonly found throughout the water lily leaf. These cells were identified by Dr. Conard, University of Pennsylvania in his intensive microscopic studies of the water lily leaf in 1905 as **idioblasts** (Weiss,1878).

41

137. Is the cleft or cut "v" found in the water lily pad the same in all varieties of water lilies?

No. The classical water lily pad with the "v" cut is not the same in all water lilies. Some clefts are a large open "v" in the water lily pad while others have an overlapping "v" which make the cut "v" seem non existent when seen lying on the water surface.

138. Were there any set rules for naming the colors of the flowers of the water lilies?

No. The early hybridizers of water lilies in the later 1890s tried to describe each new water lily by a familiar descriptive color term. There were no established rules for naming flower colors. For example, what should the descriptive term be used to describe a new yellow water lily? One may describe and view it as "lemon yellow", another as "primrose yellow" and yet another as "sulfur yellow". All may depict a different "color" in our minds.

139. When was there an attempt to standardize the descriptive color names of flowers?

In 1939 the **British Colour Council** in England collaborated with **The Royal Horticultural Society** (RHS) and produced a set of color charts that attempted to identify and provide descriptive color names to the various colors found in plant flowers. The copyright was held by a Mr. Robert F. Wilson who produced a second inclusive volume in 1941. By this time many of the wonderful water lily hybrids were already described by abstract color descriptions in the literature.

140. What is commonly used today to describe the technical colors found in flowers such as water lilies?

The original set of color charts by the **Royal Horticulture Society** (RHS) has been updated with cross-references to other existing charts and has been accepted by many botanists throughout the world and can be used with water lily flowers. The RHS not only attempts to establish a descriptive term for a particular color but also have the hues, tones and intensities of each color identified. For example, the water lily *Nymphaea* 'Sulphurea' is often described as having "sulfur yellow flowers". The term "sulphur yellow" is used by the RHS and the color charts have color prints of sulphur yellow with graduated tints. With the color charts there is no virtual mistake for the color expected of the well known water lily *N*. 'Sulphurea' if described as "sulphur yellow" as per the RHS color charts.

141. Do the water lilies from commercial sources for the public use the Royal Horticultural Society (RHS) terminology for flower color?

No. Since most people that purchase water lilies do not have the set of color charts from the Royal Horticultural Society (RHS) their color descriptions would be useless. Most individuals have to rely upon the expertise of each commercial company supplying the water lilies to define the flower colors and provide photographs as near possible the original. Many commercial aquatic companies will retain the original historic descriptions which includes the abstract flower color names. The RHS flower color terminology however is used in the scientific realm when establishing and recording a new botanical variety.

142. Do the water lily stems have hairs on them or are they smooth?

Some water lily stems have fine hair-like projections and some do not. They are very small and fine only about 1/16 of an inch in length. Whether or not the stems have hairs is characteristic of certain varieties.

143. Do the different varieties of water lilies have round shaped pads?

No. A close look at the individual water lily pads of the different varieties will show a genetic difference to the shapes of roundness. Some may appear oval and others perfectly round depending upon the variety.

144. Are all water lilies considered hardy?

No. There are two groups of water lilies: **tropical water lilies** and **hardy water lilies**. Tropical or tender water lilies are considered annuals in our northern latitudes and hardy water lilies are considered perennial in the temperate zone.

145. Do the tropical water lily flowers float on the surface of the water like the hardy water lily flower?

No. The tropical water lily characteristically will have long stems that hold the flowers well above the water surface. These stems are typically over a foot long. The hardy water lily flower generally floats on the surface of the water.

146. Does the water lily flower stay open all day and night?

No. There are two different groups of water lilies known as **day bloomers** and **night bloomers**. The water lilies that opens in the early morning and close in the late afternoon are known as day bloomers. The night bloomers open in the late afternoon and close early the next morning.

147. Are night blooming and day blooming water lilies found in both hardy and tropical water lilies?

No. Both hardy and tropical water lilies have day blooming varieties of water lilies. Only the tropical water lilies have the select group of night bloomers.

148. Do water lilies produce flowers during the entire growing season?

Yes. Unlike many other wonderful flowers that have only a few weeks of flowering each year the water lilies are known for their continual blooming during the entire growing season. Therefore, the flowers of the water lily can be enjoyed throughout the entire summer.

149. Do water lilies need stagnant or moving water?

Water lilies grow best in stagnant water or non-moving water.

150. How much sunlight should the water lily receive?

The water lily should receive at least four to six hours of direct sunlight. Water lilies perform best in sunny locations, the more sun the better growth and flowering. To achieve the outstanding descriptions found in water garden catalogs a full day of sunshine is often required.

151. Is it normal for the flower of a blue water lily to appear magenta-like after photographing?

Yes. The photographing of water lilies for true flower color is extremely difficult by the amateur. The reflection of the water is a major set back in trying to capture the water lily in its natural state. The spectacular blues and purples of the tropical water lilies are virtually impossible to reproduce by photographing with standard methods and is a challenge to the experts.

PLANTING WATER LILIES

152. How do you plant or pot a water lily?

Water lilies and other aquatics are planted in a similar fashion (figure 26). The first step is to fill a container with good topsoil and mix with a granular aquatic fertilizer. Second, a small hollow is made in the top of the soil. Third, the aquatic plant is placed into this hollow and soil is gently pressed around the plant. Fourth, a cover of gravel is placed on top. Fifth, the potted aquatic plant is now lowered into the water garden pool at the correct depth.

Figure 26. Planting or potting a water lily and other aquatics is easy.
1. Mix fertilizer into the topsoil. 2. Hollow an area on top. 3. Place aquatic plant into hollow and cover with soil. 4. Cover soil with a gravel.
5. Place into garden pool at correct level.

153. Is the muck from the bottom of a natural pond better to plant in than topsoil?

No, muck is low in nutrients and can be very acidic. Water lilies are heavy feeders and will perform better with a good organic source such as topsoil supplemented with an aquatic fertilizer.

154. What is the minimum amount of soil a water lily should be planted in?

The water lilies are heavy feeders and should be put into at least one cubic foot of soil. The more soil the better growth and flowering.

155. What type of planting containers are used for aquatic plants?

Specially designed plastic containers with lattice sides (holes) are used in planting aquatic plants.

156. What determines the size of the aquatic planting container selected?

Typically, the size of the planting container will determine the final size of the aquatic plant. The containers are made to hold different amounts of soil which will support the growth characteristics of different aquatic plants.

157. How can the correct sized planting container be chosen for the variety of aquatic plants?

Most commercial aquatic establishments recommend the correct sizes of potting containers based upon the growing attributes of each aquatic plant. Smaller marginal plants and oxygenators can be ganged into a single larger container.

158. What happens if the aquatic planting container is too small for potting the water lily or other aquatic plants?

If a container is too small for the expected growth of an aquatic plant the plant will respond by being dwarfed. Besides having smaller foliage and flowers, the actual flowering potential may not be achieved.

159. What is the advantage of having lattice (holes) sides over using a solid sided containers for planting aquatic plants?

The lattice sides will allow the roots of the aquatic plants to penetrate the surrounding water and directly derive nourishment from the water. The roots of the aquatic plants do not go deep into the soil but spread over the top few inches of soil. Thus, the ability of the roots to grow along and through the sides of the container adds more growing surface area and enhances growth. With these traits the lattice sided containers require less soil and are lighter in handling than the solid sided containers.

160. After potting the aquatic plant in topsoil, can it be placed directly into the water garden pool?

No. A pea sized gravel or sand should be used to cover the top layer of soil before it is placed into the water garden pool.

161. Can any type of gravel be used to cover the soil?

No. A river washed gravel is best. For example, the use of limestone gravel should not be used since it will leach lime (increasing the pH) into the water and may harm plants and fish.

162. How much pea gravel or sand should be used to cover the top layer of soil after potting the aquatic plant?

The soil of the potted aquatic plant should be covered with approximately one-half inch of pea gravel or sand.

163. Why is a pea gravel or sand used to cover the soil after potting the aquatic plants?

There are many reasons to add pea gravel or sand to cover the soil. The pea gravel or sand will hold the soil with fertilizer in place in the water garden as it is lowered into the water. Under the water the pea gravel or sand will help to keep unwanted weeds from growing immediately and allow the planted aquatic to better dominate the pot. The covering by gravel or sand will deter most fish from digging into the soil and making the water cloudy.

FERTILIZING

164. Are the three main chemicals (nitrogen, phosphorous and potassium) that are commonly found in most synthetic commercial fertilizers found in aquatic fertilizers?

Yes. The commercial aquatic synthetic fertilizer must have the correct amounts of the three classical ingredients: **nitrogen**, **potassium** and **phosphorous**. These are necessary for good growth and flowering.

165. Can a commercial synthetic fertilizer for lawns, roses, etc. be used to mix into the soil before planting the water lily?

It is recommended to use only a specific proven fertilizer for aquatics. There are many commercial synthetic fertilizers with different ratios of nitrogen, potassium and potash that can be purchased and may not meet the nutritional needs of aquatic plants. The ratio of nitrogen, potassium and phosphorous is formulated for a particular plant. In addition, there are different types of fertilizers that have different rates of solubility in water. An incorrect fertilizer formula applied to the soil can "burn" or kill the aquatic plants and leach excess chemicals into the water. Many commercial aquatic nurseries have proven formulas with recommended applications that will prevent aquatic root burn and promote growth and flowering. After years of research with aquatic plants, a chemical engineer, **Dr. J. T. Charleston**, working for the William Tricker company published in 1933 findings of a superior aquatic formula that is still used in the industry today known under the trade name **Praefecta**™, based upon his findings that he "perfected" it primarily for aquatic plants.

166. Is it necessary to continue to fertilize the water lilies or aquatic plants after planting throughout the growing season?

Yes. Most aquatic plants and especially water lilies are heavy feeders. They must be fertilized regularly depending upon growth. The directions on the manufacture's label should be followed.

167. What different types of aquatic fertilizer are used in the water garden?

There are two forms of aquatic fertilizer. They can purchased as a hardened pellet, about the size of a dime, or the familiar loose granular type.

168. Why are there two forms, granular and pellet, of aquatic fertilizer used in water gardening?

The two forms have different fertilizer formulas which support the different growth phases of the aquatics. The granular form is commonly used to mix into the soil before planting and will promote beginning and sustained growth into the season. During the growing season the hardened aquatic fertilizer pellets are used by pushing them directly into the soil of the submerged container in the water garden pool. This pellet of fertilizer complements the residual granular fertilizer and will promote the flowering and continued growth.

169. Is there a specific location to push the pellet of fertilizer into the container below the surface of the water?

Yes. The hardened pellet of aquatic fertilizer is pushed into the soil by a finger near the roots (figure 27).

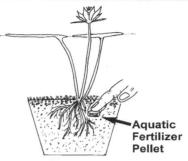

Aquatic Fertilizer Pellet

Figure 27. Special aquatic fertilizer in pellet form should be periodically added to the soil near the roots.

170. Is there a special technique that should be used when adding the pellet of aquatic fertilizer to the submerged plant in the water garden pool?

Yes. After the finger pushes the harden pellet down into the soil, the finger is slowly retracted and the hole is covered with soil by the thumb. This will prevent the fertilizer chemicals from leaching into the surrounding water where it may cause problems with either fish or algae. Under the soil the pellet of fertilizer will become moist and dissolves as it feeds the aquatic plant.

171. Can the synthetic aquatic granular fertilizer be used instead of the pellet form to fertilize the water lilies or aquatic plants after they are growing in the water garden pool?

Yes, but a method of getting the granular fertilizer under the soil without removing the aquatic planting container from the water is necessary. The amount of granular fertilizer must be determined by the commercial producer as a dosage for aquatic plants. Too much fertilizer can burn the plants roots. The proper amount of granular fertilizer can be wrapped in paper and pushed into the soil near the roots similar to the commonly used hard pellets.

172. Why should the supplemental feeding of aquatic plants be made with fertilizer covered with soil?

Pushing the fertilizer into the soil will directly add nourishment to the roots of the aquatic plants but must be covered with soil. The aquatic fertilizer should not be allowed to leach in the surrounding water since it may promote the growth of undesirable algae or harm fish. Therefore, the technique of covering the fertilizer with soil in the planting container is recommended.

49

173. Is the solubility of the nitrate in most aquatic fertilizers effected by the temperature of the pond water?

No. The nitrates will dissolve easily in water at most temperatures.

174. During a very cool spell, should the amount of aquatic plant fertilizer be reduced?

Yes. In cooler weather the water temperature will correspondingly drop and slow the growth of the aquatic plants. This slow growth will result in less of a demand for nitrogen and the other ingredients of fertilizer. Adding more fertilizer can cause fertilizer burn to the aquatic plants.

175. Can "liming" be done with the soil to plant the water lilies in?

No. It is not recommended to use lime or add calcium compounds to the soil of aquatic plants to raise the pH of the soil since it may have a very adverse effect on fish and other life in the pool. Excessive amounts of lime can drastically increase the pH of the water.

176. Is there any preparation to make to the water garden before autumn?

Yes. If there are trees in the area that will lose their leaves in the autumn, these leaves should be prevented from falling into the water. The leaves will begin to decay and release methane gas which can be harmful to fish and other life. The use of a net (figure 28) to catch the leaves can be placed across the water garden pool. It is important to not have the net touch the water's surface if the water garden contains fish. If the net is touching the surface of the pool the fish can become entangled in the net and die. The net can be supported above the surface of the water in large pools with wood frames, ropes or other similar structures.

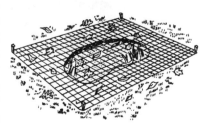

Figure 28. A net covering in the Autumn is an excellent method to keep unwanted leaves from entering the water garden pool.

IV. Water Lily Pioneers and Hybridization

* Hybridization * Water Lily Pioneers* Historic Books *

HYBRIDIZATION OF WATER LILIES

177. Why should the water gardener be familiar with water lily hybridization and the water lily pioneers?

To become familiar with our historic water lily pioneers and the hybrids they produced should be the goal of every avid water gardener. The water lily pioneers developed many water lily hybrids that are still unequaled in the industry today. Understanding water lily hybridization methods gives a true understanding of their accomplishments which, at times, seemed mystical but in reality shows their dedication and years of meticulous labor. Most aquatic authorities agree that "new" water lily hybrids introduced in the trade should be distinctly different from the former hybrids. This challenge is most difficult as seen from many "so-called" new hybrids that may have found their way in the water lily industry. Most names associated with the marvelous water lilies which continue to adorn our water gardens still carry the pioneer names: **Tricker, Marliac, Richardson, Sawyer, Randig,** etc. These names are associated with water lilies that have adorned our water gardens for decades. The beauty and labors of their success can still be enjoyed by all water

51

gardeners. To grow a water lily of a pioneer hybridizer is like having Monet paint your water garden.

178. How were the names of plants originally assigned in ancient scientific literature?

As far back as 300 B.C. man has been trying to classify and record plants. The father of botany **Theophrastus** (370-285 B.C.), who was a student of **Aristotle**, classified plants using Greek names based upon plant morphology. This method of classification stood essentially unchanged and scarcely enlarged for some 19 centuries until the development and invention of the microscope. Since that time, many noted individuals have contributed to identification and naming of plants which were recorded under different systems of classification. Much of the documentation was written in the standardized Latin. During this time the "law-less" names of plants were used, i.e. *Victoria foliis orbiculatis, margine elevato, integerrimis glabris, supra reticulato-areolatis viridibus, subtus purpureis, nervis valde prominentibus aculeisque insturctis; sepalis extus atropurpureis; oetakus exterioribus virgineis, inteioribus roseis.* This became a cumbersome and rather difficult method to cross reference to newly discovered plants. By the way, the plant name in the example is an 1840 species description of the queen of water lilies the *Victoria* which is the vegetable wonder of the world.

179. When did the classification and scientific naming of plant "genus" and "species" begin?

Many of us are familiar with the two or binomial names used by scientists indicating the **genus** and **species** of plants or animals written in botanical Latin. This system was started in 1753 by **Carolus Linnaeus** (1707-1778) in his published *Species Plantarium* and for the first time all known plants were named according to a uniform system based upon the designation of two names each consisting of one word, i.e. *Nymphaea alba*, and thus the written botanical Latin was preserved.

180. Did the entire world use the same botanical Latin nomenclatural system as devised by Carolus Linnaeaus?

No. The world needed to agree on a uniform or standard method of applying the Latin names to plants. In 1867 **Alphonse de Canolle** (1806-1893), a botanist and strong advocate of botanical Latin used in classification, was charged by the International Botanical Congress at Paris to prepare a code embodying the rules to be followed by botanical nomenclature. This is considered the first attempt at standardizing and legislating of nomenclature in the world and was known as **First International Botanical Congress**.

181. Is it necessary to use botanical Latin names for aquatic plants rather than "common names" which are more familiar?

Yes. Most of us feel that it is unfortunate that "common names" are not accepted for every plant because it appears to be a more understandable and memorable use of identification. However, the main problem lies in the fact that not all common names are uniformly understood as representing the same plant which results in confusion and lack of uniformity. The scientific botanical name is often well accepted around the world and is used for only one plant.

182. If "common names" of aquatic plants are easier to remember and used quite often, why not accept them?

There are advocates of such a "common name" system, however it would be an enormous task and require the support and agreement of botanist around the world. The system used today has many imperfections that have been revised through the decades, however a new system would more than likely take decades of revision and may be a step backward.

183. Specifically, why are the "common names" of aquatic plants a problem?

The common names that are used with aquatic plants can result in confusion with different interpretations. For example the common name "cowslip" may indicate to some the aquatic plant "Marsh Marigold" (*Caltha palustris*) while others may consider it to be a "Primrose" (*Primula veris*). Some common names may appear that the difference is subtle, possibly due to the color of the flower which may not be true. There are over 200 types of the word "loosestrifes" used in common names which are unrelated. For example, the common names of two entirely different plants such as the "purple loosestrife" is *Lythrum Salicaria* but the "yellow loosestrife" is *Lysimachia vulgaris* which are found in two different scientific genera. The common names would indicate that only the flower color differs which is totally untrue, while the scientific name indicates that the two plants differ not only by flower color but have entirely different morphological structures. There are many examples of the misinterpretations of common names of aquatic plants versus their true scientific names and can only be resolved with the genus and species.

184. What does the phrase a "water lily species" mean to the water gardener?

To have a botanist define the word "species" seems rather elementary to a layman, however after generations of definitions no single answer exists. A species generally refers to the ability of a plant to interbreed within a specific group of plants and this becomes very subjective to discussion and argumentation. In general however, the phase **"water lily species"** refers to a particular type of water lily in the context of having a Latinized "genus and species" and is often found native to a geographical area, i.e. *Nymphaea alba,* a white water lily native to England. A water lily species in not a **water lily hybrid.**

185. What is meant by a "water lily hybrid"?

The "**water lily hybrid**" is a phrase used in describing the result of genetically crossing two unlike water lilies and obtaining new genetic features. The term **hybrid** is used to designate the offspring that results from crosses between plants belonging to different species or to distinct forms of the same species. Many water lily hybrids have their origins from the crossing of the water lily species or other water lily hybrids. Thus, the crossing of two water lilies produced the pure white flowered water lily hybrid *Nymphaea* 'Alice Tricker'.

186. What set of rules were used in the 1890s for scientific naming of plants?

Even though the **First International Botanical Congress** met in Paris in 1867 to standardize the nomenclature of plants, it was only a start. In 1892 a group of Botanists in the United States, under the leadership of a N.L. Britton of the New York Botanical Garden, developed a set of rules to govern plant nomenclature was presented in Rochester, N.Y. and became known as the **Rochester Code**. It was the Rochester Code that became popular in the early 1890s with many botanists in the United States.

187. What nomenclature system did the early water lily hybrids use in the late 1800s when water lilies were being introduced for the first time?

Attempts to follow the newly introduced codes by the botanist of the world were still not uniform in the late 1800s. Many of the early hybrids included the Latinized names of the hybridizers. For example, E. D. Sturtevant named his 1884 water lily seedling *"Nymphaea Sturtevantii"*; Marliac's 1887

"Chromatella water lily" carried his name *"Nymphaea Marliaceae chromatella"*; and William Tricker's 1892 "Victoria" was named *"Victoria Trickeri"*.

188. What rules are currently used for naming the water lilies?

After many more meetings around the world it was not until the close of the Cambridge Congress in England of 1930 that accord and harmony existed among the major botanical experts of the world and is known as the **International Code of Botanical Nomenclature**. Over subsequent years of many amendments in the International Botanical Congress, the water lilies as well as other plants follow the botanical names of plants governed by an internationally accepted rules found in International Code of Botanical Nomenclature in scientific literature.

189. How are the water lily hybrids written in the literature today?

The water lily hybrid is designated by enclosing the hybrid name in single quotes following the genus which is in italics. For example, the Tricker water lily hybrid commonly called named **Panama Pacific** is written as *Nymphaea* cv. 'Panama Pacific' or *Nymphaea* 'Panama Pacific' and the Marliac hybrid **Chromatella** as *Nymphaea* cv. 'Chromatella' or *Nymphaea* 'Chromatella'. The "cv." means cultivar.

190. How are the water lily crosses indicated in the literature?

The International Code of Botanical Nomenclature allows the name to be written by a formula or name. It is the formula name that would reveal a water lily cross indicating the parents. For example, the noted Tricker water lily hybrid *Nymphaea* 'Mrs. C. W. Ward' resulting from the cross of two water lilies would be written using a multiplication sign as *"Nymphaea flavo-virens X Nymphaea zanzibariensis rosea"*. The multiplication sign or "X" is pronounced "the hybrid species" and never like the letter "X". The resulting cross would be indicated as *Nymphaea* cv. 'Mrs. C. W. Ward', whereas the "cv" stands for "cultivar" or simply *Nymphaea* 'Mrs. C. W. Ward'.

191. If someone finds a water lily "seedling" that appears to be a new "hybrid" can that person name that hybrid?

Yes, but with extreme caution. If that person is not familiar with the multitude of hybrids that exist or have existed in the history of water lilies, the hybrid may not be new but may be already credited to someone else. There have literally been hundreds of water lily hybrids named in over a century of production. Most water lily authorities agree that a "new" hybrid should show distinctive different traits over the existing hybrids.

192. When did formal knowledge of genetics become known to the plant hybridizers?

In biology class in school we learned that an Austrian Augustinian monk by the name of **Gregor Mendel** (1822-1884) conducted many genetic experiments with a variety of garden peas beginning in 1856. He was able to predict the outcome of many of his crosses or hybrids while developing an understanding of genetics. In 1866, Mendel published his findings but it soon was forgotten since the scientific community of his day was unprepared for so radical a view of heredity. In 1900, when the details of cell division was worked out, Mendel's work was rediscovered by individuals who simultaneously and independently performed experiments that led to the same conclusions. These men were **Carl E. Correns** in Germany, **Erich von Tschermak-Seysenegg** in Austria and **Hugo De Vries** in Holland.

193. Did the early water lily hybridist use the knowledge of genetics in making the new hybrids before the publishing of the laws of Gregor Mendel?

Yes. It is interesting to note that many of the early water lily hybridist before 1900 were using the fundamental genetic laws of crossing before any formal rules were specifically recognized. It gives one a true respect and admiration for the early water lily hybridists who managed to discover new and exciting water lily hybrids that have survived decades.

194. What does "cross-pollination" and "self-pollination" in water lilies mean?

Cross-pollination is when the pollen (male part) of a specific water lily is placed upon the stigma (female part) of a genetically *different* water lily and fertilization may occur to produce fertile seeds. If pollen of the specific water lily fertilizes its own stigma then this would be known as **self-pollination**

195. Is there a difference in the hybrid water lilies that are produced from self-pollination than cross-pollination?

Yes. Self-pollination by water lilies is not a desired method of hybridization. This is a form of inbreeding. Horticultural geneticists realize that inbreeding by plants will result in weakness, loss of fertility, lack of vigor or other defects. Mr. Robert Sawyer, famous hybridizer and author from William Tricker, Inc., Independence, Ohio said of the famous water lily hybridizer M. Latour Marliac of France that *"Marliac crossed and recrossed the various hardy water lily varieties back and forth until they hardly knew themselves"*. Many of M. Marliac's varieties are sterile and may prove what Mr. Sawyer was indicating. Many of the M. Marliac hybrids have survived over the decades which resulted in superior crosses.

196. If many of our excellent water lily hybrids are sterile and cannot be reproduced by seed, how are they propagated?

Nature provides an excellent way to keep the water lily reproducing the same selected traits by the ability to produce **tubers**. The tubers grow and reproduce new plants without the production of seeds.

197. Do water lilies propagated from tubers produce identical plants?

Yes. The genetic makeup of the water lily is found in the tuber. Thus, vigor and other desired characteristics in the original plant are stored in the tuber. Thus, if the water lily tuber is cut into several plants, each plant produced will be identical.

198. If self-pollination of water lilies is not a desired method of producing a new water lily, would not this be occurring in the pond all of the time?

No, not necessarily. Some water lilies can self-pollinate while many do not. Nature realizes the problems that can arise from self-pollination and in many plants attempts to prevent this from occurring in our natural lakes and ponds. Some water lilies have **pollen** (male part) that matures at a different rate than the **stigma** (female part) on the same plant. Thus, when the pollen is ripe it must find a mature stigma on another water lily that will accept this pollen. This mechanism of producing viable seeds from two different parents is nature's way to forcibly mix the genetics of the plants within a specific geographical area in an effort to select a genetically superior plant to survive in a complex ecosystem. Nature can be considered a hybridizer with a goal to produce, after many thousands of years of plant generations, a plant that has superior survival traits. After many thousands of generations of crosses within a specific geographical area often results in producing a **true breed** or a plant that will continue to show the same characteristics of the parent plant regardless of self-fertilization or cross fertilization. The hybridizer can cross these geographical boundaries, such as countries separated by water, mountains, etc. and mix the genetics of these water lilies.

199. If a pond of natural water lilies produces "true breeds" from seeds, where do the new water lilies come from?

In certain instances **mutations** may occur and produce a superior plant within a true breeding population. This mutated plant may successfully compete with the current breeds. In addition, if the genetic barrier such as a mountain or water that separates the two different populations of water lilies is crossed, new genes can be introduced and begin producing a new hybrid. This can be a result of thousands of years of erosion of mountains, changing of river beds, animal seed dispersal, etc. With the interest in water lilies at the turn of the 19th Century, the water lily hybridist collected water lilies and artificially crossed nature's geographic barriers and began to mix the genetics of water lilies. This has produced many new varieties of water lilies that have lasted over 100 years.

200. Why are found or "chance" water lily seedlings not as desirable as hybrids made by individuals?

It is well known that self-pollination in the horticultural field often produces less desirable characteristics such as a less vigorous plants. A hybridizer uses the crosses to his advantage by selecting genetic traits that are desired. For example, if both plants selected for hybridization show excellent wintering traits during extreme cold winters, the hybridizer stands a good chance that this trait will be transferred to the new hybrid. However, a chance seedling produced by self-fertilization could, for example, inherit a non desired trait of a plant that will not withstand a mild winter. Nature could eliminate this chance seedling during years of different climatic conditions. Thus, a finder may be disappointed when the trait is displayed on this newly discovered "so-called" hybrid.

201. If a chance seedling or so-called "hybrid" is found in a southern climate, could that new water lily be inferior in a northern climate?

There is no control over the chance seedlings discovered anywhere. The chance seedling can easily be from self-fertilization of a hybrid and reveal a trait that was not shown in the parent water lily. The new water lily may show exciting different traits such as color, size, blooms etc., however some of the other traits such as vigor need to be proven before this water lily can be grown year after year. For example, questions arise if a newly suspected "hybrid" is from a self-fertilized hybrid water lily: Can this newly acquired water lily withstand the severe winter of the parent? Can it resist diseases as the parent? Can it withstand hot temperatures? Can it be planted in a hotter or colder climate? And the questions go on.

202. In selecting water lilies for hybridization, is it important to select a specific proven hybrid for crossing?

Absolutely! For example, in selecting a "yellow flowered" unnamed hardy water lily or the Marliac yellow flowered hardy water lily *Nymphaea* 'Chromatella' can have some interesting and disappointing differences of chance. The unnamed yellow flowered hardy variety can carry a genetic trait that does not flower well but grows rapidly. *Nymphaea* 'Chromatella' on the other hand grows well and produces an abundance of flowers each season and has very desirable traits. Selecting a known variety gives a better chance of producing a new improved quality plant with desired genetic traits.

203. Can a newly introduced water lily hybrid describing a "so-called" different flower color and growth be considered a new quality water lily?

Possibly. Before introducing a "new" water lily hybrid it must be tested and grown in a variety of conditions. A new introduction may display a particular flower color and growth pattern dependent upon the environmental or climatic conditions. The depth and temperature of the water, fertilizer or soil quality and many other environmental concerns may make this so-called "new" hybrid appear different from its parent but can easily be the result of **acquired characteristics** which are **NOT** genetic characteristics. For example, acquired characteristics can show a deeper red color of flower than the supposed parent, smaller or larger flowers, thicker leaves, deeper mottling of leaves, etc. all of which can be derived or acquired from the growing environment. Even if the hybrid was developed and grown in the same location, it still must be grown in different environmental conditions. A mild winter may allow the new hybrid water lily to survive and a harsh winter may kill the water lily. After over 100 years of hybridization of water lilies, many varieties have proven records of superiority. This is why old favorites or the old proven hybrids are often the best water lilies to grow. Many authorities in the field will only accept distinctly different hybrids as a "new" hybrid.

204. Were the early water lily hybridizers aware of how the new hybrids were created?

Yes. In 1905 Dr. Henry S. Conard, University of Pennsylvania, addressed this concern. He considered that there were two types of hybrids with water lilies: **accidental** and **artificial**. He defined the accidental hybrid as cross-pollination or self-pollination by insects or mutation. Dr. Conard defined artificial pollination as a deliberate methodology of crossing by individuals, hybridizers, of selected varieties of water lilies.

205. Did our early authorities on water lilies believe that a found or "chance" water lily seedling is not a "hybrid in the true sense"?

Yes. It is the meticulous and tedious work of a hybridizer crossing different varieties of water lilies and not the "finding" of a water lily seedling which was considered by our early authorities a "hybrid in the true sense". As far back as 1894, one of America's first aquatic specialist **Edmund Sturtevant** admitted in the literature that his famous water lily *Nymphaea* 'Sturtevantii' introduced in 1880 was not a "*hybrid in the true sense*". He stated that there was no attempt to cross a parent plant with another water lily. In fact, Mr. Sturtevant adds that there was no other water lily growing in close proximity of the parent and since it was a "chance" seedling it can be assumed to be a product of self-fertilization.

In 1905, Dr. Henry Conard refutes that the "hybrid" water lily *Nymphaea* 'Devoniensis' by Sir Joseph Paxton introduced in 1851 is a "so-called" hybrid since it was probably produced by self-fertilization.

206. Did the early hybridists of water lilies use the basic rules of genetics in their hybridization?

Yes. The works of the early hybridists made laborious attempts to adhere to the basic rules of plant genetics. They made sincere attempts to cross only water lilies that exhibited desirable characteristics. They selected plants with good growing characteristics, reproducible qualities, flowering qualities, flower color, disease resistant, etc. and tried to "make" a new and exciting water lily hybrid. "True" hybridization required long and tedious hours with meticulous record keeping. This is required if the crosses are to be monitored for the desirable characteristics.

207. How does a water lily hybridizer select a water lily to cross?

The hybridizer will select two water lilies that have many outstanding plant characteristics or traits. These traits can be flower color, number of flower petals, hardiness, size, leaf structure, etc. The hybridizer hopes to reproduce the best desirable traits from each water lily into a single plant.

208. After the hybridizer has selected the particular water lilies to cross, how is fertilization accomplished?

The selected water lilies to hybridize are manually crossed by the hybridizer by taking the pollen from one parent water lily plant is placed upon the stigma or female part of the other plant. This is commonly done with a fine haired brush.

209. How can the hybridizer be sure that "self-pollination" does not occur?

The flower that is to produce the seed capsule will have the **stamens** (pollen producers) removed on the first day of bloom before the pollen is manually transferred. On the first day of bloom the pollen is not developed or "ripe" so any accidental dropping of pollen on the **stigma** (female part) will not effect the water lily by self-fertilization.

210. How can the hybridizer be sure that an insect does not bring unwanted pollen from another water lily?

After removal of the stamens, the seed bearing water lily flower must be covered to protect from air borne pollen or insects carrying pollen. This was done by the water lily pioneer William Tricker in the early 1890s by using a wire screen in the shape of a hood. William Tricker would select the two water lilies for hybridization, one which would provide the pollen and the other the stigma. He would either shake the pollen of one plant over the stigma of the other or cut off the stamens of the one plant and place into the nectar on the stigma of the other. The flower that was artificially pollinated is covered with a wire screen hood . If within a few weeks the cross is successful, the seed capsule will swell. Today, similar methods are used.

211. How does the water lily hybridizer know that the cross was successful?

In about a week, depending upon the water lily variety, if the cross is unsuccessful the seed pod and stem will begin to rot or decay. If the cross is successful the seed pod will begin to swell and lower into the water as the seeds develop. In another two or three days the seed pod will raise to the level of the water and burst releasing the seeds that are floating in a gel.

212. What is the size of water lily seeds?

The water lily seeds are small and round varying from the size of tiny grains of sand to the larger size of the *Victoria* which is the size of a pea.

213. If many of the well known water lily hybrids do not produce fertile seeds, what water lilies are best selected in the crosses?

Many of the native water lily species are used to produce either the pollen (male part) or used as a receptacle (female part) for crossing. For example, some of the more popular tropical water lilies used in crossing is *Nymphaea elegans, N. capensis* and *N. capensis zanzibariensis* and some popular hardy varieties that have been used is *Nymphaea odorata* and *N. alba.*

WATER LILY PIONEERS

214. When did hybridization of tropical water lilies begin in England?

In 1851 a red flowered tropical night bloomer was introduced by **Sir Joseph Paxton**, head gardener to the Duke of Devonshire at Chatsworth, England and was named *Nymphaea* 'Devoniensis'. There is some question if this was a "true hybrid" since it was assumed to be a discovered seedling. Dr. Henry S. Conard, University of Pennsylvania, in his 1905 book *The Waterlilies* questions the validity of being a hybrid or a "so-called hybrid" of a self-fertilized seedling of *Nymphaea rubra*. However, this "hybrid" is sometimes considered the beginning of water lily hybridization.

215. When did hybridization of tropical water lilies begin in America?

One of America's oldest "hybrids" is *Nymphaea* 'Sturtevantii' introduced by **E. D. Sturtevant** of Bordentown, New Jersey in 1880. In 1894 Mr. Sturtevant stated that he did not consider his tropical night bloomer a "*hybrid in the ordinary sense of the term*". He said it was a seedling from a known "hybrid" at that time, *Nymphaea* 'Devoniensis' which was produced in England in 1851.

William Tricker began to hybridized tropical water lilies in the early 1890s. These hybrids were known to be recorded with documented parentage, a classical step to true hybridization of water lilies. By 1895, William Tricker had produced and distributed five noted hybrids which were named accordingly: *Nymphaea* 'Columbiana' (1894), *N.* 'Smithiana' (1893), *N.* 'Deaniana' (1894) and *N.* 'Delicatissima' (1894).

216. What is meant by a "Tricker Hybrid"?

This refers to the water lily hybrids that **William Tricker** (1852-1916) created beginning in the 1890s and includes the hybrids produced by associated individuals of his company William Tricker, Inc.® which was established in 1895. Some of the outstanding Tricker hybridizer's were **Robert Sawyer, Albert Buskirk, Gilbert Lambacher** and **W.G. O'Brien**. Examples of some popular and well known Tricker hybrids are: *Nymphaea* 'Blue Beauty', *N.* 'Panama Pacific', *N.* 'Independence', *N.* 'Mrs. Robert Sawyer', *N.* 'Patricia', *N.* 'Firecrest', *N.* 'Mrs. C.W. Ward' and *N.* 'Shirley-Ann (color plate I). These hybrids are known throughout the world.

Figure 29. William Tricker   1852-1916.
Founder of William Tricker, Inc.®

217. Is the William Tricker, Inc.® nursery of Independence, Ohio with aquatic greenhouses on the original property?

Yes. In the 1840s the property that the historic aquatic greenhouses and ponds at William Tricker, Inc.® are located was originally owned by William Buskirk and subsequently passed on to his grandson Albert Buskirk (1874-1953), a horticulturist and businessman. Albert Buskirk had an interest in aquatics and established a nursery at the turn of the 19th century. A natural spring from the adjacent sandstone rock quarry not only supported ponds full of water lilies but was used to feed his aquatic greenhouses. In the 1920s, Albert Buskirk's aquatic nursery and the William Tricker company of Arlington, N.J. became well known for selling aquatic plants throughout the nation competing in the horticultural literature. In 1927 a milestone was made when both companies merged and incorporated as "William Tricker, Inc.®" under Ohio laws and became the largest producer and supplier of water lilies in America. All mail and advertising was directed to the main Independence location. In 1986 the branch at New Jersey was sold, however the main property of William Tricker, Inc.® at Independence, Ohio remains a historical landmark to water lily culture. The historic aquatic greenhouses, with sandstone foundations from the old abandoned adjacent 1850s sandstone quarry, are still standing and growing century old Tricker hybrid water lilies fed from the original spring. Visiting William Tricker, Inc.® today is much the same as it was during the tremendous interest that was stimulated in the 1920s when water gardening was coming into fashion.

218. How many water lily hybrids were created by William Tricker?

William Tricker himself is created over 10 worthwhile tropical water lily hybrids that were sold or distributed in the trade. The company he began in 1895, which latter became known as William Tricker, Inc.®, is still producing new water lily hybrids and has contributed over 22 worthwhile and proven tropical water lily hybrids.

219. What are the names and years of introduction of the early water lily hybrids that were developed by William Tricker?

William Tricker is credited with such tropical water lilies as *Nymphaea* 'Trickeri' (1893), *N.* 'Smithiana' (1893), *N.* 'Deaniana' (1894), *N.* 'Delicatissma' (1894), *N.* 'Blue Beauty' (1896), *N.* 'William Stone' (1899), *N.* 'Mrs. C. W. Ward' (1900), *N.* 'Mrs. Woodrow Wilson' (1914) and *N.* 'Panama Pacific' (1914).

220. Were there any other well known hybridizers before William Tricker that produced day blooming tropical water lilies that are popular today?

No. According to Dr. Henry Conard, in the early 1860s a well known German tropical water lily hybridizer by the name of **Professor Robert Caspary** (1818-1887) at the University of Konigsberg, Germany devoted much attention to the hybridization of tropical day blooming water lilies but the results were not preserved. Since Mr. Tricker went on to establish a commercial aquatic company in 1895 many of his select hybrids were preserved and are still being sold today. Therefore William Tricker was a true pioneer not only in hybridization but preservation of tropical water lilies throughout the world.

221. What is meant by "Marliac Hybrids"?

These are hardy water lily hybrids that were developed by **Monsier Bory Latour-Marliac** (1830-1911) of France that have received many awards and honors. He was the son of a distinguished French botanist. His estate was located at Temple Sur Lot in France where he had about 800 ponds devoted to water lilies and aquatic plants which were sold around the world. M. Latour-Marliac began crossing hardy and tropical water lilies in 1879. After his death, his grandson, **Monsier Jean Laydeker** (1887-1974), continued to introduce and name some of his remaining hybrids which are known as the **Laydekeri Group**. Thus, his establishment continued to introduce new hardy water lily hybrids after his death. All of his hybrids are also commonly referred to as **Marliac hybrids**. The Marliac hybrids continue to be some of the most beautiful and unusual hybrid water lilies known today.

222. What was the first water lily hybrid by M. Latour-Marliac?

In his own written testimony, beginning in 1879 M. Latour-Marliac crossed unsuccessfully the water lilies he had in cultivation. Soon afterward he successfully crossed *Nymphaea pygmaea alba* (white flower) with the pollen of *Nymphaea rubra Indica* (red flower). This resulted into a beautiful water lily with deep red flowers. However, to his disappointment the plant did not produce seed or offsets and died. Thus, the first cross of M. Latour-Marliac that produced a water lily hybrid was in 1879.

223. Is the horticultural establishment of M. Latour-Marliac still in existence?

Yes. The property of M. Latour-Marliac is located in southern France in a town known as Temple Sur Lot and is currently under ownership of Stapley Water Garden, England who renovated the property in 1995.

224. How many water lily cultivars did M. Latour-Marliac create?

M. Latour-Marliac began his aquatic establishment in 1879. It is estimated that he produced at least 90 worthwhile varieties in the next 39 years of his life. Seedlings left by M. Latour-Marliac after his death and the introduction of his cultivars by his grandson Laydeker would add another approximate 20 more cultivars.

225. What is considered the first popular hardy water lilies distributed in America from M. Latour-Marliac of France?

In 1887, M. Latour-Marliac introduced to America two hardy water lily yellow cultivars in 1887, *Nymphaea* **'Sulphurea'** and *N.* **'Chromatella'**. In 1889 the literature in American began to respond to the Marliac hybrid *Nymphaea* 'Chromatella' by giving testimonials and comments as to the growth and admiration. In August of 1889, the noted water lily specialist E. D. Sturtevant was observing the flower and growth in Bordentown, New Jersey. In 1890 Mr. Sturtevant introduced the Marliac hybrids to America in the literature and trade specifically noted as: *Nymphaea Marliacea chromatella* (yellow flower), *N. Marliacea* var. *rosea* (pink flower) and *N. Marliacea* var. *carnea* (light pink flower).

Figure 30. Reproduced plate from William Tricker's *The Water Garden* published in 1897 of *Nymphaea Marliacea chromatella*. This M. Marliac hybrid still is a leader among the hardy water lilies in water gardens around the world.

226. What was the parentage of the popular *Nymphaea* 'Chromatella'?

M. Latour-Marliac claimed in 1894 that the parentage of *Nymphaea* 'Chromatella' was *Nymphaea alba*, a hardy white flowered water lily species, fertilized by the pollen of the yellow flowered semi-hardy American species *Nymphaea flava*.

227. Was the Marliac hybrids accepted immediately in the United States?

No. In 1890 the leading aquatic experts such as William Tricker, J. N. Gerard and Edmund D. Sturtevant published their comments on the new Marliac water lily hybrid introductions in the United States. It appeared that the experts were cautious with the newly introduced hybrids of M. Latour-Marliac. William Tricker commented in 1890 that the well known yellow *Nymphaea Mexicana* was flowering more freely then the "supposed" (quotations supplied by author for emphasis) hybrid of M. Latour-Marliac's newly introduced *N.* 'Chromatella'. As *Nymphaea* 'Chromatella' became more familiar growing in the gardens at several locations it soon became known as the "handsomest" of the aquatic plants. In fall of 1891 J. N. Gerard said that *'Nymphaea chromatella' is far the best yellow 'Nymphaea', a strong grower, easily propagated from its numerous eyes, and constantly in bloom."* It was definitely on its way to become a legend around the world.

228. Did M. Latour-Marliac reveal his water lily crosses to the public?

No. Much guessing was made as to the parentage of the hybrids from Marliac. In 1893 William Tricker published guesses as to the origin of some of the Marliac hybrids. M. Latour-Marliac rejected many of the parentage guesses by William Tricker. Finally, William Tricker commented as to the origin of *Nymphaea* 'Chromatella' that *"of its' parentage, however, I cannot make a guess, and Mr. Marliac keeps it a secret"*. Later, M. Latour-Marliac does give some alleged parentages but in 1895 William Tricker still claims that many of his crosses are in *"considerable obscurity"*. In 1905 Dr. Henry Conard in his book *Waterlilies* says that *"So great was Marliac's lead in this work, and so carefully did he guard his secret of success, for trade reasons..."* and *"The parentage of the Marliac hybrids is a matter of speculation"* indicates that Marliac did keep his hybrids a secret.

229. Since William Tricker in America was concentrating on introducing new tropical water lilies in the 1890s, is there any other noted individual in America introducing any hardy water lily varieties during this time?

Yes. Of Irish decent was an individual named George Richardson (1856-1925) of Lordstown, Ohio (which is located approximately 30 miles from William Tricker, Inc.®, Independence, Ohio) who began cultivation of water lilies and other aquatic plants in 1880 on a 50 acre farm. He later began a water lily establishment which sold his aquatic plants and was known for his famous water lilies throughout the world.

Figure 31. George Richardson 1856-1925

230. What water lilies is credited to George Richardson?

George Richardson is credited with introducing two wonderful pure white flowered hardy water lilies known around the world. The first is an award winning white flowered hardy water lily that was introduced in 1894 and was named **Gladstone** (color plate IV). William Tricker named it botanically *Nymphaea Gladstoniana*. In 1911 this water lily received the distinguished Award of Merit by the Royal Horticulture Society in England. The other hardy water lily introduced in 1897 by George Richardson was a multi-petaled white flower named **Richardsonii**. William Tricker named it botanically *Nymphaea tuberosa Richardsonii*. Both are still sold and admired today.

231. Since M. Latour-Marliac became a world expert on hybridization of hardy water lilies, did his establishment have any water lilies of George Richardson?

Yes. George Richardson sent his water lilies all over the world. In the 1922 trade catalog of M. Latour-Marliac both *Nymphaea Gladstoniana* and *N. tuberosa Richardsoni* are listed with credit to Mr. Richardson. In the catalog, the description for *N. tuberosa Richardsoni* is described as a "very distinct variety of great merit".

232. What became of George Richardson and his property that grew such famous water lilies?

In the 1880s George Richardson wrote and published articles about his water lilies and lotus on his property and had received many visitors to witness these new and wondrous plants. He became known as an expert on growing aquatic plants and sent his plants all over the world. His father died when he was only a month old and his mother and only brother also passed away before his death in 1925. George Richardson never married and subsequently had no children. The property of George Richardson is currently owned by a government facility in Ohio and has since been converted to a school nature center. Interestingly, ponds with water lilies are still existing and are fed by the original spring water rushing out of the ground that nourished the truly wonderful water lilies discovered so long ago by George Richardson. The author has walked this property and can only imagine the excitement at this very location that must have occurred over 100 years ago as individuals experienced water lilies and lotus for the first time.

233. At the turn of the 19th Century, who was considered the leading water lily hybridizers in the world?

According to Dr. Henry S. Conard in his 1905 *The Waterlilies* he states that no one else has done so much for hardy water lilies as **M. Latour-Marliac** of France. As for the tropical water lilies he states that **Mr. William Tricker** is the acknowledged leader in America.

234. Who continued to hybridize tropical water lilies after the death of William Tricker in 1916?

George Harry Pring (1885-1969) of the Missouri Botanical Garden introduced his first tropical water lily hybrid in 1917 and soon became noted for his many wonderful tropical water lily hybrids that followed. His hybrids were all introduced through the William Tricker Company under the presidency of Charles Tricker (1890-1961) the son of the late William Tricker. George Pring used water lily hybrids in his hybridization program developed by hybridizers of the William Tricker Company.

235. What is meant by "Pring Hybrids"?

In 1906 George Harry Pring (1885-1969) arrived from England as a graduate of the famous Queen's School of the Royal Botanic Gardens at Kew, London and was employed at the Missouri Botanical Gardens, St. Louis, Missouri. He became superintendent in 1928 and retired in 1963. During his 57 years at the gardens he focused mainly on developing new tropical water lily hybrids which became known as "**Pring hybrids**".

236. How many significant tropical water lily hybrids did George Pring produce at the Missouri Botanical Gardens?

George Pring is credited with over 30 noted tropical water lily hybrids.

237. Did George Pring use any other water lily cultivars besides his own for his crosses?

Yes. For example, George Pring used the Tricker viviparous hybrid *Nymphaea* 'Independence' which was produced in 1927 by Mr. Robert Sawyer, William Tricker, Inc.®, Independence, Ohio.

69

238. What hybrids did George Pring produce using the Tricker hybrid *Nymphaea* 'Independence'?

The Tricker viviparous hybrid of *Nymphaea* 'Independence' (1927) which has beautiful rich pink blossoms with an abundance of petals and a very good bloomer was used by George Pring in hybridizing several of his water lilies. It was this very hybrid, *Nymphaea* 'Independence', that George Pring used to produce several good hybrids that are still popular today. The noted hybrids produced that use the parentage of *Nymphaea* 'Independence' were *Nymphaea* 'Director George T. Moore', *N.* 'Pink Platter', *N.* Bagdad, *N.* 'Rio Rita' (color plate VI) and *N.* 'Peach Blow' all introduced in 1941.

239. Did George Pring keep records of his water lily crosses?

Yes. As a leading water lily hybridizer, George Pring kept accurate records of his water lily crosses. He made many crosses and recorded his results as he attempted to produce some of the finest tropical water lily hybrids in his time. Many are still in the trade today and continue to bring beauty to our water gardens.

240. When George Pring was hybridizing water lilies, was there any other well known hybridizer?

Yes. Another well known hybridizer was **Martin E. Randig** (1897-1967) who started an aquatic nursery in San Bernadino California in 1918. He took the world of tropical water lily hybrids to a new height with spectacular significant introductions.

241. How many tropical water lily hybrids is credited to Martin Randig?

Martin Rangid is credited with 28 wonderful tropical water lily hybrids.

242. Were there any historic milestones derived from the tropical water lily hybrids by Martin Randig?

Yes. Many of the Martin Randig hybrids became popular. One of the great accomplishments by Martin Randig was the hybrid *Nymphaea* 'Mrs. Martin Randig (1931) which became the second patented water lily in history in 1938 (the first being held by George Pring's 1933 patent of *N.* 'St. Louis'). *N.* 'Mrs. Martin Randig' is a beautiful purple shaded flower that is viviparous. It has the parentage of the very popular Tricker hybrid *N.* 'Panama Pacific' along with other hybrid genetics within the plant.

243. Were there any very unusual flower colored tropical water lily hybrids developed by Martin Randig?

Yes. One of the most unusual hybrids was *Nymphaea* 'Green Smoke' (1965). The flower is a wonderful yellow-green blue which is very unusual in the tropical water lily world of flower color. Two other tropical flower colors which show autumn colors that are rare in the flower colors are *N.* 'Afterglow' (1946) which has combined colors of deep pink, light orange and yellow and *N.* 'Golden West' (1934) which is a peach-pink.

HISTORIC WATER LILY BOOKS

244. What would be considered the oldest book introduced to the public on the subject of water gardening?

The Water Garden published in 1897 by William Tricker is considered the oldest water garden text in the world that was written to inform the public on the complete topic of "water gardens". This pioneer book was very comprehensive and advanced for the 1890s. In the 120 pages, William Tricker discussed planting and growing aquatics. He wrote to inform the public of his knowledge of hybridizing water lilies, explaining the different classes and distribution of water lilies and lotus, his new variety of one of the most unusual aquatics the *Victoria*, fertilizing aquatics, enemies of the water garden, along with many other water gardening topics. Spectacular photographs were also imprinted to show the public water gardens for the first time in this informative textbook.

245. Did William Tricker publish any other water garden books after his 1897 pioneer book *The Water Garden*?

Yes. He also completed another book in 1913 titled *The Making of a Water Garden*. This was not only a very small book in size, 4.5 inches by 6.5 inches, but contained only 51 pages. During this period, water gardening was beginning to become popular. It may have been a small book, however it was a very comprehensive water garden book for the novice water gardener and was special since it was written by such a well known noted expert during this time. The book was offered as one of a collection of several other general gardening books. This was William Tricker's last text before he passed away in 1916.

246.   What would be considered the earliest English technical book written on the comprehensive subject of water lilies?

One of the earliest attempts to identify and discuss the water lilies was written by **Dr. Henry Conard**, University of Pennsylvania, who wrote a monograph published in 1905 titled *The Waterlilies*.   The book is a comprehensive technical text for the botany professional during this period and is still used today as a reference for water lilies.   In the 279 pages, the book describes in great detail the world of water lilies with historical, taxonomic, developmental, structural, microscopic and cultural descriptions. The text has many detailed drawings from cellular structures of water lily cells to the identification of the different types of water lily.   It also has 30 very detailed and rare color plates of water lilies.

247. Did Dr. Conard ever write a general book on water gardening?

Yes. Dr. Henry Conard with Henri Hus in 1907 wrote *Water-Lilies and How to Grow Them*. This fine text not only describes in 228 pages the many types of water lilies existing at that time but also goes into detail on how to make a water garden pool and the use of accessory plants.   The book was written to be included in a collection of 12 garden books on various topics. In 1914 the hardback covered book could be purchased for $1.12.

248.   What water lily pioneers are documented in the historic books as leaders of the hybridization of hardy and tropical water lilies?

According to Dr. Henry S. Conard, senor fellow at the University of Pennsylvania, who wrote one of the most complete technical text on water lilies (*The Waterlilies* published in 1905) stated that two individuals were acknowledged as leaders with water lily hybridization, **William Tricker** of America and **M. Latour- Marliac** of France. He stated that M. Latour Marliac (1830-1911) during 1885-1890 produced magnificent hardy water lilies and William Tricker (1852-1916) was the "acknowledged leader" with the tropical water lilies. Since this statement in 1905, both individuals went on to continue to produce more new water lily hybrids and become well known in the culture of water lilies in the decades that followed.

249. Did the early textbooks written on the subject of water gardening include fish?

No. The early water garden books concentrated on making a water garden pool and discussing the culture and growing of aquatic plants.

250. What would be considered one of the first water garden books that included fish in the water garden pool?

Peter Bisset of Washington, D.C, wrote a superb text *The Book of Water Gardening* first published in 1907 and revised in 1924. Peter Bisset was an authority on water lilies and worked with the United States Department of Agriculture. The over 200 pages of text was very comprehensive on describing aquatic plants and is similar in format to that of William Tricker's water garden text published in 1897 and, in fact, used the same publisher. The text of Mr. Bisset, which differed from the early writers such as William Tricker and Dr. Henry Conard, had a final chapter of eight pages which discussed fish in the water garden.

251. When did fish and water garden pools finally get established in books?

At the turn of the century many water garden authorities suggested the addition of fish to the pool. However, it was not until the later 1920s when water gardening was increasing in popularity did fish keeping with water gardens become prevalent. **Robert Sawyer**, employee of William Tricker, Inc.®, Independence, Ohio with Edwin Perkins, a fish specialist, published in 1928 the text *Water Gardens and Goldfish*. While employed at William Tricker, Inc.® Mr. Sawyer introduced many wonderful water lily hybrids, both tropical and hardy. Mr. Sawyer was an author with experience. During this time, the William Tricker company was one of the leaders in not only supplying aquatic plants but supplying fish for water gardens around the country. The fish shipped in large metal cans of water on trains. It was known that the conductor of the trains would take care of the fish and even do water changes if necessary in route as they stopped along a stream. In 1927 W.G. O'Brien, aquarist for William Tricker, Inc.® and coworker of Mr. Sawyer, invented and introduced the pH test kit, a vital need for caring for fish as the hobby began to flourish. Mr. Sawyer was known for his many articles on water gardening in national magazines. The water garden text devoted much to the subject of the fish in the water garden pool. The direction of water gardening with aquatic plants and fish was now established and would last into the decades that followed.

252. As water lily culture developed over the decades was there any comprehensive book that was written on the subject of water lilies?

Yes. One of the most outstanding books written on the subject of water lilies was *The Encyclopedia of the Water-Lily* by **Charles O. Masters** published in

1974 and contained 512 pages. Charles O. Masters received his advanced degree from Western Reserve University in Cleveland, Ohio. He spent much time and research at William Tricker, Inc.®, Independence, Ohio studying the microscopic plant and animal life within their aquatic greenhouses.

253. Is the book *The Encyclopedia of the Water-Lily* by Charles O. Masters technical?

No. It was an excellent book that covered the subject of water gardening in detail with explanations using general terms. Charles Masters approached the subject of water gardening from a biological prospective, but was simple enough to allow an avid water gardener to understand the vast world of water lilies. He listed many of the water lily hybrids that were identified up to the time of printing and included brief descriptions with historical data. This book is still used today as a historic reference, not only for descriptive historic water lily hybrids but to some of the lost and unknown varieties of water lilies. It indeed has one of the most complete listings of bibliographies and periodicals on the subject of water lilies in existence today.

254. How is the word "water lily" written in the texts over the decades: Water-Lily, Water Lily or Waterlily?

It is through the past writings that show the variety of writing of the term "water lily". Of the historic books previously mentioned: William Tricker writes "Water lily" (1897), Dr. Henry Conard writes "WaterLily" (1902) and later used "Water-Lily" (1907), Robert Sawyer writes ""Water Lily" " (1928) and Charles O. Masters writes "Water-Lily" (1974). Today the writing of the word "water lilies" is still not uniform and can be seen as any of the three types in literature and books.

V. Day Blooming
Tropical Water Lilies

* Characteristics * Care * Selected Hybrids and Species * Viviparous *

CHARACTERISTICS

255. Why should the water gardener choose a day blooming tropical water lily for the water garden?

The tropical day blooming water lily is truly the aristocrat of the water garden. It grows extremely well and blooms profusely in the sunlight. The aroma of the flowers are wonderful. They can be enjoyed in water gardens in every state of the continental United States and Hawaii.

256. What flower colors are found in the day blooming tropical water lilies?

Contrary to the hardy water lilies, the tropical water lilies are

Figure 32. *Nymphaea* 'William Stone'. Hybridized by William Tricker in 1899 and still a favorite tropical water lily. Photograph taken in the early 1930s by hybridizer Robert Sawyer of William Tricker, Inc.®

75

characteristically known for having flowers in all the colors of the rainbow: blues, purples, pinks, whites, yellows and reds.

257. How big can the day blooming tropical water lily blossoms grow?

Tropical water lilies can become spectacular in size of blooms. Some tropical flowers can reach a size of over 12 inches across.

258. Are all of the day blooming tropical water lily blossoms large?

No. Like the hardy water lilies, there is a group of tropical water lilies that are found in miniature known as **pygmy water lilies**. The flowers of the pygmy water lilies are very small, approximately 1 to 2 inches across with corresponding small floating pads about 5 inches across.

259. Do the day blooming tropical water lilies have both single and multi-petaled varieties?

Yes. There varieties that have a single row of petals and have been referred to as **star lilies** since this morphological structure resembles a star (figure 32). The multi-petaled tropical water lilies have a profusion of petals that give an unique shape and mass of color to each flower. Both have a beauty of their own.

260. Do tropical water lilies produce blooms during the entire growing season?

Yes, tropical water lilies are known for their continual and tremendous blooming characteristics. A single plant will often have multiple blooms during the growing season. It is not unusual for the water gardener to have continual blooms on the tropical water lily the entire summer. The quantities of flowers produced in a growing season from a tropical water lily by far out performs the hardy water lilies. It is highly suggested that a grower of only hardy water lilies "tries" a single tropical water lily and experiences this spectacular display of flowers.

261. How long will a single blossom last on the tropical water lily?

Most single blossoms of a tropical day blooming water lily will last three to four days. After the three or four days, the blossom will close and the stem with the expired blossom will bend down into the water. Since the tropical water lily has many blooms at one time and the expired blossoms are hidden below the water level, the continual cycle of blooming usually goes unnoticed. The water lily will appear as if it always has blooms.

262. Do tropical water lilies have strong fragrances?

Yes, this is an outstanding characteristic of tropical water lilies that is most desired by the water gardener.

263. Can tropical day blooming water lily blossoms be cut and brought indoors?

Yes. The tropical water lily flowers, preferably first day blooms, can be cut at the bottom of the long stem and brought indoors. A first day bloom can be recognized by the nectar, which is a clear water-like fluid, seen in the center of the flower. The cut flowers can be brought indoors and placed in a vase with water. The tropical water lily blossoms will continue to open and close as if outdoors. They will emit their beautiful fragrance which permeates throughout the rooms.

264. How can one keep the day blooming tropical lily cut flower to remain open in the evening?

To enjoy the cut tropical water lily in the evening, the flower must be prevented from closing during the night. This can be accomplished by putting a drop of melted wax from a candle between the petals and sepals while the flower is open. The wax will act as a door jam and keep the flower open both day and night.

265. Are cut tropical water lily blossoms placed in a vase or floated in a dish of water?

Both. Cut tropical water lily blossoms can be placed in a vase with water since they have long stout stems to hold up the flowers. By cutting the stems at the base of the flower, they can also be floated in a dish of water on a table. Both methods produce a most satisfactory and interesting addition to any home.

266. Are all of the tropical day blooming water lily pads solid green?

No. The variety of tropical water lilies have either solid green pads or **mottled** pads. Mottled varieties are green with blotches or variegation of brown to rust coloration. The solid green coloration also varies, such as bright green, dark green and olive green. The water lily pads often complement the flowers and are specific to the identification of the variety.

267. Are the margins of the tropical day blooming water lily pads all smooth?

No. The margins of the water lily pads can vary among the different hybrids. Most of the margins are smooth while some have a wavy margin which is characteristic of the variety.

268. What makes the tropical day blooming water lily blossom open in the morning?

The main opening of the flower of a water lily is associated with sunlight.

269. Does the opening and closing of the tropical day blooming water lily flowers occur at the same time each day?

No. As the flowers becomes older they will open later the next day. In addition, overcast days can delay the opening of the flowers. Therefore, if the water lily flower opens at 10:00 A.M. today and if the sky is overcast tomorrow, the same flower may open much later than 10:00 A.M.

270. What part of the plant is associated with the opening and closing of the flower?

The opening and closing of the flower is controlled by the **perianth**. The perianth is the structure that protects the developing reproductive parts of the flower and is normally made of the **petals** and **sepals**. Thus, cutting the flower below the perianth and placing in a vase will still retain the natural opening and closing of the water lily flower indoors.

271. Do tropical water lily hybrids produce viable seeds?

Yes, but not all. In fact, many of the wonderful hybrid varieties of tropical water lilies are sterile. However some hybrid tropical water lilies can produce a variety of plants from their seeds. For example, Robert Sawyer, water lily hybridizer, has stated that the seeds of the beautiful Tricker hybrid *Nymphaea* 'Panama Pacific' (Tricker, 1914, color plate VI) can produce a wonderful surprise of different water lily plants.

272. Will a tropical water lily produced from seeds be identical to the original water lily?

No. The water lily offspring or seedling produced from a water lily hybrid will have a different genetic makeup derived from both of the parent plants. It may have different plant characteristics such as blossom color, blooming frequency, size, etc.

273. How long does it take for a tropical water lily seed to sprout or germinate?

The different cultivars and native varieties of tropical water lilies produce seeds that germinate at different rates and under different environmental conditions. It is not unusual for a ripe seed to sprout within a few days, while others may germinate in a few months. It truly makes one appreciate the time and effort used to produce new varieties of tropical water lilies when working with specific crosses.

274. Can a night blooming water lily be crossed with a day blooming tropical water lily?

The noted hybridist George Pring, Missouri Botanical Gardens, has tried innumerable experiments and has proven beyond much doubt that it can not be done.

275. Do the color of the outside of the sepals on tropical water lilies all look the same?

No. Some sepals on the outside are solid green while others have slight markings or variegation on them. The markings are characteristic of the variety and is used to identify certain true hybrids. These specific traits are often used to identify similar looking varieties.

276. How can the outside of the sepals with mottling be used in differing two tropical water lilies?

Two very similar looking tropical water lilies of the same color can be differed by looking at the outside of the sepals. For example, the two blue tropical water lilies *Nymphaea* 'Blue Beauty' (Tricker, 1896: formally *N. pulcherrima,* color plate 1) and *N.* 'Blue Bird' (Sawyer, 1927) can be differed by looking at the outside of the sepals. *N.* 'Blue Beauty' has markings of black lines and dots on the outside of the sepals whereas *N.* 'Blue Bird' are plain green. This trait is used by many water lily hybridizers and technical establishments to identify the most subtle of differences.

277. Where did the tropical water lilies that were used in early hybridization originate?

Most of the early native tropical water lilies that were used to cross pollinate and make new cultivars came from tropical regions of Africa and South America.

CARE OF THE TROPICAL WATER LILIES

278. When can the tropical water lily be planted outside?

The tropical water lilies require warm water to survive. Therefore, the tropical water lilies should not be put outside until the weather is warm enough to keep the water at a temperature of at least 70 degrees Fahrenheit. Danger of frost must definitely have passed.

279. What is the earliest month in the United States that tropical water lilies can be put outside?

In the United States in the latitudes of Chicago, Cleveland and New York, the tropical water lily can be safely placed outside during the first week of June. Southern states can put the tropical water lily out earlier based upon temperatures.

280. What happens if the tropical water lily is put outside too early and the weather becomes cold?

Cold weather can force the tropical water lily to go dormant or, more importantly, can kill the tropical water lily. Even if the tropical water lily recovers from the cold, it may succumb to a disease agent such as a bacteria or fungus. This disease may severely effect growth or kill it. Thus, waiting until the weather stabilizes is very important. A brief warm spell early in the season has enticed some eager water gardeners to put out their tropical water lily too early only to be disappointed with failure when the weather turns cold again. Since tropical water lilies grow extremely rapid, a delay in planting is often rewarded by a wonderful blooming and growing season when planted at the proper recommended time.

281. Is there a special location to plant the tropical water lily in the container?

Unlike the hardy water lily, the tropical water lily does not produce a tuber that will grow across the surface of the soil. Rather, it will produce a mass of roots. Thus, it is suggested that the tropical water lily is planted in the center of the planting container.

282. How often should the tropical water lily be fertilized?

Tropical water lilies are fast growers and require a good supply of fertilizer throughout the growing season. The commercial aquatic fertilizer selected must meet this demand and adhere to the directions of the manufacturer.

283. How can you tell if the tropical water lily is not fertilized properly?

Since tropical water lilies are excellent and constant bloomers, the first indication of lack of fertilizer is the reduction of flowers. Another indication is the yellowing of the water lily pads. Lastly, a tuber will begin to form from lack of nutrition.

284. Can the tropical water lily be overfertilized and "burned" from chemical fertilizers?

Yes. Too much chemical fertilizers can burn the roots of the tropical water lily and kill it. This is why the recommended amount of fertilizer from a reputable source should be followed. Quite often the tendency is that a little more fertilizer will promote better growth only to end in disaster. Fertilizers that are designed for other uses, such as grass or roses, should be avoided since they have different chemical formulations.

285. How can one identify a tropical water lily that is producing a dormant tuber during the growing season?

Carefully feel the area in the soil where the roots attach to the crown of the tropical water lily. If there is a small round and hard formation a tuber is being made and the plant is going dormant.

286. If the tropical water lily has begun premature dormancy what can be done?

If the water lily is fed with the correct aquatic fertilizer, receives ample sunlight and is in water that is at least 70 degrees Fahrenheit, it should begin to grow and come out of dormancy.

287. Can the tropical water lily be wintered in a northern climate?

It is best to treat the tropical water lilies as annuals in northern climates that will have ice in the winter. Many techniques have been proposed in hopes of wintering a tropical water lily. Unfortunately many of these techniques only cause disappointment in the spring. And to make matters worst, the attempt often produces a tuber that decays and harbors a specific water lily fungus or bacteria which can spread to other healthy aquatic plants in the spring. The manner of growth of the tropical water lily in the pool of the water garden during the year does not favor the advantage of wintering a tropical water lily. The methods used by commercial growers are far different than occur in the water garden pool. Thus, with all the types of beautiful tropical water lilies to choose from, life is too short to miss out on enjoying as many as possible.

SELECTED TROPICAL WATER LILIES
Hybrids and Species

288. Are there any tropical water lily hybrids that do not have the stamens in the center of the flower?

Yes, and can be seen in the unusual variety *Nymphaea* 'Midnight' (color plate VIII) which has a mass of rich deep purple petals. This hybrid has the stamens replaced with modified "stamen-like" purple petals. There are large petals on the outside of the flower and as the petals progress towards the center they become smaller. This unusual tropical water lily was hybridized by Mr. George Pring in 1941 at the Missouri Botanical Gardens, St. Louis, Missouri. It is a beautiful and distinct variety among the tropical water lily hybrids.

289. What tropical day blooming water lilies grow best in reduced light or in partial shade?

The following tropical day blooming water lilies have been selectively chosen by water gardeners over the decades as shade tolerate: *Nymphaea* 'Director George T. Moore' (George Pring, 1941: color plate VII), *N.* 'Dauben' (Dr. Daubeny, 1863, color plate VII), *N.* 'Panama Pacific' (William Tricker, 1914: color plate VI), *N.* 'Patricia' (W.G. O'Brien, 1927: color plate V), *N.* 'August Koch' (August Koch, 1922) and *N.* 'Independence' (Robert Sawyer, 1927).

290. What tropical water lily is known to have the largest blossoms and spread in the water garden pool?

Many of the tropical water lilies, if fertilized properly and planted in a large container, will make enormous blooms and grow to very large proportions. In 1917 George Pring introduced *Nymphaea* 'Mrs. Edwards Whitaker' which has been considered to have the largest blossoms of the water lilies with corresponding spread of pads. The satin-like brilliant light blue blossoms are known to reach 14 inches across. A single plant can spread 10 to 15 feet across the water garden pool. Other tropical water lilies that have large blossoms and spread across the pools are: *Nymphaea* 'Mrs. C.W. Ward' (William Tricker, 1900, color plate V), *N.* 'General Pershing' (George Pring, 1920) and *N.* 'Blue Beauty' (William Tricker, 1897, color plate I).

291. What would be an example of a popular pink "star" or single petaled day blooming tropical lily?

One of the most popular star or single petaled rose-pink tropical water lilies was introduced by William Tricker in 1900 is *Nymphaea* 'Mrs. C. W. Ward' (color plate V) and sometimes erroneously called *N.* 'Red Star'. Dr. Conard in his technical book *The Waterlilies* published in 1905 stated that *N.* 'Mrs. C. W. Ward' is the finest tropical day blooming hybrid available. *N.* 'Mrs. C. W. Ward' is still a favorite among the pink star-type water lilies.

292. What would be an example of a popular blue "star" or single petaled tropical day blooming water lily?

One of the most popular single petaled or "star" shaped day blooming tropical water lilies was introduced by William Tricker in 1899 known as *Nymphaea* 'William Stone' and has been reported to be erroneously called *N.* 'Blue Star' by some. Dr. Conard in his technical book *The Waterlilies*

83

published in 1905 wrote that *N.* 'William Stone' is the finest day blooming tropical water lily. *N.* 'William Stone' is still a favorite choice by water gardeners among the blue star water lilies.

293. Are there any day blooming tropical water lilies that have single blooms that last more than the typical three or four days?

Yes, a beautiful and unusual tropical day blooming water lily *Nymphaea gigantea* or "Blue Gigantea" (color plate VI) has a blue flower that will last up to a week.

294. Is *Nymphaea gigantea* a tropical "hybrid" water lily?

No. It is a water lily species that is native to the tropical lakes and marshes of Australia and New Guinea.

295. Is there any other types of "Blue Gigantea", *Nymphaea gigantea*?

Yes. The commonly sold variety is the "Blue Gigantea" or *Nymphaea gigantea* var. *gigantea* which has sky blue blossoms. There are other varieties that have white and pink colored flowers. These different colored blossoms have been identified as distinct varieties or hybrids by aquatic plant experts such as Dr. Conard.

296. Is the flower of the Blue Gigantea similar to the other tropical water lilies?

No. The sky blue flower of Blue Gigantea, *Nymphaea gigantea* is distinctly different from any of the tropical water lily blossoms, including the hardy water lily flowers. It is cup-shaped with inward curved stamens and petals. It actually resembles a lotus flower more so than a water lily flower.

297. Who is responsible for bringing the cultivation of the Blue Gigantea in the United States?

The Blue Gigantea was reported to have been introduced into the United States from Australia in 1852. It was displayed and grown in the early 1890s in the aquatic gardens of Mr. John Simpkins, Esq. of Yarmouthport, Massachusetts by the noted gardener Mr. James Brydon. However, it was not until the early 1900s that this rare and unusual plant found cultivation for the public in the United States.

Dr. Conard in 1926 writes that *"One is almost tempted to assert that all real progress is made by the amateur-the man or woman with a hobby and who devotes time and money and thought to that hobby through long periods of fruitless endeavor. A business venture rarely permits of such profitless persistence. At any rate, the amateur does not accomplish much both in novelty and publicity; and as peculiarly concerning the pioneer days of Waterlily culture there are two armatures who very notable contributions aptly illustrates the force of the assertion"*. Dr. Conrad was writing of the contributions of a rector of a church Dr. Houghton of Colorado and E. T. Harvey of Ohio who was connected with a leading opera house. These two individuals brought the Blue Gigantea into cultivation in the United States during the early 1900s. Both were amateur collectors of water lilies and each took an interest in water lilies and the magnificent Blue Gigantea.

298. What day blooming tropical water lilies have the most outstanding variegation or mottling in the leaves?

Many of the tropical water lilies are known for their striking variegation of the water lily pads. Some of the most popular and deeply variegated are *Nymphaea* 'Evelyn Randig', *N.* 'Bagdad', *N.* 'Pink Perfection' and *N.* 'Leopardess'.

299. What distinct flower color of tropical water lily was historically the last to be discovered?

Yellow. In 1890, a yellow tropical water lily was reported by a German botanist named Stuhlmann. The yellow tropical water lily was reported to have been found somewhere in eastern Africa but no one ever obtained it's seed or the plant. As tropical water lilies gained popularity in the 1920s, all major flower colors were offered except yellow. The yellow flowered tropical water lily reported by Stuhlmann became known as the *"lost yellow water lily"*. Since there were no yellow flowered cultivars, a search was made by the Missouri Botanical Garden to find this lost yellow flowered water lily. In 1929 George Pring of the Missouri Botanical Gardens received seeds from a yellow flowered specimen discovered in Africa. He was able to germinate a single yellow flowered variety from these seeds, but it had poor growing characteristics. He continued his hybridization in an effort to find a yellow flowered hybrid.

85

300. After the first yellow flowered species of tropical water lily was discovered, when was the first yellow flowered tropical hybrid water lily produced?

After 86 pollinations, George Pring was able to produce an outstanding yellow flowered tropical water lily in 1932. He named it *Nymphaea* 'St. Louis' after the city that the Missouri Botanical Gardens are located.

301. Since water gardening grew to great popularity in latter 1920s, how was the new 1932 yellow hybrid tropical water lily introduced to the public?

The excitement of introducing this fine new hybrid produced the headlines "Lost Tropical Yellow Water Lily was Found" in the 1933 water lily mail order catalog by William Tricker, Inc.® This first yellow flowered tropical water lily of limited supply and was offered in 1933 exclusively through William Tricker, Inc.® for $50.00, a hefty price to pay during the depression years in the United States. Today, the yellow flowered varieties of tropical water lilies are now in production and can be enjoyed by all at reasonable prices. *Nymphaea* 'St. Louis' remains a popular variety and can be admired as it was introduced in 1933. In 1963 *N.* 'Eldorado' (color plate VII) was introduced by Martin E. Randig and has wonderful lemon yellow flowers with mottled leaves.

302. What was the first patented water lily in the United States?

In 1930, the Congress of the United States passed a plant patent law that provided for the granting of patents to new and distinct varieties of asexually propagated crops that are not used in human consumption. It was not long after this law passed that the first patented water lily was the George Pring hybrid, the rare yellow flowered *Nymphaea* 'St. Louis' in 1933. William Tricker, Inc.® proudly became the exclusive distributor of this water lily.

303. Are there any blue flowered tropical water lilies found native to the United States?

Yes. There is a blue flowered tropical water lily *Nymphaea elegans* which was first collected in 1849 near Waco, Texas. The water lily is also commonly found through Mexico to Guatemala.

304. Are there any pygmy species (not hybrid) water lilies suitable for small water gardens or tub gardens?

Yes. One highly selected species is the *Nymphaea colorata* or commonly called Colorata. It produces purple to lilac flowers that are about four inches across with dark green, four inch leaves. It is most suitable for small water gardens or tub gardens. Colorata was used by George Pring in hybridization of tropical water lilies and has produced some fine varieties such as *N.* 'Director George T. Moore' (color plate VII) and *N.* 'Midnight' (color plate VIII).

305. What would be considered the deepest purple flowered tropical water lilies?

The water lily *Nymphaea* 'Director George T. Moore' (George Pring, 1941) and *N.* 'Royal Purple' (Buskirk, 1927) represents two of the deepest purple blossoms produced.

306. Are there any hybrid pygmy tropical water lilies?

Yes. There are a few popular hybrid tropical pygmy water lilies available for the small water garden or tub garden. *Nymphaea* 'St. Louis Gold' (Pring, 1956) and *N.* 'Royal Purple' (Buskirk, 1927) tops the list for two excellent pygmy tropical water lilies.

307. Were there any species (not hybrids) of a pure white flowered tropical water lily?

Yes. A Mexican species that has large star-shaped white flowers is *Nymphaea gracilis* (*N. flavo-virens*) was sold in the early 1900s. Until better hybrids were produced, this species was considered the only white day blooming water lily in cultivation. Hybrids such as the popular *N.* 'Mrs. C. W. Ward' (rosey pink flowers, color plate V) and *N.* 'William Stone' (rich violet-blue) were developed by William Tricker from *N. gracilis*.

308. When was the first pure white flowered tropical water lily produced?

George Pring produced the first pure white flowered tropical water lily in 1922 and named it *Nymphaea* 'Mrs. George H. Pring'. He crossed the species *Nymphaea ovaliflora* with another of his creations from 1917, the many petaled hybrid *N.* 'Mrs. Edwards Whitaker'. When *N.* 'Mrs. George H. Pring' was introduced into the trade, it was introduced as a plant that produces pure white flowers of good size, 13 inches, and can bloom in close quarters like one of the parents *N.* 'Mrs. Edwards Whitaker'.

309. Were there any other improved pure white flowered varieties of tropical water lilies produced after the introduction of *N.* 'Mrs. George Pring'?

Yes. An improved version of the *Nymphaea* 'Mrs. George H. Pring' was introduced by the William Tricker company in 1937 named *N.* 'Alice Tricker' (color plate V). It was named after the wife of Charles Tricker, the president of William Tricker, Inc.® It differs mainly by having larger blossoms and wider petals.

310. What is considered one of the best selling and oldest "blue" flowering tropical water lily sold today?

In 1896 William Tricker introduced one of the most popular light blue flowered hybrids, ***Nymphaea* 'Blue Beauty'** (previously named *N. pulcherrima*, color plate I). It is by far one of the most beautiful grown, spicy fragrant blue flowered tropical water lilies today. The contrasting dark green leaves are lightly speckled with markings and the sepals are irregularly striped dark red. The flower opens very early and remains open late into the afternoon, long after other water lilies have closed. If given enough space, *N.* 'Blue Beauty' can spread to great proportions in the water garden pool.

Note: Current literature may confuse the original 1896 hybrid of William Tricker's *Nymphaea pulcherrima* or *N.* 'Blue Beauty' with a 1901 hybrid of Dr. Henry Conard named *N.* 'Pennsylvania'. Both are very similar in appearance which reflected their common African native parents used in the crosses: *N. caerulea, N. capensis* and *N. capensis* variety *zanzibariensis*. Historical documentation clearly supports the existence of two different water lilies. William Tricker sold both *N. pulcherrima* and *N.* 'Pennsylvania' in the early 1900s under a description that *N.* 'Pennsylvania' had deeper blue flowers than *N. pulcherrima*. William Tricker selected the name *N. pulcherrima* from the botanical Latin ***pulcher*** meaning ***beautiful*** (with a superlative). Since many gardeners can not translate Latin, the translated English name 'Blue Beauty' would be more fitting and in the 1920s, *N. pulcherrima* was changed to *N.* 'Blue Beauty'. This name change was made according to the *Standardized Plant Names,* an attempt during this time to use English rather than Latin nomenclature. Thus, gardeners would now choose between either *N.* 'Blue Beauty' or *N.* 'Pennsylvania'. During thc tremendous increase in the popularity of water gardening in the 1920s, the William Tricker company introduced many of their new tropical water lily hybrids along with exclusive tropical water lily hybrids of George Pring. The subtle differences between the two water lilies, *N.* 'Blue Beauty' and *N.* 'Pennsylvania', were overshadowed by these distinctly different introductions and both began to be sold under either name. Within the last several years, however, *N.* 'Pennsylvania' has been reintroduced and the existence of these two historic water lilies can still be enjoyed.

311. What is the name of the first hybrid "red" flowered tropical water lily?

George Pring introduced what is considered the first of his red flowering group of tropical water lilies in 1941 named *Nymphaea* 'American Beauty'. It was a cross with the Tricker hybrid '*N.* 'William Stone' (a pink flower) and the species *Nymphaea colorata* (a blue flower). *N.* 'American Beauty' has reddish-pink petals in the flowers. Another beautiful deep red blossom was also hybridized by Mr. Pring in 1941 and named *N.* 'Rio Rita' (color plate VI). Both of these tropical water lilies display a brilliant red coloration. However, the deep apple red flower coloration found in their cousins the hardy water lilies is lacking. More work in hybridization of the red tropical water lilies is necessary to achieve the deep red flowers that are found in the group of hardy water lilies. The pink varieties, such as the beautiful *N.* 'Pink Pearl' (Koch, color plate VIII), demonstrate the transition from red coloration.

312. Besides the red, white, blue and yellow flowered tropical water lily hybrids, are there any other colors?

Yes. There is a yellow-green blue flowered hybrid developed by Martin Randig in 1965 known as *Nymphaea* 'Green Smoke'. This is a very unusual hybrid standing alone in its class. It not only produces a most beautiful colored flower but is a good grower.

313. Is there any sunset flower color of tropical water lily flowers?

Yes. There are a few tropical water lily hybrids that can be considered having "autumn" colors in their flowers. Two wonderful autumn flowered hybrids produced by Martin Randig is *Nymphaea* 'Afterglow' (1946) which has colors of deep pink, light orange and yellow similar to a beautiful sunset and *N.* 'Golden West' (1934) which has peach-pink blossoms. Another wonderful hybrid was developed by Dr. Birdsey and named after the "father of aquarium plants" is *N.* 'Albert Greenberg' (1969).

VIVIPAROUS TROPICAL WATER LILIES

314. What is meant by a "viviparous" tropical water lily?

The tropical water lilies have a group known as **viviparous.** This means that the water lily produces a new plant, called a **plantlet**, from the center of the water lily pad. Old literature also referred to these types as "leaf propagating" types. A few examples of viviparous tropical water lilies are: *Nymphaea* 'Dauben' (color plate 89), *N.* 'Blue Bird', *N.* 'August Koch', *N.* 'Independence', *N.* 'Panama Pacific' (color plate VI) and *N.* 'Janice' (color plate II).

315. When can the viviparous water lily plantlet be transplanted?

When there is at least three to four strong roots and the leaves are beginning to be developed the viviparous water lily can be transplanted to a container with soil.

316. How deep should the viviparous plantlet be submerged in the water garden pool?

There should never be more than a few inches of water over the top of the plantlet. Once the water lily becomes larger, it can be moved to a deeper location.

317. Can the viviparous plantlet become a new hybrid or different plant than its parent?

No. The plantlet will be genetically identical to the parent plant. If the water lily had blue flowers the plantlet will also have identical blue flowers; if the water lily had mottled leaves the plantlet will also develop mottled leaves, etc.

318. When should the newly transplanted viviparous plantlet be fertilized?

Once growth commences and the plantlet appears to have established a root system fertilization should begin. Since the plantlet is small, one-half dose of fertilizer should be used until it reaches full size.

319. Will the new water lily developed from the viviparous plantlet also be viviparous?

Yes, since it is genetically identical to the parent plant it will also become viviparous.

320. What is the name of the first hybrid purple flowered viviparous tropical water lily?

This honor goes to William Tricker for introducing the wonderful purple flowered *Nymphaea* 'Panama Pacific' (color plate VI) tropical water lily which was introduced through his company in 1914. It was named after the *Panama Pacific International Exposition* held in San Francisco from February 20 to December 4, 1914. As the buds of the flower come out of the water they are a bronzy green spotted with a reddish brown, opening rich, rosy red, which is quite pronounced in the full sun. When *N.* 'Panama Pacific' was first introduced, it held the claim of having a new and distinct flower color in water lilies. After decades of growing in water gardens all over the world it still remains one of the most attractive of all tropical water lilies.

321. What is the name of the first hybrid blue flowered viviparous tropical water lily (not pygmy)?

This honor goes to William Tricker for introducing the hybrid *Nymphaea* 'Mrs. Woodrow Wilson' in 1914. This water lily is the parent of other popular water lilies such as *Nymphaea* 'August Koch' (August Koch) which has a beautiful lavender blue flower which and was introduced in 1922.

322. What is the name of the first hybrid white flowered viviparous tropical water lily?

This honor goes to the Tricker hybrid *Nymphaea* 'Janice' (color plate II) produced by hybridizer Robert Sawyer of William Tricker, Inc.® and introduced in 1928. The introductory description as indicated in the William Tricker, Inc.® catalog is as follows: *JANICE: An exquisite pure white flower, bell shaped with many stamens. This tropical day bloomer is the finest achievement of modern nymphaea culture, being the first white lily to bear plants on its leaves as well as being superior to both the present white tropical lilies. The shape of the leaves is different from the star shaped 'Mrs. Pring' which was crossed with 'Independence' in producing this new variety."* It was introduced in 1928 for $5.00 a plant. Not only was this a major accomplishment with water lilies, but the first hybrid white flowered tropical water lily (not viviparous) was just introduced in 1922 (*N.* 'Mrs. George H. Pring').

323. What is the name of the first hybrid viviparous pink flowered tropical water lily?

This honor goes to the 1927 Tricker hybrid *Nymphaea* 'Independence' produced by hybridizer Robert Sawyer of William Tricker, Inc.® He named it after the small city of Independence, Ohio where he worked in the nurseries of William Tricker, Inc.® The 1927 introductory description in the William Tricker, Inc.® catalog is as follows: *INDEPENDENCE: It typifies our first and perhaps greatest novelty, a viviparous nymphaea of deep pink coloring instead of the regulation blue of its class. It has a gorgeous, full petaled flower that opens earlier and closes later than other day bloomers. The plant is vigorous in growth and free-flowering.* It was introduced for $5.00 per plant.

324. Are there any viviparous hybrid pygmy tropical water lilies?

Yes. The *Nymphaea* 'Dauben', which was introduced in 1863 by the German **Dr. Daubeny**, has light blue flowers that are one to three inches across. Another wonderful viviparous crimson flowered tropical hybrid was introduced by **W.G. O'Brien** of William Tricker, Inc.®, Independence, Ohio in 1927 and named *N.* 'Patricia' after his wife who had auburn hair. The flowers are very dainty ranging from one to three inches with complementing deep green leaves.

VI. Night
Blooming Tropical
Water Lilies

* Characteristics * Selected Hybrids and Species*

CHARACTERISTICS

325. Why is the night blooming tropical water lily known as the "working man's pleasure"?

The night blooming tropical water lilies are excellent for the day working person. By the time the day working person comes home to enjoy the water garden, the day blooming tropical and hardy water lilies are closing or have closed. It is the night blooming tropical water lilies that show their large blossoms in the late afternoon and can be enjoyed throughout the night. Sitting by the edge of the water garden in the evening moonlight is an experience beyond compare.

326. How does the moonlight effect the appearance of the night blooming tropical water lilies?

The moonlight or any artificial light make the appearance of the open night blooming tropical flowers a different hue or color than seen in the afternoon sunlight or early morning sunlight. A very mystifying color change is due to the reflective wavelengths produced by the moonlight or artificial light on the petals of the night bloomers with the dark surroundings. They often are described as glowing.

327. Of the night and day tropical water lily bloomers, which has a more aggressive growing habit?

The night blooming tropical water lily will outgrow a day blooming tropical water lily. If the two are planted in close proximity in the water garden pool, the pads of the night bloomer will typically crowd and cover the pads of a tropical day bloomer. The blossoms produced, however, are produced in great profusion by both. It should be noted that the night bloomer still needs full sunlight in the day time to achieve the spectacular growth and flowering traits in the night.

328. What mechanism effects the nightly opening of the night bloomers?

The reduction of sunlight will begin the opening of the night blooming water lily flower. Intense artificial light, such as outdoor lighting, can effect this opening.

329. Are the tropical night blooming water lily pads different from the day blooming water lilies?

Yes. The night bloomers characteristically have serration on the water lily pad edges and the leaves are much thicker with a leather-like texture. There is no mottling found in night bloomers.

330. Are there any blue or purple flowered tropical night bloomers?

No. There are only red blooms with accompanying shades of pink and pure white flowers found in the tropical night blooming family. Thus, it also can be stated that there are no yellow flowered night bloomers.

331. How long does a single flower last on a tropical night bloomer?

The flowers of the tropical night bloomers have similar flowering patterns like their cousins the day blooming water lilies. A single bloom will open and close for about three to four days before dying. There are constant blooms on the night bloomers during the growing season.

332. Are there any "pygmy" tropical night blooming water lilies?

No. The entire group of night blooming water lilies produce large plants with correspondingly large blossoms and spreading leaves. There are no pygmy types as found in hardy and tropical day blooming water lilies.

333. Do the night blooming water lilies produce more than one flower at a time?

Yes. Like the tropical water lilies they will produce a spectacular display of several blooms on single plant at one time.

334. Are there any tropical night bloomers that have mottled water lily pads?

No. The tropical night blooming water lilies characteristically have deep green and very leathery pads with serrated edges. There is no distinctive mottling of the leaves as found in the tropical day bloomers.

335. Are there any viviparous tropical night blooming water lilies?

No. There are no viviparous tropical night blooming water lilies.

336. Do the night blooming water lilies make dormant tubers similar to the day blooming water lilies?

Yes. Once dormancy is stimulated, the night bloomers will produce a tuber similar to the day blooming water lilies. The tuber of the day bloomer is generally a single bulb-like structure whereas the night bloomer will commonly produce a group of attached bulbs.

337. Are night blooming water lilies recommended for tub gardens?

No. The night blooming water lilies are aggressive growers and large plants. They will grow out of a tub garden and require more space.

338. Can tropical night blooming water lilies be used as cut flowers?

Yes. The night blooming tropical water lilies can be cut and brought indoors using the similar techniques as with the day blooming tropical water lilies (see question 264). They are extremely attractive in that they seem to take on a different mystical color in artificial light. Also, like the tropical water

95

lilies, can be waxed open so they do not close during the day. Unfortunately, the tropical night blooming water lilies do produce the aroma of a tropical day blooming water lily.

SELECTED HYBRIDS AND SPECIES OF TROPICAL NIGHT BLOOMERS

339. Did the ancient Egyptians have night blooming tropical water lilies?

Yes. The species tropical night bloomer *Nymphaea lotus* is the well known "Egyptian lotus" that is recognized in the over 5000 year old ancient Egyptian paintings and hieroglyphics. This plant should not be confused with the familiar named "lotus" of the genus *Nelumbo*. The Egyptian lotus has large six to ten inch white flowers and produces an abundance of fertile seeds.

340. Are "species" of night blooming water lilies the preferred plant of choice for the water gardener?

No. The night blooming species were first sold with the new hybrids in the early 1900s but have been replaced by improved hybrids. The Egyptian Lotus, *Nymphaea lotus*, was sold in the 1940s but was dropped in favor of the new improved night blooming hybrids that were produced.

341. Were there any night blooming hybrids derived from the species of the Egyptian lotus, *Nymphaea lotus*?

Yes. The well known and popular *Nymphaea* 'Juno' is a result of the hybridization of the Egyptian lotus species, *Nymphaea lotus*. It was introduced in 1906 under the name of *Dentata superba* referring to the fact that at one time the *N. lotus* was synonymous with another species *N. dentata*. The former species name was later discontinued in 1941 because of the standardization of names and remains as *N.* 'Juno'. This improved white night blooming water lily continues to be known as the "*most perfect flower developed by cultivation from the sacred Lotus of the Egyptian tradition*". The flowers, from 8 to 12 inches, have very broad, heavy petals that open widely revealing flat, saffron yellow stamens.

342. What is considered the largest hybrid tropical night bloomer?

The largest tropical night bloomer is *Nymphaea* 'Missouri' (color plate VII) which has huge pure white flowers ranging from 10 to 14 inches across and a single plant can spread over 8 feet across a pond. This night bloomer has been recognized for decades as the "largest" tropical night bloomer. *N.* 'Missouri' was introduced by George Pring in 1932 and named in honor of the state of Missouri where the Missouri Botanical Garden is located.

343. What would be considered one of the most popular tropical night bloomers?

The water lily *Nymphaea* 'Emily Grant Hutchings' introduced by George Pring in 1922 is considered one of the most popular night bloomers. This night blooming water lily has a rose-pink flower and is easy to grow.

344. What is the deepest colored red flowered night blooming water lily?

There are two popular red flowered night bloomers that have very deep red colored petals. The first, *Nymphaea* 'Red Flare' was developed in 1938 by Martin E. Randig of California and has very deep red colored blossoms. The second deep red variety is *N.* 'Antares' (color plate III) which was introduced by Mr. Patrick Nutt, Longwood Gardens, Kenneth Square, Pennsylvania in 1962. *N* 'Antares' was named after the largest star and red heart of the constellation Scorpius. The deep red blossoms of *N.* 'Antares' appears to glow in the moonlight. Both tropical night bloomers have proven to be excellent growers and bloomers.

345. What would be considered the oldest hybrid night blooming tropical water lilies in trade today?

The night bloomer *Nymphaea* 'Sturtevantii' (E.D. Sturtevant) introduced in 1884 and *N.*'Trickeri' (William Tricker, color plate I) introduced in 1893 represent some of the oldest night blooming water lilies sold today. Both of these have pink flowers and have adorned water gardens for decades.

346. Do all tropical water lilies follow the basic opening and closing pattern relative to the sun's rise and fall?

No. A very unusual "night blooming" tropical water lily *Nymphaea Amazonum* has a different blooming pattern of opening and closing than other tropical night bloomers. It blooms for two days. On the first day the flower

97

VI. Night Blooming Water Lilies

opens at approximately three o'clock a.m. and closes approximately six o'clock a.m. The second night the creamy white flower opens at 6:30 p.m. and stays open until approximately 6:00 a.m. the next morning.

VII. Hardy Water Lilies

*Characteristics * Care * Selected Hybrids and Species *

Figure 33. A clear glass bowl full of hardy water lilies. The flowers gently float on the surface of the water. Note the variety of distinctly different shapes of flowers that were chosen by Robert Sawyer, hybridizer. Photograph by Robert Sawyer, William Tricker, Inc.® circa 1930 (see questions 355 and 356).

CHARACTERISTICS OF THE HARDY WATER LILIES

347. Do the hardy water lilies bloom during the entire growing season?

Yes. The hardy water lilies will provide blooms all summer. In the autumn, the water lilies will reduce the blooms and develop a tuber for winter.

348. Do all hardy water lily flowers float on the water surface?

Not necessarily. In one situation, when the hardy water lily becomes crowded with other aquatic plants the **petiole** (leaf stalk) will elongate and cause the flower to rise a few inches above the surface of the water. There are a few varieties that attempt to keep the flowers a few inches above the water surface without a crowded condition, i.e. the yellow flower of *Nymphaea* 'Charlene Strawn'. Flowers held on stems high above the surface of the water, 12 inches or more, is a characteristic of tropical water lilies.

349. Does the color of the water lily pads of hardy water lilies look the same?

No. There are plain green water lily pads and **mottled** water lily pads. The mottling, blotches of brown and maroon on the green pad, is not as intense as found in the tropical water lilies. A good example of mottling in the hardy water lilies can be seen in *Nymphaea* 'Chromatella'. Most hardy water lilies have plain green pads.

350. Do hardy water lily flowers stay open throughout the night?

No, the flowers open in the early morning and close in the late afternoon. There are no night blooming hardy water lilies as found in the tropical water lilies.

351. Are there small varieties of hardy water lilies?

Yes, these are known as hardy **pygmy** water lilies. They produce smaller flowers and water lily pads that are only a few inches in size. The Marliac hybrids *Nymphaea* 'Yellow Pygmy', *N.* 'Sioux' and *N.* 'Aurora' are a few examples of the hardy pygmy water lilies.

352. What colors of flowers are found in the hardy varieties?

The color of the hardy water lily blossoms are red, white, pink and yellow with corresponding shades. There are no purple or blue hardy water lily blossoms as found with the tropical water lily blossoms.

353. What is meant by a "changeable" hardy water lily?

A special group of hardy water lilies are referred to as **chanageables**. These have blossoms that open as one color and gradually "change" or fade to another color in the successive days during the single bloom.

354. Do the changeable hardy water lilies depend upon certain environmental conditions in displaying their descriptive flower colors?

Yes. The temperature, sunlight intensity and fertilization appear to effect the pronounced changes seen in any of the changeable hardy water lilies. It has been observed that the same variety will show different color patterns and shades growing in different ponds.

355. What flower shapes are found within the hardy water lily group?

The shapes of the blossoms of the hardy water lily differ mainly by the number of petals. There can be a few single rows of petals or multiple rows of petals that make up the flower of the hardy water lily. Examine figure 33 and note the multiple petals in the flowers at the top and bottom of the photograph whereas the rest are considered to have single row of petals. Beginning at the top is the multi-petaled white *Nymphaea* 'Richardsonii' and continuing clockwise is *N.* Attraction, the multipetaled *N.* 'James Brydon' (color plate III), *N.* 'Gloriosa (color plate III) and a pygmy *N.* 'Aurora'.

356. Do hardy water lilies make good cut flowers?

Yes, they can be cut and placed into a bowl of water indoors (figure 33). They make an extremely attractive and an unusual display on a table. The cut blossoms will, however still maintain the opening and closing traits as displayed outdoors, that is, at night the blossoms will still close.

357. Since hardy water lily blossoms close at night, can the cut hardy flowers be kept open in the evening floating in a bowl of water?

Yes, using a simple age old technique. The water lily blossoms are collected during the day when they are open. A few drops of melted wax from a candle is dripped at a point where the stamens, sepals and petals are joined. The blossom can now be floated in the bowl of water. This wax technique will keep the blossom open and prevent it from closing in the evening.

358. Does the hardy water lily have any fragrance?

Yes, but not all have fragrances. The hardy water lily blossoms are not as well known for the fragrances as the tropical water lilies. Some hardy varieties have been described with a faint sweet licorice or apple smell.

359. Do all rootstocks appear the same in the hardy water lilies?

No. There are three distinct morphological types. The **tuberous type** which is similar to the root of a tree, being long and slender and has buds that develop into new plants as it grows. This type of rootstock is commonly found in our native species of water lilies which has been used to hybridize many new varieties that retain this rootstock. The rootstock of the well known hardy white *Nymphaea* 'Richardsonii' has a tuberous rootstock. Another rootstock is the **odorata type** rootstock which is similar to the tuberosa but has tuber-like branches. This is commonly found in the white species *Nymphaea odorata*. The final tuber is a mass of roots that are tightly packed together originating from a central rootstock and can be referred to as the **Marliac type**. These are commonly found in many of the Marliac hybrid water lilies such as *N.* 'Chromatella'.

360. Are there any "viviparous" hardy water lilies?

Yes, but not of the common leaf producing type found within the tropical water lilies. A viviparous hardy water that produces plantlets directly from the flower is *Nymphaea* 'Colonel Welch'. *N.* 'Colonel Welch' is known for its foliage and not flowering ability and thus not a widely desired water lily.

361. Is the viviparous trait in hardy water lilies the same as that of tropical water lilies?

No. The tropical water lilies are known for the "viviparous" ability of producing plantlets from the center of the leaves whereas any hardy water lilies

102

that are viviparous produce plantlets directly from the flowers. The water lilies that were able to produce a new plant directly from the flower were referred by horticulturists as **bulbels** and were described as similar to the bulbels of growth found in the familiar Easter Lily or Tiger Lily.

CARE OF THE HARDY WATER LILIES

362. When can the hardy water lilies be planted outside in the spring?

The hardy water lilies can be planted safely outdoors in the spring when the danger of frost is over. In the United States, the hardy water lilies can be placed outside in the latitudes of Chicago, Cleveland and New York safely in May. Southern states can put out hardy water lilies earlier.

363. Can hardy water lilies be planted anytime during the growing season?

Yes. It is best to allow the water lily to establish itself by planting in the spring, however plants with tubers can be planted late in the growing season.

364. Should the hardy water lily be planted differently than the tropical water lilies?

Yes. As the tropical water lily grows, it will make a mass of roots and is planted in the center of the container of soil. Whereas, as the hardy water lily grows, the tuber will tend to creep along the surface of the soil. Therefore, the hardy tuber should be planted skewed to one side of the planting container with the growing tip facing across the soil. It is not abnormal for the hardy water lily to grow completely outside of the planting container.

365. What happens to the hardy water lily plant when it is going into dormancy for the winter?

In the late fall the hardy water lily will begin to prepare for winter. This can be identified by the decrease in the production of flowers and leaves. In addition, below the water level the hardy water lily has been preparing for the winter by making a "winter tuber" that contains the stored food for new growth the following spring.

366. What should the water gardener do in the winter to protect the hardy water lily for next year?

The container with the hardy water lily tuber should never be frozen. Freezing the tuber may kill it. The container with the dormant water lily should be placed on the bottom of the water garden pool at the lowest point where freezing will not occur. Removing any dead leaves, by carefully cutting off approximately a few inches from the tuber, can be done and will not harm the tuber.

367. After wintering the hardy water lily in the planting container on the bottom of the pool, when should it be returned to the correct growing depth?

The wintered hardy water lily container can be placed back to the original location the following spring as soon as frost is no longer expected. Once the water warms up and sunlight increases in the spring, the dormant tuber will begin to grow.

HARDY WATER LILY SPECIES AND HYBRIDS

368. What makes a specific hybrid hardy water lily "popular" or a good grower?

To be a "popular" or a good growing hardy water lily, it should have many successful years of successful growing in a variety of geographical areas where they are subject to different environmental conditions. For example, a newly introduced hardy water lily that successfully grows in a particular state may not grow well in another state. The other state may have a different climatic winter or summer which can either suppress the newly found hybrid characteristics or even worst, kill the hybrid. There are available many proven hybrids that have adorned water gardens for decades in a variety of climatic conditions. The water gardener should be familiar with these proven varieties which are "popular" or "good" growers.

369. What is the name of the hardy white flowered water lilies seen growing in natural ponds or lakes in the United States?

In the United States there are two commonly found native hardy white flowered species (or subspecies) of water lilies located mainly in the eastern half. One is the **Sweet Scented Water Lily**, *Nymphaea odorata* (or *N. odorata* subspecies *odorata)* and the other is the **Tuberous Water Lily**, *N. tuberosa* (or *N. odorata* subspecies *tuberosa*), which is also found in the north western United States. Both are excellent seed producers and have produced a variety of similar water lilies that have been identified and named over the years as varieties.

370. Can the two native species of white flowered hardy water lilies be differed by looking at them growing in a pond?

It is difficult to look at the two native water lilies floating in the same pond and differentiate by an untrained eye. A close comparative observation and smell of the flowers can reveal the main differences of these type species. *Nymphaea tuberosa* characteristically has odorless flowers from four to nine inches in diameter whereas the *N. odorata* has sweet scented flowers which are smaller, approximately four inches in diameter.

371. Are there any other colors of native water lilies found naturally in the lakes and ponds in the United States?

Yes. From the natural crossing of the two white species of *Nymphaea odorata* and *N. tuberosa* produces pink varieties (i.c. *N. odorata* var. *rosea*) and other similar white varieties (*N. odorata* var. *gigantea* Tricker). Therefore, it is not abnormal to find a variety of pink and white water lilies growing naturally in our ponds and lakes throughout the United States.

372. What would be the first pink flowered hardy water lilies hybridized in America?

The famous French water lily hybridizer M. Latour-Marliac had produced a number of hybrid pink flowered hardy water lilies by the early 1900s. American hybridizers began to produce some wonderful pink flowered hardy varieties at the turn of the century. A most attractive pink hybrid water lily was introduced in 1913 by Mrs. Helen Fowler, Washington, D.C. named *Nymphaea* 'Rose Arey' (color plate IV) after her cousin. In 1928 Mr. Robert Sawyer of William Tricker, Inc.®, Independence, Ohio introduced a beautiful pink flowered hardy named *N*. 'Fire Crest'. The name is derived from the fact that the tips of the stamens were colored "fire-red". Since this time, other pink hardy water lilies have been introduced and many await the proven quality as compared to these proven reliable varieties.

373. What native hardy white flowered water lily species is widely distributed in Europe?

The English Water Lily, *Nymphaea alba* is the most commonly grown native species of white flowered water lilies grown in Europe. The pure white flowers are typically four to five inches across and are virtually scentless. The first recording of this species was in British literature in 1562.

374. Is there a yellow flowered hardy species found naturally in the ponds and lakes of the United States?

Yes, but it is considered semi-hardy. The yellow flowered semi-hardy *Nymphaea mexicana* or commonly called Mexicana is found mainly throughout Florida and Mexico. This is a water lily species and not a hybrid.

375. How far north will the Mexicana Water Lily survive a winter?

The Mexicana Water Lily can survive mild winters in the northern United States. Since weather is unpredictable, the Mexicana Water Lily should be treated as a tropical water lily or semi-hardy in attempting to grow in the northern United States.

376. What is the most popular hybrid yellow flowered water lily?

The most popular and proven variety is *Nymphaea* 'Chromatella'. M. Latour-Marliac produced this spectacular variety in 1887 and received the Award of Merit by the Royal Horticultural Society in 1895. It still stands alone in the most often chosen hardy yellow water lily. *N.* 'Chromatella' is easy to grow and makes an abundance of flowers in a single season.

377. Does the popular *Nymphaea* 'Chromatella' have very fragrant flowers?

No. The fragrance of the blossoms of *Nymphaea* 'Chromatella' is very faint.

378. Did M. Latour-Marliac produce any other yellow flowered water lilies after the popular *Nymphaea* 'Chromatella'?

Yes. M. Latour-Marliac produced another yellow flowered hardy in 1888 called 'Odorata Sulphurea Grandiflora' or shortened to *N.* 'Sulphurea'. The water lily received the Award of Merit in 1898.

379. How does the popular yellow flowered hardy *N.* 'Chromatella' differ from *N.* 'Sulphurea'.

When M. Latour-Marliac introduced *N.* 'Sulphurea' shortly before *N.* 'Chromatella', it was referred to as "that other yellow". But upon close observation it proved to become a popular variety with different traits. The flowers of *N.* 'Sulphurea' are not cup-shaped like *N.* 'Chromatella' but have longer slender petals. The blossoms stand out of the water a few inches which is not characteristic of *N.* 'Chromatella'. And, most import to some is the fact that the fragrance of *N.* 'Sulphurea' is more odorous than *N.* 'Chromatella'.

380. Are there any popular American yellow flowered hybrid water lilies?

Yes. In the early 1930s a popular American variety was introduced named *Nymphaea* 'Sunrise'. This variety is very similar morphologically to *N.* 'Sulphurea'. The blossoms are huge varying from 9 to 10 inches and are fragrant. The name was derived from the fact that it opens very early in the day when the sun rises.

381. Are there any recent popular American hybrid yellow flowered water lilies?

Yes. In 1969 Dr. Kirk Strawn of College Station, Texas introduced a hardy yellow flowered variety *Nymphaea* 'Charlene Strawn' named after his wife. It is a wonderful yellow flowered water lily and has some resemblance to a tropical flower. The flowers are held slightly above the surface of the water.

382. What hybrid red flowered hardy water lily has the largest blossoms?

The water lily *Nymphaea* 'Attraction' has been considered to have one of the largest red flowers. It has blossoms characteristically over 8 inches in diameter. The water lily *Nymphaea* 'Attraction' was hybridized and introduced in 1910 by M. Latour-Marliac of France. It received the Award of Merit by the Royal Horticultural Society, England in 1912 and is still one of the favorites in the trade today.

383. What hybrid hardy red flowered water lily is desired for tub gardens or small pools?

An excellent choice for small water gardens or small pools is the deep red flowered hardy water lily *Nymphaea* 'Gloriosa'. It has flowers approximately six or seven inches across but has smaller water lily pads that make it ideal for smaller spaces in the water garden or in a tub garden. M. Latour-Marliac produced this hybrid in 1896 and received the Award of Merit by the Royal Horticultural Society, England in 1898.

384. What hybrid red flowered hardy water lily has small blossoms suitable for tub gardens?

The water lily *Nymphaea* 'Ellisiana' is a favorite choice for producing small red flowers that are attractive in a tub garden or small water garden pool. This hybrid was produced by M. Latour-Marliac and given the Award of Merit by the Royal Horticulture Society in 1897. *N.* 'Ellisiana' was listed in the William Tricker, Inc.'® 1934 catalog as a "recovered variety". The catalog stated that the collection of M. Latour-Marliac was depleted due to the "great war" (1914-1918) and William Tricker, Inc.® had this choice variety in their collection and were able to propagate them in numbers for sale. The effort by William Tricker, Inc.® was not in vain, since this beautiful bright red flowered water lily is still offered today and has become a favorite of water gardeners.

385. What hybrid red flowered hardy water lily has a distinct different shape and color that can be differed from the group of red flowered water lilies?

One of the most outstanding water lilies that has a distinct different shape and color from the group of red flowered water lilies is the American hybrid *Nymphaea* 'James Brydon' (color plate III). The multi-petals are a deep reddish-green with a touch of mottling. The cup shaped deep "watermelon" colored blossoms are unequaled in beauty. The water lily was developed in 1900 by the Dreer Nurseries of Philadelphia in association with William Tricker. It was named after Mr. James Brydon who was a cultivator and grower of water lilies in the early 1890s. He was the gardener of the estate of Mr. John Simpkins, Esq. of Yarmouthport, Massachusetts. Mr. Brydon was known to grow the "newest and most costly" specimens of M. Latour-Marliac. In 1906 *N.* 'James Brydon' was given the award of Merit by the Royal Horticultural Society, England. This water lily often stands alone as a favorite among the red flowered hardy water lilies.

386. What hybrid white flowered hardy water lily is considered the "King of the Whites"?

The hybrid white water lily *Nymphaea* 'Gladstone' (color plate IV) is considered the "King of the Whites". It is one of the easiest to grow and flower in the water garden. This water lily was produced by George Richardson of Lordstown, Ohio in 1894. The water lily received the Award of Merit by the Royal Horticultural Society in 1911. It is still a favorite hardy white water lily and a truly proven variety.

387. What are the names of the multi-petaled hybrid white flowered water lilies?

There are two well known white multi-petaled hybrid water lilies: *Nymphaea* 'Richardsonii' and *N.* 'Gonnere'. *N.* 'Richardsonii' was developed and introduced by the American George Richardson of Lordstown, Ohio in 1894. This wonderful pure white multi-petaled water lily was referred to as a **snow ball** when describing the appearance floating on the surface of the water. *N.* 'Gonnere' (color plate III) was introduced in 1914 from the French horticultural establishment of the late M. Latour-Marliac (1830-1911) which was under direction of his grandson M. Laydeker. *N.* 'Gonnere' was reported to be hybridized from a stock seedling from George Richardson. In 1932 Albert Buskirk, hybridizer and secretary of William Tricker, Independence, Ohio reported that these two plants were very similar.

388. What is the most popular changeable flowered hardy water lily for the water garden pool?

The water lily *Nymphaea* 'Comanche' produced by M. Latour-Marliac in 1908 is one of the most popular changeables grown in the water garden pool. The flowers open on the first day a yellow or rose-apricot and gradually changes to a coppery-red on the successive days of blooming. However, like all changeables, the distinct color changes are influenced by many conditions such as sunlight, temperature, soil nutrients, etc.

389. Are there any changeable flowered water lilies available for tub gardens or small pools?

Yes. In 1895 M. Latour-Marliac introduced one of the best changeable pygmy water lilies for tub gardens, *N.* 'Aurora'. The colors of these small flowers begin in the flower as a rosy-yellow and progress to red on the third day of blooming. The word "aurora" refers to the redness of the sky just before the sun rises in the morning. *N.* 'Aurora' is a pygmy hardy water lily represented not only by two to four inch flowers but correspondingly small leaves about six inches across.

390. Is there a pygmy yellow flowered hardy water lily for small pools or tub gardens?

Yes. In 1879 M. Latour-Marliac produced a miniature yellow flowered hardy water lily that stands unequaled in this category, *Nymphaea* 'Yellow Pygmy' or also called *N.* 'Helvola'. The star-shaped canary yellow blossoms are only a few inches across with complementing five inch olive-green mottled leaves. The entire spread of the water lily is limited to a foot or less. Since 1879, no hybrid even remotely similar to *N.* 'Yellow Pygmy' has been introduced. This single plant can be used as one example of a unique hybrid that was achieved by the master hybridizer of hardy water lilies, M. Latour-Marliac who died with many of his secrets.

391. In summation, what are the differences and similarities between the tropical and hardy water lilies?

There are many differences between the hardy and tropical water lilies. The tropical water lily has many more desirable traits than the hardy water lily. However, both are wonderful additions to any water garden. To be able to have both water types growing in a single water garden pond is having the best of both worlds. It is highly recommended that the grower of only hardy water lilies "tries" tropical water lilies to demonstate first hand the differences. The following chart compares the general characteristics of tropical and hardy water lilies:

General Characteristics	TROPICAL WATER LILIES	HARDY WATER LILIES
AROMA	Strongly Aromatic	Slight to No Aroma
NUMBER OF FLOWERS	Many Flowers per Plant	Single to Many Flowers per Plant
LOCATION OF FLOWERS	Flowers held on stems high above the water level	Flowers float on water surface
COLOR OF FLOWERS	All colors	No blue or purple shades
NIGHT BLOOMERS	Many Varieties	None
MOTTLED LILY PADS	Many Varieties light to strongly mottled	Varieties light to moderately mottled
WINTERING	Can be wintered, however treated as an annual. Will continue to bloom until frost.	Perennial, plant tuber prepares for winter, reduces flower production before frost.
LEAF VIVIPAROUS	Many Varieties	None

Chart showing the similarities and differences between the two major groups of water lilies: TROPICAL and HARDY.

VIII. Victoria and Eurayle

* History * Characteristics * Planting and Care * Eurayle *

"There are two books from whence I collect my divinity: besides that written by God, another of his servant Nature, that universal and public manuscript that lies exposed unto the eyes of all. Those that never saw him in the one have discovered him in the other."   **Sir Thomas Brown, 1851**

Figure 34. Photographs taken during the early introduction of the *Victoria* often showed a child sitting on the large floating leaves. This photograph was in William Tricker's book *The Water Garden* published in 1897 and is labeled as "*Victoria regia* (Tricker's Variety) with fully opened flower and bud showing".

HISTORY OF THE
VICTORIA

392. What is considered the largest of the water lilies?

A member of the water lily family, Nymphaeaceae, the genus *Victoria* are considered the largest of this group. The *Victoria* are known for their enormous floating leaves that reach sizes over seven feet across. The leaves are perfectly circular with the margin upturned four to eight inches at right angles to the water surface. The leaves resemble a giant pizza pan with the upturned sides. The huge flowers are often over a foot wide. Virtually the entire plant has sharp spines on the stems, sepals and floating leaves. The *Victoria* are also known as the Giant Water Lily, Water Platter or Royal Water Lily. The history of the discovery of this most unusual plant in the early 1800s has been documented from expeditions and can be translated into a fascinating story that can only conjure feelings of excitement when it was first seen for the first time and the attempts that were made to bring it to the public. The statement on the previous page by Sir Thomas Brown in 1851 was in response to the discovery and marvel at this plant wonder as it was beginning to be introduced to the world.

393. Who discovered the *Victoria* water lily?

It was suspected that the early Spanish traders and missionaries in South America would have been the original identifiers of this "vegetable wonder". However, the first European discover of the *Victoria* water lily was by a famous Spanish botanist known as **Thaddeus Haenke** (1761-1817) in 1801 on the Mamore' River (Rio Mamore') which is one of the great tributaries of the Amazon River in South America, Bolivia. He was accompanied by a Spanish missionary named Father La Cueva who later gave testimonial of their discovery. Haenke died in the Philippines without formally recording his discovery and thus the plant remained botanically unnamed. Because of his credit of discovery, but unable to botanically name this marvel of nature he was known as a *"famous but unfortunate botanical traveler"*.

394. How did the *Victoria* get its' name?

In 1832 a German botanist by the name of **Edward F. Poeppig** (1798-1868) found this spectacular plant growing on the Amazon river in South America and named it *Euryale Amazonica*. In 1837, specimens were sent by an English botanist **Sir Robert Schomburgh** from the Berbice River in Guyana (formerly British Guiana), South America to London, England. Guyana is in the northern part of South America slightly above the equator. In 1837 an English professor by the name of **Dr. John Lindley** (1799-1865) established the genus *Victoria,* published in 1838, by naming it after the reigning British Queen at the time, Queen Victoria (1819-1901) with the species *regia* (royal), thus **Victoria regia**. Later it was found in 1832 that this specimen was already named *Euryale Amazonica* by the German botanist, Edward F. Poeppig. Therefore, according to the International Rules of Botanical Nomenclature, since the species was first named *Amazonica* the correct nomenclature for this plant would be **Victoria Amazonica**.

395. When was the first *Victoria* grown in the United States?

The first *Victoria* was successfully grown in the garden of a Caleb Cope, Esq., at Philadelphia, Pennsylvania by a Professor Thomas Meehan (1826-1901) as the gardener in 1851. Caleb Cope was the president of the Pennsylvania Society and was well known for introducing rare and beautiful plants in the United States. The first flower of the *Victoria* opened on August 21, 1851.

396. How many species or varieties of *Victoria* are there?

The classification and recording of the *Victoria* dates over 150 years ago. The genus *Victoria* has been since transcribed from past literature and currently indicates two recorded species: **Victoria Amazonica** and **Victoria Cruziana** or **Victoria Trickeri**. This classification is not agreed by many botanists. Some advocate a single species, *V. Amazonica*, with more than one variety and others suggest more than one species. The problems of classification began during the discovery and identification of *Victoria Amazonica* in the 1800s. Once *V. Amazonica* was established as a genus, botanists did not agree that a proposed second species of D'Orbigny named *V. Cruziana* was a not a new species but possibly a "mere" variety of *V. Amazonica*. The botanist had no distinct botanical evidence from D'Orbigny to make a new species. From reviewing the past documentation and records, it appears that it would have been most appropriate to have listed *V. Cruziana* as intended, as a mere variety of *V. Amazonica*. It was not until the early 1890s, when William Tricker introduced a distinctly new morphological *Victoria* that exhibited different growth characteristics from *V. Amazonica,* that a new species could have been considered. Upon introduction, the new plant was provisionally listed by William Tricker as a variety, *V. Amazonica* variety *Trickeri* and was later listed as new species, *Victoria Trickeri*. For very vague reasons, such as geographical location of seed origin, it was assumed by some that *V. Cruziana* and *V. Trickeri* were the same plant and have since been listed together in botanical entries.

397. How did *Victoria Cruziana* get its' name?

In the early 1800s an individual by the name of **M. A. D'Orbigny** spent many years exploring South America and claimed the discovery of two species of this "vegetable wonder" which latter became known as *Victoria*. His written testimony of discovery brought criticism to a proposed "so-called" second species that he was to name. The first of these two species was discovered in 1827 on the Parana River near Corrientes, Argentina and had specimens sent to Paris, France. In 1832, while exploring in Bolivia, he rediscovered a second species, which was previously found by Thaddeus Haenke in 1801 on the same Mamore' River. It was not until 1840 that D'Orbigny attempted to name these plants. The plant from Boliva was already named and recorded *Victoria regia* (later changed to *V. Amazonica*) by Dr. Lindley of England in 1838. The second specimen, which was claimed to be found in a more southern part of South America in Corrientes, Argentina than the previous specimen of Bolivia, D'Orbigny selected the name *Victoria Cruziana* in honor of General Santa Cruz of Bolivia who contributed to his successful journey with his discoveries.

However, many botanist would not accept the "so-called" new species *N. Cruziana* named by D'Orbigny. **Sir William Hooker**, Vice-President of the Linnean Society and Director of the Royal Gardens of Kew, England, responded to his claim of a "second" species of *Victoria* in the 1847 *Curtis's Botanical Magazine*. Sir William Hooker referred to *Victoria Cruziana* as a "so-called" second species based upon the fact that D'Orbigny claimed it to be different than *Victoria regia (Amazonica)* by two distinct characteristics: the flower color and underside of the leaf. Sir William Hooker believed that there was little, if any, differences that D'Orbigny cited from the flowers and undersides of the leaves from *V. regia (Amazonica)*. In response to his findings, Sir William Hooker wrote that *"we may, I think, without doing violence to nature, or showing any disrespect to M. D'Orbigny, consider V. Cruziana as a mere variety, if it even deserve such a distinction, of V. regia"*. Another criticism of the "so-called" new species can be found in the 1850 text, *Lawson on Water-Lilies, The Royal Water-Lily of South America* by George Lawson, F.B.S. Mr. Lawson writes in detail about the discovery of *Victoria regia (Amazonica)* and the exploration and naming of the "so-called" *V. Cruziana* by D'Orbigny. In reference to the claim of a new species by D'Orbigny, Mr. Lawson concludes that he is *"inclined to follow the general opinion of botanists in considering it (Victoria Cruziana) a variety only"* since

115

Figure 35. The geographical discoveries of the *Victoria* spp. in South America.

others have observed different color of flowers on the same root of *Victoria regia* (*Amazonica*). Since this time, little has been done on classification of these vegetable wonders and is only left to scientific dispute.

398. How did *Victoria Trickeri* become introduced in the United States?

William Tricker introduced to the world a new "distinct" variety of *Victoria* to the trade in 1894 which he named *Victoria regia* variety *Trickeri* grown from seeds sent to him from a source in Europe that were reported to have originated from the Corrientes, South America. William Tricker writes in his text *The Water Garden*, published in 1897, that his new hybrid has distinct well-marked morphological, physical and growing characteristics that differ it from the well known *Victoria regia* (*Amazonica*). He is fully aware of the exploration and discovery of the *Victoria* in South America by D'Orbigny and includes this fact in his book, but accepts the position that the "so-called" *V. Cruziana* is not a new species nor a variety and omits this entry in his 1895 text. William Tricker lists the "*distinct and well marked characteristics*" of *V. Trickeri* in his text which differs it from the existing single species *V. regia* (*Amazonica*). He identifies one of the most "striking" morphological characteristics of *V. Trickeri* in describing the distinctive absence of spines on the sepals of *V. Trickeri* which are found on *V. Amazonica*. This very obvious observation was never indicated by D'Orbigny in the alleged *V. Cruziana* from Corrientes. In addition, William Tricker claimed that *V. Trickeri* produces flowers much earlier in the season and can be successfully grown at lower temperatures than *V. Amazonica*. With these traits, the newly introduced plant soon became known in the trade as **Victoria Trickeri**. Later, it was "assumed" that the plant came from the same geographic location in South America as that of the so-called *Victoria Cruziana* and, therefore was alleged the same plant. This assumption apparently came from comparing the over 60 year old dried specimen, stored seeds and the general botanical description by D'Orbigny of the previously claimed *V. Cruziana* that was sent to Paris, France in the early 1800s. Interestingly, the sample sent to Paris in the early 1800s from D'Orbigny is currently labeled as "*Victoria Cruziana*, Bolivia", the location where he reportedly found *V. regia* (*Amazonica*). D'Orbigny wrote that he was unable to send any specimens from Boliva but sent specimens from Correnties of South America.

Until the death of William Tricker in 1916, *Victoria Trickeri* was listed in his world renown water garden establishment, never referring to the alleged duplicate nomenclature of *V. Cruziana*. He proudly sent specimens of *V. Trickeri* around the world. In 1924, Peter Bisset, in his text *The Book of Water Gardening*, continued to credit the new variety of *Victoria* by William Tricker with a photograph and label as *"Victoria regia* 'Tricker's variety'" and separately described *V. Cruziana.*

After many decades of growing *Victoria Trickeri* (color plate II) for trade at William Tricker, Inc.® Independence, Ohio, the claims by William Tricker of a distinctly new marvel of nature is demonstrated. It does flower much earlier than reported specimens of *Victoria Amazonica* and is extremely hardy in the northern parts of the United States. In the greenhouses at William Tricker, Inc.®, Independence, Ohio the *Victoria Trickeri* has been in full bloom in June. Morphologically, the sepals of the *V. Trickeri* are smooth as reported by William Tricker in 1897 whereas *V. Amazonica* has spines. *Victoria Trickeri* has endured over a century of propagation and is still being offered in the trade. It is this very plant that has been sent to many reputable water garden and botanical establishments around the world for over 100 years.

Figure 36. The above photograph shows a greenhouse propagating pool for *Victoria Trickeri*. This photograph was shown in the 1928 William Tricker, Inc.® mail order water lily catalog with two children of the Gowing family supported upon the spectacular floating leaves. See color plate II, the photograph taken in same greenhouse aquatic tank in 1998 at William Tricker, Inc.®

CHARACTERISTICS OF THE VICTORIA

399. Can the *Victoria* floating leaf support the weight of a person?

Yes. Each leaf of the *Victoria* is a veritable boat and has been estimated that it can support approximately 150 to 200 pounds.

One could only imagine the excitement that the discovery of a plant of this magnitude brought in the 1800s. The plant was introduced into the United States in the late 1890s as a true marvel of nature and was commonly photographed with a child supported on the floating leaf. William Tricker's book *The Water Garden,* published in 1897, showed a photograph of a small child sitting with her legs crossed on a large *Victoria regia* (Tricker's variety) leaf as it floated among the other giant leaves and flowers in a quiet lagoon of a pond (figure 34). The William Tricker, Inc.® catalog displayed a photograph in 1928 of a small child on the *Victoria Trickeri* in a greenhouse propagating pond (figure 36). The leaf is not rigid however, and often the child had to be placed upon a supporting structure such as a piece of cardboard or flat of wood so as not to tear through the leaf.

400. How fast does the *Victoria* grow?

The *Victoria* continues to be a marvel of nature in its growing habit. **Robert Caspary** (1818-1887) from the University of Konigsberg, Soviet Union (today known as Kaliningrad, Russia which is about 15 miles northeast of Moscow), who is known for writing many exhaustive treatises on water lilies from 1855 to 1887, reported that the maximum growth in *Victoria* leaf length is about one inch an hour when the leaf is just expanding. In addition, the leaf surface increases four or five square feet in a 24 hour period and is able to produce in 21 to 25 weeks 600 or 700 square feet of leaf-surface.

401. Is the *Victoria* considered tropical?

Yes. *Victoria* need very warm temperatures similar to those of their native habitats of South America. They can be grown in our northern states in the United States, however it will be killed with the cold weather that comes with northern winters.

119

402. How does *Victoria Trickeri* differ from *V. Amazonica*?

Victoria Trickeri differs morphologically and requires different growing temperatures than *V. Amazonica*. *Victoria Trickeri* has spines only at the base of the sepals while *V. Amazonica* has spines which are longer and more needlelike to the tips. Since *V. Trickeri* can withstand growing in cooler temperatures, it is more adaptable to outdoor water gardens than *V. Amazonica*. The seeds of *V. Trickeri* germinate better at a lower temperature, approximately 70-75 degrees Fahrenheit, whereas *V. Amazonica* require a temperature of 85-90 degrees Fahrenheit. And finally, *V. Trickeri* flowers earlier than *V. Amazonica*.

403. In relation to the globe of the World, what latitudes of the southern hemisphere were each of the noted *Victoria* species growing in relationship to the latitudes in the northern hemisphere?

Victoria Amazonica was discovered in Brazil in association with the Amazon River and near Georgetown, Guyana (formerly British Guiana) which represents latitudes near the equator. *Victoria Trickeri* was reported from Corrientes, Argentina which is at a southern latitude of approximately 27 degrees. The corresponding degrees that the *Victoria Trickeri* is found in the northern hemisphere is West Palm Beach, Florida.

404. How far apart geographically were the two geographic species of *Victoria* found growing in South America?

The specimen named *Victoria Amazonica* by Dr. Lindley was discovered in the northern part of South America near the equator. Approximately 1000 miles south of this area *Victoria Trickeri* was reported growing near Corrientes, Argentina. Thus, the hardier of the two would be *Victoria Trickeri* because of the cooler climate in this geographical location. It was reported in the early 1900s by Henry Conard that the seeds of *Victoria Trickeri* can winter under ice in a pond. Decades later, investigation in the early 1990s at William Tricker, Inc.®, Independence, Ohio has also proven that the seeds of *V. Trickeri* will germinate after wintering under ice conditions.

405. What is the climate like in South America where the *Victoria Amazonica* are found growing naturally?

The *Victoria Amazonica* are growing in what is considered a "tropical rain forest" climate. This climate has heat and heavy rainfalls throughout the year. The annual temperatures range from 75 degrees to 80 degrees Fahrenheit, usually with less than a five degree difference between the warmest and coldest months. The average temperatures of a month does not fall below 65 degrees Fahrenheit. There are no long periods of dry temperatures, only some that are less wet. Annual rainfall is seldom below 50 or 60 inches.

406. What is the climate like in South America where *Victoria Trickeri* were reported growing?

Victoria Trickeri was reported to have been growing in a general "humid, mild winter temperate climate". This classification, derived from the Australian geographer W. Koppen known as the Koppen System which has been used as a basis for many other classifications, describes the climate as characterized by seasonal variations of temperature. Plant dormancy is usually due to cold rather than drought. The weather conditions are likely to be due to conflicting masses of air from tropical and polar sources. The chief characteristic is that the coldest month is between 65 degrees and 32 degrees Fahrenheit.

407. How does the climate of the United States compare to the climates that the *Victoria* species are found growing in South America using the Koppen System?

The United States does not have a climate such as the "tropical rain forest" of South America which supports the life of *Victoria Amazonica*. The tropical rain forest climate is found within five and ten degrees from the equator. However, the "humid, mild winter temperate" climate which can be found in the United States will support the growth of *Victoria Trickeri*. The humid, mild winter temperate climate is found in the south eastern part of the United States. This climate is classically found on the eastern sides of continents lying between the latitudes of 30 to 40 degrees north and south of the equator. Classically, tropical hurricanes in this area add to the rain fall, especially in the United States and Asia. This climatic zone begins approximately in the center of the United States to the Atlantic Ocean. The northern latitude of 40 degrees in the United States would approximately represent central Ohio to a southern 30 degree latitude of central Texas or northern portion of Florida.

408. Were there any hybrids or varieties of *Victoria*?

Yes. In 1886 an early importation of seed of *Victoria* from South America was by Edward Rand, Jr. of Para, Brazil and given to Mr. Sturtevant of Bordentown, N.J. Mr. Sturtevant grew this seed and reported a new variety which had a description very similar to *Victoria Amazonica*. The plant was reported as a new variety, ***Victoria regia*** variety ***Randii*** in some literature and in others, as a new species named *V. Randii* (**Tricker**). However, as fate would have it, other experts during this time such as Caspary and Conard, refuted *V. Randii* as being a new variety or species from the well known *V. Amazonica* and was dropped from the trade.

In 1961 a proposed hybrid of *Victoria* was developed by Patrick Nutt at Longwood Gardens, Philadelphia, Pennsylvania. The reported cross was performed between *Victoria Cruziana* (pistillate parent, received from William Tricker, Inc.® via the Missouri Botanical Gardens) and *Victoria Amazonica* (staminate). A year later, in 1962 Patrick Nutt reported that the new proposed hybrid (which was named *Victoria* **'Longwood Hybrid'**) produced more and larger flowers than either parent. In addition, he claimed that it proved to be just as hardy as *Victoria Cruziana* and surpassed the tender parents in adverse weather. It was from these characteristics that a new variety was proposed. Since *Victoria* 'Longwood Hybrid' must be propagated by crossing two different parents each year, the difficulty of production would be most difficult. Seeds from the parent of this cross would be variable and any resulting offspring would be questionable.

409. What species of *Victoria* is sold in the trade today?

At the turn of the 19th century, both *Victoria Amazonica* and *Victoria Trickeri* were offered to the public. William Tricker listed both plants in his water garden catalogs in the early 1900s. Botanical gardens required special large outdoor tanks that were heated with pipes to grow *V. Amazonica* or simply grew them within the intense heat of a greenhouse. *V. Trickeri* proved that it was able to grow and bloom in lower temperatures than *V. Amazonica*. This opened the door for growing a spectacular aquatic plant, such as the *Victoria,* in conditions found in outdoor water gardens without special heating provisions. *Victoria regia* was subsequently dropped from trade. Thus, today *V. Trickeri* remains the plant of choice for the water gardener in outdoor water garden pools around the world.

410. Are the flowers of *Victoria* considered a day or night bloomer?

The flowers of the *Victoria* are night bloomers. The flowers open late in the afternoon and close early the next morning similar to the night blooming tropical water lilies.

411. What is the color of the flowers of the *Victoria* and do they have a fragrance?

On the night before opening the large flower head will rise above the water line and will give off a powerful pineapple scent. It has been estimated that the smell will permeate the air for over 100 feet. The flower will open late in the afternoon into a beautiful multi-petalled creamy white. The numerous petals appear delicate almost like chiffon. As the sun rises the following morning, the flowers will close. On the second night the flowers open a light pink (color plate II) and have lost the powerful fragrance. After the second bloom, the flower will close and the entire flower with sepals and petals will bend and drop into the water.

412. How are the flowers of the *Victoria* pollinated in nature?

The *Victoria* is pollinated by the scarab beetles, either *Cyclocephala castanea* or *C. hardyi*. The beetles are attracted to the flowers and are often trapped within the closing flower in the morning.

413. How many seeds can a single *Victoria* flower produce?

The *Victoria* is known to produce upwards to 300 seeds per flower.

414. Does the *Victoria* make flowers continually all season?

Yes. Once the *Victoria* begins to flower, it will flower continually sending up new flowers until it succumbs to death in the late fall.

415. Does the *Victoria* make a tuber similar to the common water lilies?

No. The *Victoria* does not make a tuber like the water lilies. It can only be grown each year from seed.

416. How big are the seeds of the *Victoria*?

The seeds are small, being the size of a garden pea or approximately 1/4 to 3/8 inch in diameter (figure 37). It is quite amazing that the genetics for a plant with floating pads of seven feet and flowers over a foot wide to be derived from such a small source.

A   **B**

Figure 37. Actual size of: A. *Victoria* seed B. *Euryale* seed.

417. Since the *Victoria* have upturned edges with spines on the floating pads, do frogs sit on the pads?

Yes. The frog will leap from the water garden pool up into the air, over the edges of the side spines and land on the pad of the giant *Victoria*. The frog will sit there contented, waiting for an insect meal or if disturbed will leap back into the water.

418. What month does the flowers begin to bloom on the *Victoria Trickeri*?

The flower can be expected to begin to bloom by July or August in the northern United States and continue blooming into September.

419. Do the first leaves germinating from the seeds of the *Victoria* look like the classical pizza pan floating leaves with upturned edges?

No. The first emerging structure from the seed is a thin stem-looking structure that will grow to "feel" the surface of the water (figure 38). Once this "feeler" touches the surface of the water a small arrow-shaped leaf will begin to grow from the seed towards the surface. When this arrow-shaped leaf touches the surface of the water a new rolled leaf will now appear out of the

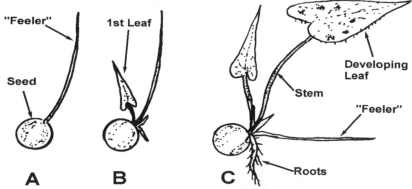

Figure 38. The sprouting of a *Victoria* seed is very fascinating: A. The seed first produces an unusual stem-looking "feeler" into the water that will deteriorate when the seed plant develops leaves and roots. B. The first leaf is small and triangular in shape. C. The "feeler" drops and begins to deteriorate as the triangular leaf will begin to float on top of the water surface. This leaf still does not have upturned sides. Roots will find the soil. Following the triangular leaves the production of miniature round shaped leaves similar to the adult leaves will begin to appear with the characteristic upturned sides.

seed and the arrow-shaped leaf will deteriorate. The new leaves will unroll and appear as small (approximately one to two inches) oval leaves that will float on the water surface. As the plant matures, the leaves will begin to develop new immature leaves with the classical upturned sides that are only a few inches in diameter. The plant will continue to produce the classical upturned leaves similar to a pizza pan, when each leaf is only a few inches in diameter. It is a special sight to watch the growth of this giant water lily from a small pea-sized seed into a plant that defies all imagination.

420. How sharp and strong are the spines on *Victoria Trickeri*?

The spines are found virtually on every part of the plant except on the top of the floating leaves and rarely on the sepals on the flowers. The bottom and sides of the leaves are loaded with sharp spines up to an inch long. Also, the stems of the flowers and leaves have many spines. These spines are extremely sharp and strong which can easily penetrate leather or rubber gloves. Once the accidental piercing of the skin is done, it is a most memorable experience.

421. Since the *Victoria* have upturned edges on the floating pads, do the pads fill up with water and sink when it rains?

No. On the sides of the floating leaves are two notches (figure 39) located across from each other that allows the excess rain water to flow out from the leaf into the surrounding pond water. In addition, there are innumerable tiny depressions on the surface of the leaf which contain small holes that can be seen with a common hand lens. These holes are named **stomatodes** (Planchon) and allow not only water to pass but any gases rising from the bottom mud such as methane to pass through and not lift the leaves. Nature has already figured this one out in her plan.

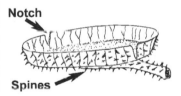

Figure 39. The *Victoria* has many spines on the underside and sides of the leaves and stem. There are two characteristic notches located across from each other on each leaf.

422. Since the *Victoria Trickeri* is tropical, will it produce flowers in the northern United States without special heated pools?

Yes. The flowers of the *Victoria Trickeri* will definitely bloom in the northern United States. In extreme northern states the water should be shallow to allow the sun to heat the water. Cold water will prevent blooms.

125

423. Since the *Victoria* is so spectacular as shown in books, has it ever made its way in movies?

Yes. In the classic 1939 version of the *Wizard of Oz* starring Judy Garland the *Victoria* can be seen . When Dorothy first enters the Munchkin Land and the program becomes colorized, the spectacular *Victoria* can be seen in the streams around the yellow brick road. The plant was probably chosen to dwarf the Munchins and give a mystical surrounding to the scene.

CARE AND PLANTING
OF THE VICTORIA

424. What is the size of *Victoria* when received in the mail from the nursery?

The *Victoria* received in the mail will have a few leaves approximately a few to several inches across with small roots. It will have small developing prickers on the stems and leaves. This size will travel well and transplant readily. There is no tuber.

425. How should the *Victoria Trickeri* be planted when received from the nursery?

Since there is no tuber, the roots should be carefully planted into a good topsoil with an aquatic fertilizer as recommended by the manufacturer. The larger the container the better. Many spectacular displays at botanical gardens use containers three to four feet across with a depth of two feet. The water gardener should plant the *Victoria* in a container that holds at least a few cubic feet of soil. After planting, the container with the plant should be placed in the warm shallow water of the water garden pool with only a few inches of water over the crown. The small immature leaves of the *Victoria* should be floating on the surface of the water and not totally submerged. Once the plant begins to grow and the leaves become progressively larger, the plant can be lowered to a deeper depth from six to 24 inches. The plant will thrive in warm water and strong sunlight.

426. How large of a water garden is necessary for growing a *Victoria*?

A single *Victoria Trickeri* planted in a large container can be a spectacular sight in a water garden pool of approximately 400 square feet or 20 feet by 20 feet. However, if the planting was done in a smaller container (for example, a one square foot container) the flowers will be smaller, approximately a few inches across with corresponding one to two foot leaves. Since the spread of the *Victoria* growing in a smaller container does not take as much surface area, it can be enjoyed in a 10 foot by 10 foot water garden pool in miniature.

427. When should the *Victoria Trickeri* be planted outside?

The *Victoria Trickeri* should not be planted outside until the weather is warm and the water can maintain at least 70 degrees Fahrenheit. This is usually not until the first week in June in the northern United States for many water garden ponds. Planting in a lake or large pond should be delayed until the water is warmer. The larger amount of water in a lake or large pond is cooler in early June and can slow the growth or kill the plant. Intense heat and sunshine will greatly enhance the growth of the plant.

428. How often should the *Victoria* be fertilized?

The *Victoria* demands more fertilizer than water lilies. The *Victoria* should be fertilized with a proven aquatic fertilizer. Depending upon weather, if the growth is very fast and flowering profusely, additional fertilizer should be used. Care should be taken during fertilization not to be hurt by the spines on the plant.

429. Do the large floating leaves of the *Victoria* need pruning?

Not necessarily. As the large leaves grow out into the water will naturally deteriorate by becoming yellow and literally dissolve in the water. If the decaying leaves begin to breed aphids, they should be removed by washing off with a strong stream of water. Pesticides, as well as any algicides, should be avoided since the *Victoria* is sensitive to chemicals. The plant will continually send out new extraordinary large leaves. It is a marvelous and unique experience to watch this happen. The plant will mysteriously and constantly send new leaves into open areas on the water surface left from the decay of the spent leaves. It does this as if it could "see" these open areas from under the surface of the water.

430. How are the large floating leaves of the *Victoria* pruned?

The leaves of the *Victoria* can be pruned by using gloves and pliers. The pliers are used to cut through the stems of the older yellow leaves and lifting the large leafs by the stems into the air and removing them from the pond. Extreme care is taken not to pierce the skin with the spines on the plant.

EURYALE

431. Is there any other aquatic plant that is similar in size to the *Victoria*?

Yes. The aquatic plant that is similar to the *Victoria* is found in the genus *Euryale ferox* and is known as the **Gorgon Plant** or **Prickly Water Lily**. The plant name "Gorgon" originated from Greek mythology which referred to one of the three Gorgons. The Gorgons were monstrous daughters of the sea god who had venomous snakes of hair of which only Medusa was mortal. The portrayal of the plant to a Gorgon more than likely referred to the thorns or prickers found over the entire plant.

432. What is the native county of the *Euryale*?

The *Euryale* is native to tropical parts of eastern Asia and has been cultivated for centuries in China. It was entered into the genus *Euryale* in 1809, eight years after the discovery of the *Victoria* (Lindley, 1837) by Haenke in 1801. It was Richard Anthony Salisbury (1761-1829) of England that named the single species as *Euryale ferox*. Another synonym that has been reported in older literature was *Anneslia spinosa*.

433. Does the *Euryale* have floating leaves as large as the *Victoria*?

No. The floating leaves of the *Euryale* are often one to four feet across. The prefix "*Eury*" is derived from the Greek meaning "wide" or "broad" referring to the leaf.

434. Are the floating leaves of the *Euryale* similar to *Victoria*?

No. The leaves of the *Euryale* have spines on the top of the floating leaves whereas the *Victoria* have no spines on the top of the leaves. Also, the *Euryale* does not have upturned margins on the edges of the leaves and thus does not have the pizza-pan look of the *Victoria*. The *Euryle* has a deep purple color, similar to cabbage, under the leaf.

435. How does the flower of the *Euryale* compare to the *Victoria*?

The two flowers are distinctly different. The day blooming flower of the *Euryale* is smaller, rarely larger than two inches across, than the one foot night blooming flower of the *Victoria* spp. The *Euryale* flowers are a beautiful deep blue-violet in color, whereas the night blooming Victoria flowers have a creamy white first day and a light pink second day flower. The flowers open both above and below the water surface whereas the flower of the *Victoria* opens only above the surface of the water.

436. Is the *Euryale* hardy in the northern United States?

Yes. The plant will die in the fall when winter arrives. The seeds of the *Euryale* will survive under a pond with an ice covering in the northern parts of the United States. In the spring the seeds can sprout (figure 39) and develop into a new plant. There is no tuber formed for the winter.

437. How large is a *Euryale* when sent in the mail?

The *Euryale* are small plants when shipped in the mail. They will have a few floating leaves that are a few inches in diameter. They, like the *Victoria*, do not produce a tuber and will have roots.

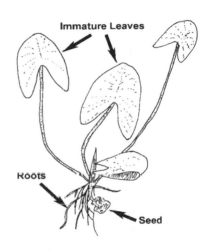

Figure 40. The sprouting of the seed of a *Euryale* is similar to the *Victoria* seed in that it first produces triangular leaves.

438. How is the *Euryale* planted in the water garden pool?

The small plant without a tuber is carefully planted similar to the *Victoria* by placing the roots into a large container. The larger the container the better. At least a container that holds 2 to 3 cubic feet of soil should be used. Once placed into the water garden the small leaves should float upon the surface of the water. As the plant gets larger the container can be moved up to a depth of 24 inches.

439. Since there are spines on top of the floating pads of the *Euryale* do frogs sit on these?

Yes. Interestingly, the frogs will climb onto the pads of the *Euryale* regardless of the spines. It appears that the spines do not hinder or hurt the frogs.

IX. Lotus

*Characteristics * Selected Lotus Species and Hybrids*
* Planting and Care*

Figure 41. A historic photograph of lotus from William Tricker's book *The Water Garden* published in 1897. The lotus are shown in full beauty with many blooms and leaves. Note how the flowers and buds typically reach high above the circular leaves.   A beautiful sight that should be seen by all.

CHARACTERISTICS OF LOTUS

440. Are there any purple or blue lotus flowers?

No. The hybrid or species lotus flowers are found in shades of yellow, red and white. There are no blue or purple lotus flowers.

441. How large are the flowers of the typical lotus?

The lotus flowers typically range 8 to 10 inches across but is not uncommon to have lotus blossoms over a foot across.

442. How do the flowers of the variety of lotus differ structurally?

There are single and double petals found in the lotus flowers. The flower structure has very thin sepals with petals and a central receptacle for the development of the seeds.

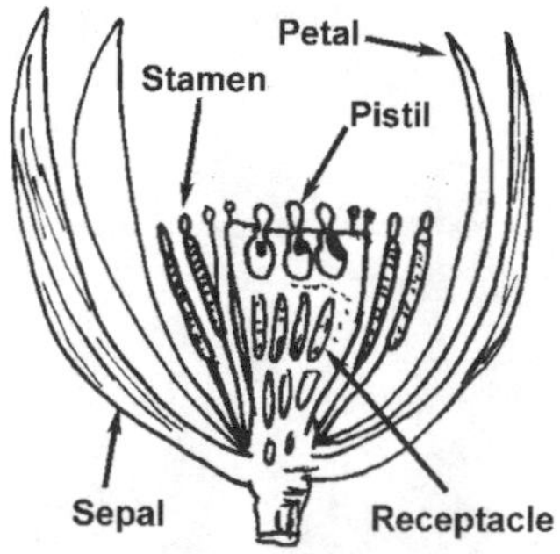

443. How many lotus flowers are found on a single stem?

There is a single lotus flower found on each stem. It is typical, however, to have multiple flowers in bloom at one time on a single plant.

Figure 42. The cross section of a lotus flower reveals the common structures found in flowers.

444. Do the lotus flowers have an aroma?

Yes, a very mysterious and distinct aroma. The aroma is so unusual that no comparison to another plant can be made. Smelling a lotus blossom is a first time experience.

445. What makes the flowers of the lotus very fragrant?

An interesting fact is that the lotus is able to regulate the temperature of its flowers. It has been reported that the sacred lotus, *Nelumbo nucifera*, has the ability to regulate the temperature of its flowers, similar to a warm blooded

132

animal, between 86 to 96 degrees Fahrenheit even if the air is as cool as 41 degrees Fahrenheit. The reason for this temperature regulation is thought by many botanists to better disperse the scent of the lotus blossom to attract insects for pollination. Others suggest that the added temperature helps the pollinating insects by warming up their muscles in colder temperatures which would "jump start" them on cold days. What ever the reason, temperature regulation of the lotus is an odd feature that only adds to the mysterious nature of such a plant and enhances the aroma permeability.

446. How long does a typical single blossom bloom?

A single typical lotus blossom will bloom for about three or four days which is similar to the blooming duration of water lilies.

447. When does the classical "funnel-shaped" seed pod develop that is often seen in dried flower arrangements?

Once the lotus flower is fertilized by an insect or artificially fertilized by hand, the internal cone-shaped seed pod (figure 43) will begin to develop into the classical funnel-shaped seed pod. After the third day of blooming all of the petals drop off and the fertilized seeds will begin to enlarge or swell. Within a few weeks the entire seed pod will soon resemble the classical funnel-shape that is so often seen in dried flower arrangements.

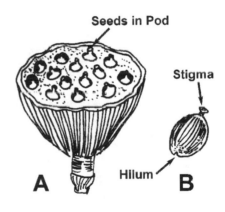

448. Do all of the flowers of the lotus in the water garden develop into the classical looking funnel-shaped seed pod?

Not necessarily. Typically, if the flower is fertilized or pollinated the classical funnel-shape seed pod develop.

Figure 43. A. The characteristic seed pod of the lotus is commonly found in flower arrangements. B. The seed, shown as actual size, has a hard coat and a protrusion that is the "stigma" where the pollen will enter and a "hilum" or notch where it was attached to the seed pod.

449. What happens if the lotus flower is not fertilized or pollinated?

Typically, the cone-shaped structure left after the petals fall will turn brown and dry with a series of wrinkles. It will remain in this form on the stem without any developed seeds. Under certain instances, the pod will still develop without producing fertile seeds.

450. How many seeds can be produced by a lotus flower?

The amount of lotus seeds per single pod vary in different varieties, but a typical lotus flower can produce about 20 to 25 seeds per flower.

451. How big are the fertilized seeds of the lotus?

The oval seeds of a lotus after fertilization will become about 3/4 of an inch in length and about 1/2 inch wide.

452. If only a few seeds are fertilized in the lotus flower, will a classical funnel-shaped seed pod still develop?

No. If only a few **stigmas** (female part) are fertilized only a partial funnel will develop. Partial fertilization will produce an abnormal irregularly looking funnel-shaped seed pod. This is common in a water garden with a single lotus plant that was unable to attract insects during the fertility period.

453. What is inside of the seed of the lotus?

The seed of the lotus (figure 43) has similar internal parts to other seeds. The cross section of the lotus seed shows the female **stigma** where the pollen will land and make a small opening called the **micropyle**. The pollen will grow through the **style** and into the **ovary**. An **embryo** will develop which will grow into a new plant utilizing the **endosperm** which is made of sugars and starches. It is the endosperm that has been consumed by man as food. The **hilum** or notch is where it was attached to the seed pod.

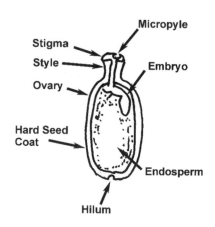

Figure 44. The internal structure of a lotus seed is similar to other seeds.

134

454. What does the lotus seed look like when it sprouts?

The sprouting of the lotus seed is very similar to other seeds that sprout which is simply a marvel of nature. The first sign of the seed sprouting is the splitting (figure 45) of the hard seed coat. After the hard seed coat splits the first immature leaf will begin to arise. The tip of the leaf is rolled together into a point which can push through the soil above. Soon a second immature leaf will grow, followed by the developing immature roots. Under ideal conditions the first recognized leaf can reach the surface of the water within a few days from when the seed coat splits. The pointed shaped leaf will unroll into the classical round leaf at the surface of the water.

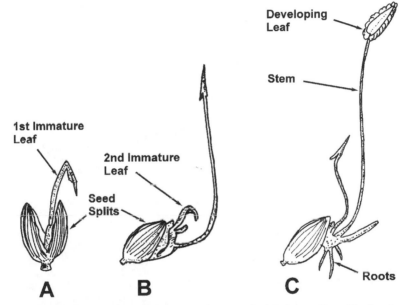

Figure 45. The sprouting of a lotus seed is a wonderful observation. The hard seed coat will split and the immature leaves will begin the growth to the surface. Roots will develop and nourish the plant to the full size.

455. What do the seeds of the lotus plant feel like?

Once the fertilized seeds of a lotus plant are dried they have a smooth hard seed coat that feels like a hard piece of plastic. This hard outer coating of the seed has enabled them to survive long periods of time under the water as well as outside of the water.

456. How long have the seeds of the lotus survived?

Since the seed coat of the lotus is very hard, it can survive many years before germinating or sprouting. In 1924 a researcher reported to have sprouted lotus seeds that were lying in moist peat beds of South Manchuria for at least 1000 years. In addition, on July 17, 1939 it was reported in a garden magazine that a pink blossom lotus bloomed from a seed at least 300 years old at Garfield Park, Chicago. These seeds were brought to the United States 12 years prior and were also from peat beds of Southern Manchuria.   It was indicated that a lake once existed were the lotus seed was collected and trees as old as 120 years now grow in this location.

457. Are lotus aggressive growers?

Yes. They will grow rapidly and can easily take over a shallow earth bottomed pond. They are known to spread more than 50 feet across an earth bottom pond in one season.

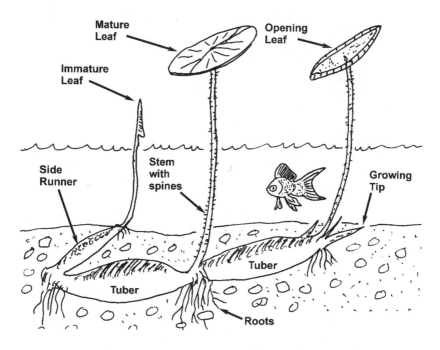

Figure 46. The lotus can grow a great distant in a pond. The tubers develop from the underground runners.

458. Are all lotus hardy?

Yes, there are no tropical lotus.

459. How tall are the stems of the lotus?

The lotus plants will commonly have stems that grow five feet above the water. The dwarf varieties of lotus are around two to three feet tall.

460. Who discovered that the lotus "tubers" could survive in the northern winter climates of the United States?

In the February 1896 Meehan's Monthly (a magazine of horticulture and botany founded and published in 1891 in Philadelphia, Pennsylvania) published a letter written by a Edward Tatnall of Wilmington, Delaware. The letter was in response to a past article that described how the lotus grew and made dormancy in the form of tubers and gives credit to a number of naturalists for this discovery. Mr. Tatnall wrote *"Honor to whom honor is due"* and responded that he had a letter from a Dr. Engelmann in 1860 which he quotes *"the tubers of Nelumbium are the only part of the plant living over winter"*. Thus, Dr. Englemann in 1860 would be the identifier of the lotus tuber being responsible for its successful dormancy.

461. Do the lotus flowers follow the same pattern in opening and closing as the water lilies?

Yes. They open quite early in the morning and close late in the afternoon. This pattern is repeated for approximately three days whereas the petals fall from the flower.

462. Are there any night blooming lotus?

No. All the lotus flowers resemble our hardy water lilies which open and close only during the day.

SELECTED LOTUS SPECIES AND HYBRIDS

463. Are the lotus in the same genus as the water lilies?

No. The lotus are in the genus *Nelumbo* while the genus of the water lilies are *Nymphaea*.

464. How many species of lotus are there?

There are two recognized species of lotus: *Nelumbo lutea* and *N. nucifera*. Botanist are not in agreement with only two species, however more work is needed in this category which may be expanded.

465. How many hybrids of lotus are there?

There are hundreds of hybrid lotus plants found around the world. Most of the known hybrids are found in China.

466. Where are the native origins of the two species of lotus and what color are the flowers?

Nelumbo lutea is the common yellow flowered American Lotus which is native to America. The yellow American Lotus has received many common names: **Water Chinquapin, Yanquapin, Wonkapin** and **Pond Nuts** to mention only a few. *Nelumbo nucifera* is known as the **Sacred Lotus** or **Egyptian Lotus** (Color Plate III) which is native to Asia, specifically China and Japan and has a pink flower.

467. Was the yellow flowered lotus ever found to be native in China or Japan?

No, America is very proud to claim the origin of such a fine aquatic plant as *Nelumbo lutea*.

468. Is the American Lotus a true native plant found in the United States?

Yes. The American Lotus, *Nelumbo lutea* is truly a native plant found in the United States. A spectacular sight of American lotus is near Huron, Ohio along Lake Erie which is located approximately 50 miles Northwest from William Tricker, Inc.®, Independence, Ohio. There are literally millions of American lotus growing and dotting the shoreline with their beautiful sulfur yellow flowers and huge round leaves. At the turn of the century William Tricker wrote that the American Lotus was found in abundance along the shores of Lake Erie but was scarce in the Middle Atlantic and eastern states and said *"when the American lotus is well established it is a magnificent plant, when in blossom it is a sight well worth traveling miles to see"*.

469. Are there any lotus flowers that bloom longer than three days?

Yes. A most popular miniature or dwarf lotus, *Nelumbo* 'Mono Botan' is noted for a longer blooming period than the other lotus. A single flower bloom can last up to a week. The seed pods that develop are not as large and typical as the other lotus seed pods.

470. Did the early American Indians use the native American Lotus as food?

Yes. Over five centuries ago the American Indians cultivated this yellow lotus in the Tennessee and Cumberland Rivers and was abundant in the tributaries of the Mississippi. The Indians used the tubers and seeds of the American lotus as food. It is thought that the Indians carried it towards Connecticut.

471. Were the early horticulturist in the 1890s interested in the American lotus?

Definitely. In the early horticultural writings the American lotus received much attention. In the 1890s much was written on how the lotus survived through the severe winters in the northern United States. For example, in the January 1888 issue of *Popular Gardening* a H.E. Van Deman responds to a previous publication of the fact that the lotus southern limit of growing is at latitude of 40 degrees. He writes that he has witnessed the American lotus, *Nelumbo lutea* growing as far south in acres of ponds in *"Kansas, Missouri and Indian Territory. In fact it is so common that as far south as 36 degrees that the Indians use the seeds and the tubers as food. I have tried them myself but prefer Corn and Potatoes"*.

472. If the American lotus was native to America, who introduced the other species of lotus, *Nelumbo nucifera* or Egyptian Lotus to the United States?

In 1876 E.D. Sturtevant of Bordentown, New Jersey saw a specimen of *Nelumbo nucifera* growing at Jardin des Plantes, Paris, France. He wondered if this plant would winter over in the United States. During the next few years Mr. Sturtevant cultivated this lotus on his property in Bordentown, New Jersey without subjecting to freezing. Now the test was to come, will it survive in an open pond subjected to a winter of freezing? The rest was history. Not only did the Egyptian or Sacred Lotus winter under ice but flourished in an open pond in New Jersey. On April 10, 1889 Mr. E. D. Sturtevant published his findings in *Garden and Forest* with a photograph of this pond full of thousands of Egyptian Lotus as proof. Thus, Mr. E. D. Sturtevant is credited with the naturalization of the Egyptian or Sacred Lotus in northern America.

473. When did the other hybrids besides the American Lotus and Egyptian Lotus (Sacred Lotus) enter the United States?

In the early 1880s not only were there only the two species, *Nelumbo nucifera* and *Nelumbo lutea*, of lotus grown in American, but knowledge of other hybrids were virtually unknown. It was not until the mid 1890s that other lotus hybrids from outside the United States gained popularity.

474. What were the names of the newly introduced lotus that gained popularity in the United States in the mid-1890s?

The hybrids of *Nelumbo nucifera* showing different shades of colors and petal structures were being introduced into the United States in the latter 1880s. The lotus hybrids arrived from China/Japan introduced with names such as *Nelumbo album grandiflorum* (or *Nelumbium nucifera album grandiflorum*), which bears exceedingly large white flowers, *Nelumbo roseum*, the blooms of which are of a deep rosy pink, *N. Kermesinum*, which shows a more delicate shade of pink, *N. striatum*, the buds of which look striped, owing to a crimson margins on the white petals, and a number of other sorts from Japan arrived in the United States.

475. Were the new hybrids from Japan in the mid-1880s considered new species?

No. There still remained only two species of Nelumbo. The newly introduced hybrids had Latin names but were considered hybrids of *Nelumbo nucifera*. Many of the Latin names remained in describing these hybrid types, i.e. the Japanese Lotus *Nelumbo nucifera* var. *Album Grandiflora* would become *Nelumbo* 'Album Grandiflora' or *Nelumbo nucifera* 'Album Grandiflora'.

476. What lotus were popular in the 1920s when water gardening was gaining popularity?

By the 1920s the two species of lotus, Egyptian Lotus (*Nelumbo nucifera*) and American Lotus (*Nelumbo lutea*) were grown by water gardeners. The selected hybrids that found their way to the water gardeners had such names as the Chinese Red Lotus (*Pekinesis rubrum plenum*), Flavescens (yellow flower), Japanese or Magnolia Lotus (white flower, *Album grandiflorum*), Shiroman (white flowered double petals), Pekinese Rose (double pink flower) and others.

477. Of the old proven lotus hybrids, what are still available in the trade today?

After over 100 years of successful selection of the beauty of growing lotus, water gardeners still find some of their traditional favorites offered in the trade today: Shiroman (*Nelumbo nucifera* 'Alba Plena' or *N. nucifera* 'Shiroman') a beautiful large Japanese white flower which is double, Asiatic Lotus (*N. nucifera* 'Alba Grandiflora', color plate III) a pure white flowered lotus, Flavescens (*N. lutea* 'Flavescens') a yellow flower, Empress (*N. nucifera* 'Alba Striata') a white flower with edges stripped pink and Double Dawn (*N. nucifera* 'Rosea Plena') a double rosy-pink flower.

478. Did the early American water lily hybridizers in the 1890s work with the lotus?

Yes, the American hybridizers produced double flowered varieties of lotus but was under much criticism and not well accepted. William Tricker prior to 1895 produced a double flowered lotus which was rose-pink in color. E. D. Sturtevant also produced a pink flowered lotus that had eighty petals and a pure white flowered lotus with over 100 petals. The criticism in 1895 was indicated in the horticultural literature as these double flowered varieties "*lacks the ethereal grace of the single varieties*". Therefore, the hybrid lotus that were multi-petaled were not well accepted.

479. Did the famous hardy water lily hybridizer from France, Latour Marliac experiment and grow lotus?

Yes. He is known for the yellow flowered lotus hybrid known as *Nelumbo* 'Flavescens'.

480. Is the ancient "Blue Lotus of the Nile" a true lotus of the genus *Nelumbo*?

No. The "Blue Lotus of the Nile or Egypt" is referring to *Nymphaea caerulea* which is a blue tropical water lily and not the "lotus" of the genus *Nelumbo*. The water lily was named in 1802 by Marie Savigny based on specimens collected near Cairo, Egypt. This plant is sometimes referred to as the "Egyptian Lotus" which also should not be confused with the commonly used name of *Nelumbo nucifera*. The Egyptian lotus, *Nelumbo nucifera*, was cultivated along the Nile during the Roman period more likely for food.

PLANTING AND CARE
OF THE LOTUS

481. How are lotus plants purchased in the mail to be transplanted?

The lotus purchased in the mail is transplanted by using dormant tubers. A bare rooted lotus plant, with stems and roots, can not be transplanted. In special circumstances a harden runner can be transplanted.

482. Why are lotus tubers selected for transplantation?

Once the lotus becomes a grown plant it must not be disturbed. Transplanting by removing a growing lotus plant from the soil will disturb the delicate root structure and more than likely kill or set back the plant.

483. What is the recommended type of soil that the dormant lotus tuber should be planted in?

A good topsoil is necessary with a the correct amount of aquatic fertilizer as specified by the manufacturer.

484. What does the dormant tuber of a lotus plant look like?

Delicate Growing Tip

Figure 47. The lotus tuber has a delicate growing tip.

The dormant tuber of the lotus classically resembles the shape of a banana (figure 47) with a delicate growing tip at one end. The color of the dormant lotus tuber vary in shades of colors. They typically have shades of creamy-white, dull yellow or light to dark brown in color. The dormant lotus tuber has a smooth texture and is typically firm. It can easily be bruised and will decay at the point of damage.

485. If the growing point on a dormant lotus tuber is broken, is the tuber dead?

Not necessarily. It is possible that a broken growing point will survive and still sprout.

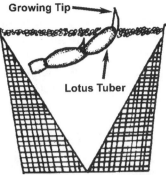

Growing Tip

Lotus Tuber

Figure 48. The lotus tuber is planted with great care not to break the delicate growing tip.

486. How are dormant lotus tubers planted?

Great care should be used not to break the growing tips in planting a dormant lotus tuber. After mixing the correct amount of manufacturer's recommended fertilizer in a good topsoil and compacting into the selected planting container, a trough or groove is made on the top of the soil. The lotus tuber is placed into this trough with the growing tip extended upwards. The tuber in the trough is carefully covered with loose topsoil and the entire container covered with a layer of pea gravel. The lotus growing tip should extend above the top layer of pea gravel (figure 48). The container is placed into the water garden pool with apporximately four to six inches of water over the top of the container. After growth is established a depth of approximately eight inches is appropriate.

487. How long does it take for a dormant lotus tuber to sprout after it is placed in the water garden pool?

After placing the container with lotus in the water garden pool, the sprout should occur within a few weeks depending upon temperature of the water and amount of sunlight.

488. How large should the container be for planting a lotus tuber?

Lotus plants demand a great deal of soil and space to grow in. The larger the container the better for a lotus tuber. The lattice sided aquatic containers of at least 15 inches square by 11 inches deep is appropriate.

489. What happens to the plant if the planting container selected is too small for the lotus?

If the container is too small, the lotus will dwarf and not grow as intended and may fail entirely. The flowering ability will be restrained and leaves will be small. Also, the lesser amount of soil will quickly be exhausted and stunt the plant or force it into a premature dormancy.

490. Since lotus are hardy do they grow better in deep cooler water and cooler temperatures?

No, the hybrids of lotus thrive in intense heat and do extremely well with only a few inches of water over the crown where the water is warmest.

491. What care for the lotus is necessary at the end of the growing season?

A tuber will be made by the lotus plant at the end of the season. As long as this tuber in the soil will not freeze it will sprout the following spring.

492. How can the lotus tuber be protected from freezing in the water garden pool in the winter?

To insure that the tuber will not be frozen in the winter, the planting containers can be sunk down to the bottom of the water garden pool.

493. When should the planting container with the dormant tuber be restored to the proper location after winter storage in the water garden pool?

In the spring, after the last frost, the planting container can be relocated to the original growing location. As the sun light increases and the water warms, the winter tuber(s) will sprout.

494. How can I tell if my lotus is going dormant at the end of summer?

The flowers will stop being produced and the round leaves will turn brown.

495. Can the lotus plant with leaves and flowers be brought indoors and be prevented from going dormant in the fall?

No. Mother Nature has an agreement with the lotus that it must go dormant late in the fall.

496. Can the dormant lotus tuber be brought indoors for the winter and not be sunk to the bottom of the water garden pool for storage?

Yes. If the pool is in danger of freezing solid, the container can be brought indoors for storage in the winter. It can be placed in a dark and cool cellar or basement that is not subject to freezing. It should be kept moist all winter. In the spring, after the last frost, the dormant tuber in the container can be restored to the original place in the water garden pool.

497. Since the lotus grows extremely well, does it become pot bound?

Yes. In a few years the lotus must be re-potted. This can be accomplished in the early spring before growth appears by removing the dormant tubers and replanting them. Extreme care should be used in not breaking the growing tips found on the tubers.

498. When can the lotus tuber be planted outdoors?

A completely dormant lotus tuber can be planted at any time in the early spring. This is typically around April in the northern climates of the United States and earlier in the southern states.

499. Will a lotus tuber that has sprouted or coming out of dormancy in the spring and transferred to a colder climate be harmed?

Yes. By transferring a sprouted lotus tuber or one that is coming out of dormancy from a warm climate to a cold climate may not only stunt the growth but may eventually harm the tuber and kill it. If the weather conditions that brought the lotus tuber out of dormancy were warm, then the same conditions must be met in the new climate. The temperatures should be equal to or at least warmer than the temperature of the sprouted or coming out of dormancy lotus tuber. This is why many successful aquatic nurseries put a tremendous value on the time of shipping lotus tubers, as well as other aquatic plants, to different climates during specific times.

500. Can a completely dormant lotus tuber be easily differed from a tuber coming out of dormancy?

No. It is very difficult to tell when the lotus tuber is coming out of dormancy. The tuber will begin to come out of dormancy when the temperature and sunlight signal the tuber that it is safe to grow. There are many physiological functions that begin to occur in the tuber before the growing tip begins to sprout or grow. Since the identification of dormancy is questionable, it is important that not only the sprouted tubers but the dormant tubers are not transplanted into a colder temperature that may shock or kill the plant.

501. If the dormant lotus tuber does not sprout within a few weeks after planting, is it dead?

Not necessarily, it has been found that carefully removing the potted dormant tuber and floating it in the water will stimulate growth. Do not place the floating tuber in direct sunlight but in a semi-shaded area. As soon as the growing tip begins to show growth the tuber should be carefully replanted in the original planting container.

502. Does the lotus need to be fertilized throughout the growing season?

Definitely. The lotus needs a great amount of fertilizer and a rigorous program should be adhered to throughout the growing season.

503. Are fungal infections of the leaves of the mature lotus plant common?

No, fungus appears not to be a major problem with the leaves of the lotus plant. The highly pathogenic water lily fungus *Helicosporium nymphaearum* has been directly inoculated onto the Egyptian lotus leaves with no effect. However, any weakened plant can be subjected to a fungal infection.

504. Does the leaf cutter or cutworm attack the lotus similar to water lilies?

Yes. It is most prevalent when the leaves are floating on the surface of the water and have not yet become aerial. If infected with leaf cutter, there can be found the classical oval cuts in the leaves with the floating "boats" containing the larva of the cutworm , similar to the water lilies.

505. Do aphids attack the lotus like water lilies?

Yes. The aphids can cause a lot of destruction if not treated. They can be treated by hosing them off which will become food for any fish.

X. Hardy Aquatic Shallow Water Plants

INTRODUCTION

506. What are the "shallow water plants"?

As in nature the **shallow water plants**, sometimes referred to as "bog" plants, will line the margin or a selected shallow area of the water garden with a profusion of flags, rushes, reeds and small flowering plants which delight the eye. They complement the water lilies and add color to the margins. Animal life, such as birds, dragonflies, frogs, etc., will interact with the shallow water plants as if they were put in the water garden specifically for them. When the wind blows, the plants will give life to the pool by moving ever so slowly in a gentle breeze.

507. How deep are the shallow water plants in the water garden pool?

Depending upon the specific type of plant, the shallow water plants will vary in planting depth from approximately two to six inches of water over the crown. These planting depths can generally be used as guidelines for most shallow water plants. The correct depths can be attained by placing the potted plant on a shelf or supported by rocks.

PLANTING DEPTH:
2 INCHES WATER OVER CROWN

508. How many species of native Arrowhead are there?

The arrowhead, *Sagittaria* species, are made up of over 30 recognized species.

509. How does the arrowhead reproduce?

During the growing season, the arrowhead will produce an abundance of seeds and develop vegetatively from new plants from underground runners. By the end of summer, the arrowhead will produce a multitude of plants by these runners. In the fall, each arrowhead plant will develop a small round tuber in the soil. In the spring, the tuber will sprout and make a new plant.

510. Can the arrowheads be used as food?

Yes. In the Orient the tubers of the arrowhead *Sagittaria sagittifolia* are eaten as food. In North America the American Indians used the arrowhead *Sagittaria latifolia*, known as the Duck Potato, for food.

511. Are there any hybrid arrowheads?

Yes. A very attractive hybrid is the **Double Flowering Arrowhead**. In the early 1900s, William Tricker described this hybrid as *"one of the most ornamental of the arrowheads, double form of Sagittaria japonica"*. It has been sold using the old name *Sagittaria japonica* 'Flore Pleno' or the botanical *Sagittaria sagittifolia* cultivar 'Flore Pleno'. The double white flowers, which resemble a miniature chrysanthemum, are infertile and do not produce seeds. The double white flowers stands out admirably against the dark green arrow-like foliage. It is a plant that has adorned water garden for decades.

512. When does the Hardy Calla bloom?

The Hardy Calla, being only one species *Calla palustris,* blooms a white arum-like flower May through June in the Northern latitudes in the United States. In the fall the seeds become a beautiful red color (figure 49).

513. If the Hardy Calla begins to creep out of the planting container into the water, should it be cut back?

The Hardy Calla can be left to creep out of the container. As the creeping rootstock begins to produce new roots that dangle into the water the plant can be cut and re-potted as a new plant.

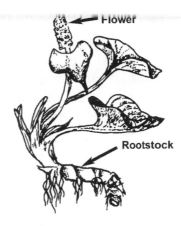

514. Will the Hardy Calla grow in full sun or shade?

The Hardy Calla can grow in either full sun or shade. In the shade, the leaves will become larger due to the limited sunlight.

Figure 49. Hardy Calla produces a unique flower and grows by a rootstock.

515. What does the flower structure of the Cardinal Flower, *Lobelia cardinalis*, look like?

The very attractive red flower of the Cardinal Flower (color plate IV and figure 50) is a narrow tube-like structure that is approximately one and half inches long and visited routinely by hummingbirds. The flower has an unusual male part or **stamen**. The pollen producing structure, called an **anther**, is fused to the structure that holds the anther, called a **filament**, and appears as a single tube. This arrangement is not typical of flowers since most flowers have distinct and identifiable anthers and filaments. The **stamen** (term which refers to the filament and anther) of the Cardinal Flower can be seen curled outside of the **corolla** (term for the collection of petals).

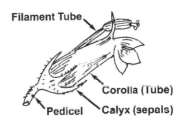

Figure 50. The Cardinal Flower has a very attractive and unusual flower.

516.   How many Cardinal Flowers need to be planted to attract hummingbirds?

A single plant of Cardinal Flower, *Lobelia cardinalis*, will attract hummingbirds. The hummingbirds are seen taking nectar from deep within the bright red flowers blooming in the fall.

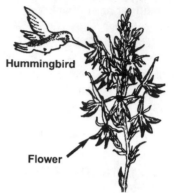

517.   Are the long narrow tube-like flowers of the Cardinal Flower only adapted to and visited by hummingbirds?

No. The flowers of the Cardinal Flower are definitely attracted by other insects, especially the bees. The long narrow tube-like flower has a split on top which allows the bees to enter. As the bee enters, it will brush

Figure 51.   A single Cardinal Flower plant will attract hummingbirds. See color plate IV.

against the **stigma** (female part) and push up the column of **stamens** (male part which contains pollen) by which it is dusted with pollen. This is a perfect mechanism for pollination by insects and insures many seeds in the fall.

518. Are all "Cardinal Flowers" the same?

No. Of the over 250 species of *Lobelia*, caution must be made in selecting the hardy red Cardinal Flower for water gardens. There are two groups of Lobelias, the annuals and the perennials. *Lobelia cardinalis* is the Cardinal Flower (red flower) native to North America and is the hardy type. *Lobelia fulgens* (or correctly *Lobelia splendens*) is a species native to Mexico and is sometimes incorrectly purchased as the "hardy" Cardinal Flower intended for the water garden.

519. Where are the Cardinal Flowers, *Lobelia cardinalis*, found growing in nature?

The Cardinal Flower, *Lobelia cardinalis*, is found growing naturally in ditches, besides streams and in wet meadows. Cardinal Flowers were once a very common roadside and meadow plant. Destruction of their habitat in the name of progress and the indiscriminate picking has led to a decline in numbers. A wet land meadow of Cardinal Flowers, with thousands of tiny deep red blossoms with contrasting green foliage, is a sight that is beyond description.

520. When does the Cardinal Flower, *Lobelia cardinalis*, produce flowers?

The Cardinal Flower, *Lobelia cardinalis,* will produce the beautiful red flowers late in the growing season. It will flower in late July in the northern United States and well into October.

521. If the Cardinal Flower did not produce seeds in the autumn, will the plant still return next year?

Yes. The plant reproduces asexually by a spreading rootstock and develops into a "clump" of cardinal flowers. Next year, the cardinal flower will grow from this spreading rootstock.

522. After the Water Plantain dies in the fall, should the dead vegetation be removed from the water garden?

No. In the northern climates with snow in the winter, the remaining foliage that held the flowers of the Water Plantain (*Alisma* spp.) should remain in the water garden. As the winter snow falls, it will be caught by the remaining dried pyramidal **inflorescence** (flower structure) stems and make a beautiful sight. It will also be a pleasant reminder of the beauty and charm that was experienced during the summer months around the water garden pool.

523. Is the Water Plantain eatable?

Yes. The thick, bulb-like rootstocks which grow below the ground can be eaten. To lose the arid taste, they are first dried and then cooked like potatoes.

524. What does the genus and species of Flowering Rush, *Butomus umbellatus*, mean?

The genus and species of Flowering Rush, as represented by the single species *Butomus umbellatus,* is derived from the Greek *buos* meaning "ox" and *temno* meaning "to cut; leaves too sharp for the mouths of cattle". This

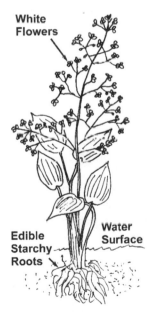

White Flowers

Water Surface

Edible Starchy Roots

Figure 52. Water Plantain has an attractive Inflorescence that will catch snow in the winter to make a very attractive sight.

151

derivation makes one focus on the stems which are characteristically triangular in cross section, which is a good identification of such a plant but hard to imagine how these soft stems could cut the mouth of an ox (color plate IV).

525. Is the Flowering Rush eatable?

Yes. The thick, fleshy underground rootstock can be eaten. It is prepared by peeling the underground rootstock and boiled like potatoes.

526. Do the flowers of the Blue Iris, *Iris versicolor* and Yellow Iris, *Iris pseudocorus* bloom all summer?

No. The flowers of the Blue and Yellow Iris will bloom once in the early spring and last for a few weeks. In the northern United States the Iris will begin to bloom in the early month of May. After blooming, the foliage will remain green the entire summer and add a continued beauty to the water garden.

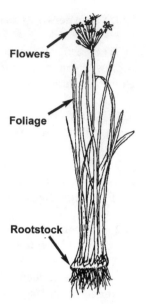

Flowers

Foliage

Rootstock

Figure 53. Flowering Rush has attractive flowers and grows from a rootstock that produces many plants.

527. Does the Blue Iris and Yellow Iris produce seeds?

Yes. After blooming, seeds are produced in large pods. The seed pods will dry later in the summer and split releasing the seeds into the water garden. Collecting the seeds and sowing them in soil will bring new plants the next season.

528. Can the Watercress, *Nasturtium officinale,* be eaten?

Yes. The Watercress, *Nasturtium officinale* is a member of the mustard family and has been used to garnish many foods. It is a plant that is known to be a supplier of vitamin C, iron, iodine, sulfur, copper and manganese. It can be picked at any time of the year, however when it is flowering it may have a bitter taste. Care should be taken to wash the plant before eating.

152

529. Why is the plant Horsetail called "scouring rush"?

The texture of the plant has a very rough texture made of silicon. The plants were used by the pioneer families in bundles to "scour" floors, table tops, etc. and thus its common name. Another common name for Horsetail in the 1800s was "Dutch Rush". The Dutch cabinet makers used the plant extensively to smooth and polish their work until the advent of sand paper.

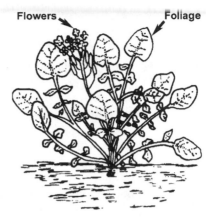

Flowers   Foliage

Figure 54. Watercress makes small white flowers in the green foliage.

530. Are the strange looking Horsetails primitive plants?

Yes. The Horsetails first appeared in the Devonian period, 400 million years ago, in fossil records. They were once a major component of the land flora and were as large as 40 foot trees but later declined to our present day horsetails that do not rise more than a few feet in height. Today much of our coal was formed from these plants.

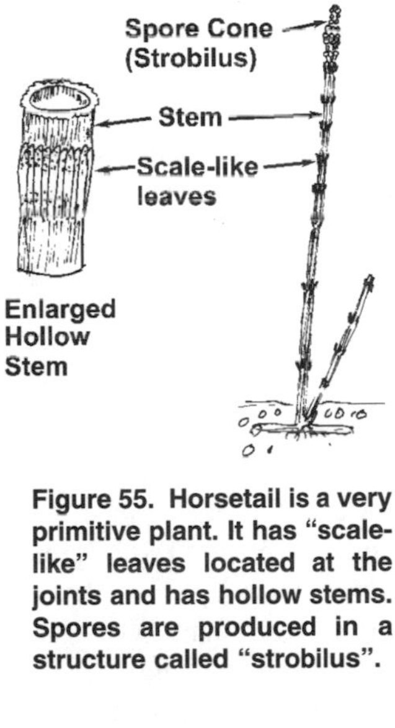

531. Do the Horsetails have leaves?

No. A close look at the Horsetail will reveal a hollow stem that is joined and around each joint is a whorl of very small and inconspicuous "scale-like" leaves (figure 55).

532. Do the Horsetails produce seeds?

Spore Cone (Strobilus)

Stem

Scale-like leaves

Enlarged Hollow Stem

Figure 55. Horsetail is a very primitive plant. It has "scale-like" leaves located at the joints and has hollow stems. Spores are produced in a structure called "strobilus".

No. The Horsetails produce spores and is known by botanist as a **cryptogam**, referring to the spore producing trait. These spores are produced at the tip of the stems or cone in a structure known as a **sporangia**. The life cycle of the Horsetail is similar to that of a fern.

533.   Since the stems are green in Horsetails are they capable of photosynthesis?

Yes. The green color produced by chlorophyll in the stems are capable of photosynthesis.

534. Are Horsetails very hardy?

Yes. Horsetails will survive a harsh winter under ice and snow.

535. Why does *Acorus Calamus* have a common name known as "Sweet Flag"?

A characteristic of *Acorus Calamus* is when the leaves are crushed they will emit a spicy "sweet" citrus scent similar to oranges, thus its common derivative name became "Sweet Flag".

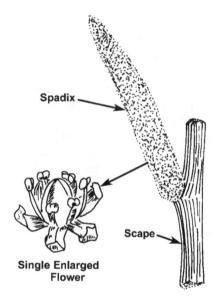

536.   Does the Sweet Flag produce flowers?

Yes, but they are not noticeable to the untrained eye. The flowers are very unusual looking and consist of a green **spadix** (figure 56) or spike of small flowers about four inches long located towards the top of the leaf. Since the spadix and leaves are both green, the observation of this structure is often overlooked by many water gardeners.   Once the water gardener identifies this fascinating flower structure, it will become a special feature in the water garden pool.

Figure 56. Sweet Flag has a very unusual flower that grows from a leafless stalk that arises from the ground. The spadix contains many tiny flowers.

537. How many species of Sweet Flag are there?

There are two species of Sweet Flag, *Acorus Calamus* and *A. gramineus*. They can readily be separated by the characteristic heights. The species *A. Calamus* grows to six feet and *A. gramineus* grows to a height of only 18 inches.

538. Are there any cultivars of Sweet Flag?

Yes. A well known cultivar is the variegated *Acorus gramineus* 'Variegatus'. It has leaves that are green stripped with white.

539. Why is *Saururus cernuus* called "Lizard's Tail"?

The name "Lizard's Tail" is named after a fascinating and unusual flower structure which has a curve that appears similar to a lizard's tail. The Lizard Tail will begin to bloom the lizard-like flowers from June through August in the northern United States.

540. Why are the flowers of the Lizard's Tail "unusual"?

The flower of the Lizard's Tail was a typical example used by botanist since the 1800s as a flower that is **naked** or **achlamydeous**. These terms were used by a well known American botanist, Professor Asa Gray (1810-1888) in his 1858 text, *How Plants Grow,* which he taught "young people botany". Professor Gray is best known for presenting the first edition of his *Manual of the Botany of the Northern United States* in 1848 which is still published today in an updated version. The terms "naked" or "achlamydeous" meant that the individual flowers have no **calyx**, a collective term for all the sepals of the flower, nor **corolla**, collective term for all the petals of a flower. Thus, the Lizard's Tail has a flower without the typical parts of flowers, the sepals and petals or more specifically, a flower without a **perianth**, a term referring to the calyx and corolla (figure 57).

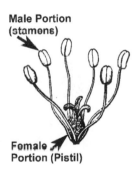

Male Portion (stamens)

Female Portion (Pistil)

Figure 57. The flower of the Lizard's Tail, *Sauraurus cernuus,* as shown in Professor Asa Gray's 1858 *How Plant's Grow* with authors label s. Note that there are no petals or sepals found in the Lizard's Tail.

541. How does the Lizard's Tail propagate?

The Lizard's Tail will reproduce by seeds or divisions of the creeping rhizome.

542. How tall does Wild Rice, *Zizania aquatica*, grow in the water garden?

Wild Rice, *Zizania aquatica*, can easily reach a height of eight to nine feet. The beauty of the developing seeds (figure 58) is a spectacular sight and the towering height has been described as the handsomest of tall hardy grasses for the margins of water gardens.

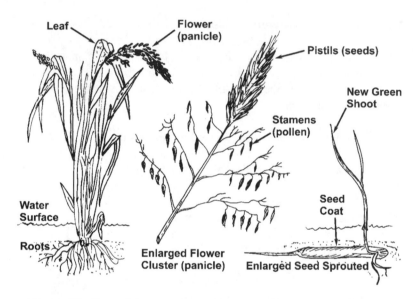

Figure 58. One of the most attractive plants for the water garden is Wild Rice. As the flower develops the stamens dangle from the flower panicleand produces a very beautiful sight. The seeds that develop will drop or can be collected and will sprout the following year to produce a new plant.

543. Can the seeds of the Wild Rice be eaten?

Yes. It was a common food as a cereal by the North American Indian and is also known as **Indian Rice**. The plant is commonly used to plant in marshes as an excellent feed and shelter for waterfowl. Fish also consume the grains as they fall into the water garden.

Nymphaea
'Blue Beauty'
Tropical Day Blooming
Water Lily

Hybridized by:
William Tricker
1896.
Introduced originally
as ***Nymphaea
pulcherrima.***

Nymphaea
'Trickeri'
Tropical Night
Blooming Water Lily

Hybridized by:
William Tricker
1893

Nymphaea
'Shirley-Ann'
Tropical Day Blooming
Water Lily

Hybridized by:
Gilbert Lambacher and
Dr. Charleston of
William Tricker, Inc.
1963

Plate I

Victoria Trickeri

Introduced into the United States in 1894 by WilliamTricker.

The pads will grow to six to seven feet across and produces a creamy white blossom up to a foot across.

Victoria Trickeri

Showing a second day flower that has changed to a pink color.

Nymphaea
'Janice'
Tropical Day Blooming Water Lily

The first white blooming viviparous tropical water lily

Hybridized by: Robert Sawyer of William Tricker, Inc. 1927

Plate II

Nymphaea 'James Brydon'
Hardy Water Lily

Nymphaea 'Antares':
Night blooming tropical water lily

Nymphaea 'Gonnere'
Hardy Water Lily

Nymphaea 'Gloriosa'
Hardy Water Lily

Nelumbo nucifera 'Asiatic Lotus'

Nelumbo nucifera 'Egyptian Lotus'

Plate III

Nymphaea '**Rose Arey**'
Hardy Water Lily

Botomus umbellatus
Flowering Rush

Nymphaea '**Gladstone**'
Hardy Water Lily

Lobelia cardinalis
Cardinal Flower

Caltha pulustris
Marsh Marigold

Aponogeton distachyus
Water Hawthorn

Nymphoides species
Giant Water Snowflake

Nymphoides species
Variegated Snowflake

Plate IV

Nymphaea
'Mrs. C. W. Ward'
TropicalDay
Blooming Water Lily

Hydridized by:
William Tricker
1900
Note the characteristic
dropping of the sepals

Nymphaea
'Alice Tricker'
Tropical Day
Blooming Water Lily

Hybridized by:
William Tricker, Inc.
1937

Nymphaea
'Patricia'
Tropical Pygmy
Day Blooming
Water Lily

Hybridized by:
W. G. O'Brien of
William Tricker, Inc.
1927

Plate V

Nymphaea gigantea
'Blue Gigantea'

Tropical Day
Blooming Water Lily

Introduced into the
United States in
1852.

Nymphaea
'Rio Rita'

Tropical Day
Blooming Water Lily

Hybridized by:
George Pring
1941

Nymphaea
'Panama Pacific'

Tropical Day
Blooming Water Lily

Hybridized by:
William Tricker
1914

Plate VI

Nymphaea 'Eldorado'
Day blooming tropical water lily

Nymphaea 'Dauben'
Day blooming tropical water lily

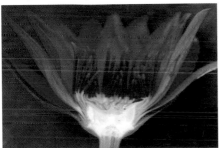

Flower cross section of
Nymphaea (Water Lily)

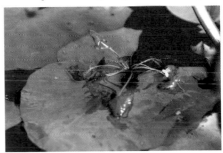

Viviparous leaf with growing
plantlet in center.

Nymphaea 'Director Moore'
Day blooming tropical water lily

Nymphaea 'Missouri'
Night blooming tropical water lily

Plate VII

Nymphaea 'Pink Pearl'
Day blooming tropical water lily

Pontederia paniculata
New Pickerel Rush

Nymphaea 'Midnight'
Day blooming tropical water lily

Completed Water Garden. This water garden is made with a durable rubber liner. It has two shelves, one with a cap of bricks and the other for placement of the shallow water plants. Coping is made of slate. A waterfall is made at the top. Plants are water lilies (both night and day blooming), floating plants, shallow water plants, oxygenating plants and includes fish with scavengers.

Plate VIII

544. How many species of Forget-Me-Not's, *Myosotis* spp. are there?

There are over 50 species of plants known as Forget-Me-Not's. The genus *Myosotis* is Greek for "mouse ears" referring to the shape of the delicate leaves resembling the ear of a mouse. The species *Myosotis scorpiodes* is the plant of choice for the water gardener. Aquatic nurseries sell this species.

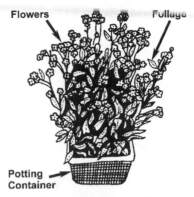

Flowers   Foliage

Potting Container

Figure 59. A planted group of Forget-Me-Nots makes a pleasing amount of dainty blue flowers.

545. Of the many different species of Forget-Me-Not's, why should the species *Myosotis scorpiodes* be selected for a water garden?

The species *Myosotis scorpiodes* is known to be tolerant of the abundance of water that is found in the water garden. The blooming characteristic begins in early spring and continues throughout the growing season. Other species may not be tolerant of the amount of water in the water garden pool and may not have these long blooming characteristics.

546. What is one of the earliest blooming marginal plants for the water garden?

The Marsh Marigold, *Caltha pulustris*, will display its wonderful bright yellow blossoms in early March in the northern United States. This trait makes it one of the earliest blooming signs of spring. It is not unusual to see a patch of marsh marigold blooming through a light covering of snow in early spring.

547. Does the Marsh Marigold bloom during the entire growing season?

No, unfortunately the bright yellow flowers of the Marsh Marigold bloom only during the early spring (color plate IV).

548. How does the Marsh Marigold reproduce?

The Marsh Marigold reproduces vegetatively in clumps and by seeds. The seeds are produced in small pods that ripen during the summer. The seeds are very small approximately the size of grains of sand.

549. Where is the Marsh Marigold found growing in nature?

The Marsh Marigold is found growing in cool wet places, near running streams and surrounded by trees in partial shade. When walking in a wet land area the bright yellow flowers of the Marsh Marigold will stand out in the early spring.

550. Is the Marsh Marigold eatable?

Yes. The young stems and leaves of the Marsh Marigold taste very good when cooked.

551. How many petals does the bright yellow flower of the Marsh Marigold have?

None. The Marsh Marigold has no petals. The yellow flower color is from the sepals that have a petal-like appearance (color plate IV).

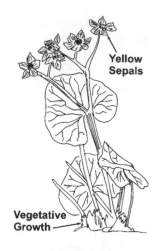

Yellow Sepals

Vegetative Growth

Figure 60. Marsh Marigold is one of the first to flower in the water garden pool. Interestingly the plant does not have petals but the attractive yellow flowers are from the color of the sepals.

552. Since the Marsh Marigold does not have petals, does it attract any insects for pollination?

Yes. The female carpel found in the center of the flower secrets nectar. This nectar attracts small bees and flies intent on breakfasting as these flowers open in the morning sun. Conspicuous among the flowers of the Marsh Marigold is the brilliant colored *Syrphidae* flies (figure 61).

553. What does the insect *Syrphidae*, conspicuous among the flowers of the Marsh Marigold, look like?

The family *Syrphidae* contains a large group of flies known as the **Syrphus Flies** or **Flower Flies** (figure 61) and comprise many of the most interesting of the two winged insects that are commonly found around flowers. The Syrphus Fly does a great deal of hovering among flowers and are often seen on a sunshiny day. They vary greatly in color. Some are metallic greenish, while others are banded in yellow in different ways. This group of flies have evolved a special type of survival known as **protective mimicry**. Protective mimicry is a term used by the entomologist (insect specialist) which means that the

Syrphus Flies have evolved into different species over thousands of years to resemble or mimic in body color and flying habits almost all types of bees and wasps. Thus, any feared potential predator to a bee or wasp would not challenge the Syrphus Fly since it could not differ the two and would be afraid of the danger of being stung, bite or attacked by this insect. Interestingly, none of the syrphids can bite man. Many gardeners cannot tell the difference between the syrphids as a mimicked bumble bee, honey bee or wasp.

554. If the syrphus flies resemble stinging and biting insects, can the water gardener tell the difference?

Barely. The resemblance to mimicked bees and wasps is astonishing (figures 61 and 62). An entomologist (insect specialist) can tell you that if the suspected wasp bites you, it is not a syrphus fly since the syrphus fly cannot bite. Without going through such a traumatic experience of being bitten, the main difference between any flies and bees or wasps is that flies have one pair of wings and the bees or wasps have two pairs of wings. A close observation of a bumble bee and a mimicked syrphus can be differentiated by counting the number of wings. Be careful in getting too close when attempting to identify the unknown insect by counting the number of wings, or an unsuspected bite will make the effort conclusive.

Single Pair of Wings

Figure 61. The Syrphus fly does not bite and can be seen visiting the Marsh Marigold. The Syrphus fly has a single set of wings but resembles a bee for protection.

Two Pair of Wings

Figure 62. A bee has characteristicly two pair of wings while a fly has only one pair.

555. Do Marsh Marigolds make good cut flowers?

Yes. The Marsh Marigold was once a highly desired bright yellow flower that was sold as a cut flower at the turn of the century. It is known to last a long time as a cut flower.

556. Is the Marsh Marigold in the same family as that of the common garden variety "marigold"?

Absolutely not. These are two distinct groups of plants and the Marsh Marigold is not a "true marigold". The common garden variety marigold and other "true marigolds" are found in the Composite Family (botanically, Compositae Family) while the Marsh Marigold is in the Buttercup Family (botanically, Ranunculaceae family). An old favorite double flowered "marigold" is the *Calandula officinalis* known as the Pot-Marigold. The Marsh Marigold genus *Caltha* means "marigold" in Latin.

557. Why is the Marsh Marigold in the Buttercup Family and not classified with the true marigolds?

Since the 1800s, children, as did the botanical taxonomist, noticed the similarities of the Marsh Marigold and the common meadow buttercup. In old literature the common reference with "buttercups" was that children held the shinning golden flowers of the common meadow buttercup under the chin to test their fondness of butter. This test was done with the common meadow buttercup and also with the similar shining golden flowers of the Marsh Marigold. The botanist classified the Marsh Marigold within the **Buttercup Family** due to the similarity to the common meadow buttercup: by flowers and other morphological structures. It by far does not belong in the **Composite Family** that contains the "true marigolds" since it does not have morphological similar flowers or other taxonomic characteristics.

558. Why is the Marsh Marigold called a "cowslip"?

The word "cowslip" is a common name without scientific basis. It is an Anglo-Saxon word *cuslyppe* where *cu* means "cow" and *sylyppe* means "cow-slop" or "cow-dung". Thus, it has been derived from a barnyard meaning in that the flower will be found in cow pastures. In England the cowslip refers to the common Primrose and in America several plants have acquired such a term: American Cowslip (Shooting stars), Virginia Cowslip (Virginia Bluebell) and most commonly the Marsh Marigolds have been called cowslips.

> # PLANTING DEPTH:
> # 6 INCHES WATER OVER CROWN

559. How many species of cattail are there?

There are over 15 recognized species of cattails of the genus *Typha*.

560. How do the many species of cattail differ?

The many different species of cattails differ in plant height, width of leaves and spikes (flowers at top or catkins).

561. Are there any hybrids of cattails?

Yes. A popular hybrid is *Typha latifolia* 'Variegata' which is the variegated cattail. This cattail has a beautiful stripped pattern of longitudinal stripes of green and white in the leaves.

562. Is the Variegated Cattail hardy?

Yes. The Variegated Cattail is extremely hardy and can easily withstand a harsh winter of snow and ice.

563. How do the cattails reproduce?

The cattails reproduce by seeds and underground runners. If the cattail is not transplanted within a few years, it will become pot bound with a tangled mass of underground runners. It is best to transplant the potted cattails every few years by cutting the underground runners into individual plants and repotting. Repotting will prevent the underground mass of tangled roots.

564. Are cattails pollinated by insects?

No. The cattails rely upon wind dispersal of the pollen for fertilization. This is possible by the location of the female and male parts of the plant.

565. Where is the male and female flower parts on the cattail?

The flower parts of the cattail (figure 63) are separated into female and male flower parts. The lower part of the spike (catkin) is the female flower and is composed of close packed flowers which is the most familiar part of the cattail. The top part of the spike is the male part which produces the pollen. The wind that moves the cattail gently back and forth allows the pollen not only to fall from the top portion of the spike onto the bottom female portion but to disperse to other plants. Thus, the cattail uses wind as a method of pollination and does not need to attract insects.

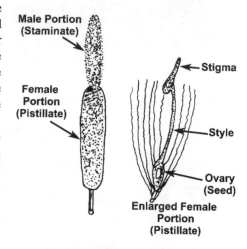

Figure 63. The Cattail produces pollen in the staminate portion and falls upon the pistillate portion to produce seeds.

566. Are cattails eatable?

Yes. Euell Gibbons, an American naturalist, has been quoted to say *"For the number of different kinds of food it produces there is no plant, wild or domesticated, which tops the common cattail."*

567. What parts of the cattail are prepared as food?

The cattail is a excellent survival plant that has been taught to military personnel. The edible rootstocks grow up to one inch thick and contains about 46 percent starch and 11 percent sugar. In preparing to eat the rootstocks, the outer covering is peeled off and the white inner portion is grated. They then can be boiled or eaten raw. In addition to the rootstocks, the yellow pollen from the flowers can be mixed with water and steamed as bread and the young growing shoots are excellent when boiled like asparagus.

568. Besides the Marsh Marigold, what other marginal aquatic plant blooms early in the season?

The Bogbean, *Menyanthes trifoiata*, is one known to bloom very early in the spring season in the northern United States. It is known to begin blooming in April and continue to midsummer.

569. What does the genus and species of Bogbean "*Menyanthes trifoliata*" mean?

The name *Menyanthes* is Greek for month flower, possibly referring to the fact that the Bogbean blooms for only a month. The species, *trifoliata*, name of Bogbean refers to the foliage which is found in groups of threes (figure 64), thus referring to "tri" meaning three and "foliata" meaning foliage.

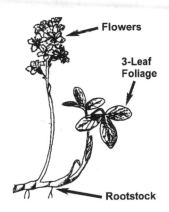

Flowers

3-Leaf Foliage

Rootstock

Figure 64. Bogbean makes a cluster of attractive flowers in the early spring with characteristic 3-leaf foliage and grows by a rootstock.

570. Does the Bogbean produce roots as it creeps across the water garden?

Yes. As the Bogbean grows across the water garden they will send down a series of roots from the rhizome seeking the bog-like bottom of the water garden. These rhizome outgrowths with roots can be cut and replanted to make new plants in other parts of the water garden.

571. What is the color of the flowers of the Bogbean?

The attractive flowers are a delicate fringed pink outside with pure white centers. The redness of the stamens gives this a beautiful overall appearance to the flowers of the Bogbean.

572. Is the Floating Heart a small water lily?

No, in fact it is not a water lily of the genus *Nymphaea* but in the genus *Nymphoides*. The small two inch, heart-shaped, mottled floating pads do resemble a miniature or pygmy water lily plant, however the delicate yellow fringed buttercup-like flowers do not. Like the true water lilies, the Floating Heart prefers still water and is extremely floriferous.

573. How does the Floating Heart spread in the water garden?

After the Floating Heart is planted in a container with top soil and placed into the water garden pool at a depth up to 18 inches, the plant will grow rapidly producing many blooms that last but one a day. The plant can grow or spread by three ways: sending out surface runners, runners from the bottom of the container and from seed pods.

574. Is the Floating Heart a prolific grower?

Yes, exceptionally prolific. In fact, in earth bottom ponds the Floating Heart can be very invasive by taking over much of the marginal areas.

575. How many species of floating heart, *Nymphoides* are there?

There are about 20 species of *Nymphoides.*

576. Are all the species of *Nymphoides* hardy?

No. The North American species *Nymphoides peltata* is an excellent hardy species commonly grown in water gardens. The tropical species are commonly referred to as **snowflakes**, i.e. *Nymphoides indica* (color plate IV).

577. What is the color and appearance of the flowers and floating leaves of the Floating Heart, *Nymphoides peltata*?

The flowers are yellow and stand approximately two to three inches above the water surface. The two inch floating leaves are heart shaped and mottled.

578. Why are the stems of the Arrow Arum so delicate?

There are no stems in the Arrow Arum, *Peltandra virginica.* A close look will reveal the leaves are directly from the stout rhizomes in the soil. What one would think is a stem is, in reality, only leaves.

579. What are the color of the berries produced by Arrow Arum?

The berries produced by the Arrow Arum are green.

560. What marginal plant produces flowers the latest in the season?

The Water Hawthorn, *Aponogeton distachyus*, (color plate IV) is known to

164

bloom late in the year and continue all winter if protected from ice. Even if the plant is found in temporary freezes of ice, the flowers and plant recovers rapidly only to continue to bloom and grow after thaw.

580. Since the Water Hawthorn blooms continually throughout the spring and during a cold winter, what happens in the heat of summer?

The Water Hawthorn can become dormant in the heat of summer. The increase in temperature of the water will begin to reduce flower production and the plant will produce a tuber. Later in the season, as the weather becomes cooler, the Water Hawthorn will begin growing and blooming. This wonderful plant was identified for water gardens at the turn of the century. William Tricker in 1897 recommended the Water Hawthorn as a plant for winter blooming (figure 65).

Figure 65. The Water Hawthorn as shown from William Tricker's *The Water Garden* published in 1897. The flowers are extremely fragrant and are very attractive. See color plate IV.

581. Does the flower of the Water Hawthorn have an aroma?

Yes, and the aroma is why many water gardeners choose the Water Hawthorn. It has a lovely delicate vanilla fragrance similar to the Hawthorn permeates the air a great distant. Many have suggested that the Water Hawthorn has one of the strongest aromas of the aquatic plants.

582. What is the flower color of the Water Hawthorn?

The flowers are white with jet black anthers. Occasionally a pink or rose-hued flower will be produced.

583. Since the flower of the Water Hawthorn smells so good, can it be eaten?

Yes. In the Western Cape where it is indigenous, the Water Hawthorn is eaten as a true vegetable. It is when the seeds begin to develop shortly after the flower opens it can be added to a salad or eaten raw.

584. How does the flower of the Hardy Thalia become fertilized or pollinated?

The Hardy Thalia, *Thalia dealbata*, has a very unusual method of fertilization and botanist have reported the Thalias as "explosive mechanisms for pollination". The purplish flowers are grown on stems four to five feet high. Looking closely at the flower a style or stem-like center structure that receives the pollen appears curved in the center of the flower. Upon insect visitation to collect nectar a sensitive portion of this trigger-like **style** activates and snaps down upon the insect. This brings the **stigma** (female pollen receptor) and the **stamen** (male pollen) into contact. Quite often this mechanism traps the insect. It is not unusual to find a trapped butterfly or ant within the flowers of a Hardy Thalia.

585. Can the unusual "explosive mechanism of pollination" of Hardy Thalia be observed?

Yes. During the later part of summer when the Hardy Thalia is in full bloom the water gardener can pull down one of the long stems with flowers into one hand. With the other hand, a toothpick or similar small object is placed into a single flower on the Hardy Thalia. When the **style** or center structure of the flower is touched, the trigger mechanism should react and snap close. A true marvel of Mother Nature's invention.

586. When does the Pickerel Rush bloom?

The Pickerel Rush, *Pontederia cordata*, blooms in the Northern United States from late June through October.

587. Why is the *Pontederia cordata* common name "Pickerel Rush"?

In the early 1900s the pickerel fish, *Esox* spp., were reported by back woodsmen to lay their eggs on these plants thus its common name. The pickerel fish are commonly found in clear grassy and weedy streams. The flowers of the Pickerel Rush attracts many insects and this fact alone would also attract many fish to this area of plants.

588. How long does a single flower of the Pickerel Rush bloom?

The Pickerel Rush (fig.66) will bloom small blue flowers continually, but interestingly a single blossom only lasts a single day. The spike on the Pickerel Rush will continually produce flowers and as the spike lengthens producing an uninterrupted succession of blooms for months. This blooming characteristic has made the Pickerel Rush a very desirable and attractive pool side plant.

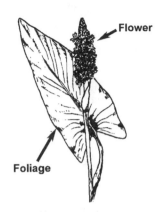

589. Does the Pickerel Rush make seeds?

Yes. However, self pollination does not occur and the need of an insect is necessary. The Pickerel Rush are visited during the summer mainly by bees. The English naturalist Charles Darwin (1809-1882)

Figure 66. Pickerel Rush has a very attractive blue flower with complementing foliage.

experimented with the essential cross pollination of Pickerel Rush by insects in relation to the morphology of the different types of flowers found on each plant. He proved how the three morphological types of flowers found on different plants (trimorphic plants) were cross pollinated by insects. The main difference in these flowers are the three different lengths of the stigmas and two sets of stamens bearing pollen grains of different size and value which involved the insects method of cross pollination.

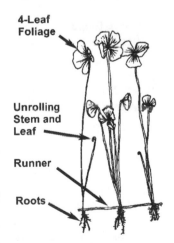

590. Does the Four Leaf Water Clover make flowers?

No. The Four Leaf Water Clover, *Marsilea* spp., (figure 67) is a water fern and like ferns, reproduce by **spores** in a structure known as a **sporocarp**.

591. Can the sporocarp of the Four Leaf Water Clover be seen?

Yes. The sporocarps that produce spores are found at the base of the petiole near the roots. It is a small round structure.

Figure 67. Four Leaf Clover produces four leaves on each stem.

592. If the Four Leaf Water Clover becomes pot bound what happens?

The leaves of the Four Leaf Water Clover normally float on the water surface. If the plant becomes pot bound, the leaves will become aerial. The leaves of the four leaf clover will rise a few inches out of the water on short stems. Interestingly, at night the aerial four leaves will close and in the morning will open again.

593. Does the Water Pennywort make flowers?

Yes. The Water Pennywort, *Hydrocotyle* spp., makes small dainty white flowers in **umbels** or umbel-like clusters (figure 68). The umbel is a flower arrangement that arises from the center axis of many short **pedicels** (stalks).

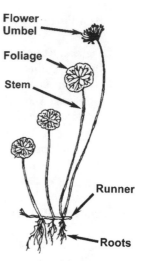

Figure 68. Water Pennywort makes small dainty flowers in a structure known as a "umbel". The plant grows by runners.

WINTERING HARDY SHALLOW WATER PLANTS

594. What should be done with the hardy shallow water plants in a winter that experiences ice and snow?

In the late fall, the hardy shallow water plants will begin a dormancy as evident from the browning of leaves and reduction of blooms which may have resulted in seed production. It is suggested to move the container of hardy shallow water plants to slightly lower location in the pool that will ensure a few inches of water over the crown during the winter. The hardy shallow water plants can withstand a great deal of harsh freezing temperatures in winter without being moved to another location in the pool. Many water gardeners have experienced the successful wintering of hardy shallow water plants without moving them from the original summer shelf growing location. The dead stems and brown foliage can be pruned, however, the remaining dead stems and foliage will catch snow and give a picturesque winter attraction to the pool (i.e. Water Plantain). In the spring, the hardy shallow water plants should be relocated to the original place in the water garden pool.

XI. Tropical Aquatic Shallow Water Plants

PLANTING DEPTH: 2 INCHES OF WATER OVER CROWN

595. Is the papyrus plant, *Cyperus papyrus,* **the paper plant that was used by the ancient Egyptians to make the ancient paper of Egypt?**

Yes. The first known writing paper is derived from the papyrus plant *Cyperus papyrus.*

596. What part of the plant did the ancient Egyptians use to make paper from the Papyrus plant?

The ancient Egyptians made thin strips from the **pith** (center) of the stem of the papyrus to make the paper.

597. Can the water gardener make paper from the papyrus plant?

Yes. Obtain the stems of a full grown papyrus plant, *Cyperus papyrus* and follow these steps:

Procedure for Making Paper From Papyrus

a. Cut off approximately a foot and half of the papyrus triangular stem with sides of approximately one-half inch. The stems should not be allowed to dry out.

b. Using a knife, peel off and discard the hard green outside cover (figure 69) to expose the white inside pulp or pith. Make "paper" thin longitudinal or lengthwise slices of the white inside pulp. The strips should be at least six inches long.

c. Place the papyrus strips in a jar of water and soak overnight.

Figure 69. Using a knife peal the hard outer cover of the papyrus.

d. The next day, the strips of papyrus are removed from the jar. If white paper is desired the strips can be soaked in a 20 percent solution of bleach. Using a rolling pin or round jar the pieces are smashed flat and lined in a row slightly overlapping (figure 70).

e. In the original formula, Nile water was used to sprinkle over the strips, however a "flour and water" mixture can be substituted for the Nile water. A second layer is made by laying additional flattened papyrus strips transversely across the original flour-watered strips. The entire papyrus layers should be rolled as flat as possible into a "sheet" (figure 70).

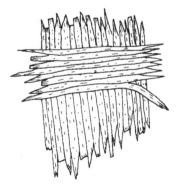

f. The "sheet" of flattened papyrus (figure 70) is then placed between two paper towels and compressed by placing something heavy on top such as a pile of books or other heavy objects. When the papyrus "sheet" is dry, usually overnight depending upon humidity, the books or heavy objects can be removed and the piece of "Papyrus Paper" is completed.

Figure 70. The flattened strips of papyrus are laid in a rows

598. Did the ancient Egyptians use the papyrus for other things besides paper?

Yes. The ancient Egyptians used the papyrus for making rafts, especially since the papyrus was thought to be abhorred by the crocodiles. Thus, when Moses needed a cradle to float down the Nile River, the best material to use would be the Bulrush Papyrus.

599. After the papyrus grows for most of the summer and the green tops begin to become spindly and brown, is it dying?

No, not necessarily. When the papyrus begins to make seeds, the green top will begin to appear brown and spindly. If seeds are being developed, the brown and spindly structures are normal.

600. How does the New Pickerel Rush, *Pontederia paniculata*, differ from the common Pickerel Rush, *Pontederia cordata* ?

The New Pickerel Rush is tropical while the common Pickerel Rush is hardy, therefore the New Pickerel Rush will not survive a winter of snow and ice. They are distinctly different in appearance. The New Pickerel Rush is taller and makes two shades of blue flowers. The New Pickerel Rush grows more rapidly and flowers profusely. Due to this fast growth, the New Pickerel Rush requires extra aquatic fertilizer during the growing season.

601. Why is the *Hymenocallis caribaea* called a Spider Lily?

Seeds

Hymenocallis caribaea has a very unusual and attractive flower which resembles a spider. The white tube-like petals have extending filaments that hang down from the flower and resemble a spider's legs.

602. Can the Umbrella Palm, *Cyperus alternifolius*, be brought indoors for the winter?

Yes. The Umbrella Palm can be removed from the water garden pool before frost in the Northern United States and brought indoors. The plant can be

Figure 71. The Umbrella Palm has very attractive leaves and makes seeds on the top.

placed in a dish of water and made sure that the soil is kept moist. A window with direct sunlight is recommended.

603. Is there a cultivar of the Umbrella Palm?

Yes. There is a dwarf or smaller cultivar *Cyperus alternifolius* 'Gracilis' or commonly known as the Dwarf Umbrella Palm. The Dwarf Umbrella Palm grows to 18 inches tall whereas the Umbrella Palm, *Cyperus alternifolius*, is usually grows to three to five feet.

604. Does the Primrose Willow, *Jussiaea longifolia*, make flowers?

Yes. The Primrose Willow, *Jussiaea longifolia*, makes bright yellow primrose-like blossoms.

605. How can the Primrose Willow be propagated?

The Primrose Willow propagates by cuttings or seeds.

606. How does the Velvet Leaf, *Limnocharis flava*, reproduce?

The plant makes very attractive yellow flowers on stems which slowly drop into the water and send up a shoot that will become a new plant. The seeds are produced in a very unusual pod and are also very fertile.

607. Why is the common name of *Limnocharis flava* called "Velvet Leaf"?

The leaf has a "velvet" green appearance. The Velvet Leaf is one of the most attractive and unusual looking plants for a water garden pool.

608. What are the water-looking droplets that form on the margins of the leaves of the Velvet Leaf?

These droplets are excess water from the plant. These are often formed when the humidity of the air is high. The botanist term for this is **guttation**. It is a similar process that occurs in dew on the grass in the morning.

609. Where is the native county or the Velvet Leaf?

Being a tropical aquatic plant, the Velvet Leaf is native to the West Indies and South America.

PLANTING DEPTH:
6 INCHES OF WATER OVER CROWN

610. How does the Tropical Thalia, *Thalia geniculata* (formerly *Thalia divaricata*) differ from the Hardy Thalia, *Thalia dealbata*?

Besides one being tropical and the other a hardy, the Tropical Thalia does not have the characteristic white powdery leaves. The **bracts** (leaf that holds the flower) are pale blue in the Hardy Thalia while the bracts are red or purple beneath in the Tropical Thalia.

611. How does the Purple Water Hyacinth, *Eichhornia azurea*, spread in the water garden pool?

The Purple Water Hyacinth spreads by submerged shoots. As the plant grows across the surface of the water it will begin to produce underwater roots. At this point it can be cut and re-potted. The shoots will develop roots as it spreads across the water garden.

612. How long do the flowers of the Water Poppy, *Hydrocleys nymphoides* last?

The Water Poppy (figure 72) produces an abundance of beautiful yellow flowers that last but only one day each. Since the plant produces such an abundance of flowers, the one day bloom often goes unnoticed in the water garden pool. William Tricker referred to the Water Poppy in the early 1900s as producing "bright cheery yellow flowers".

Figure 72. The Water Poppy from a original plate of William Tricker's *The Water Garden* published in 1897.

173

613. Why are Mellon Swords, *Echinodorus osiris,* selected for the water garden?

The Mellon Swords are selected for their beautiful foliage. The Mellon Swords are often considered one of the most beautiful of the 50 species of *Echinodorus.* The young leaves are an intensive red color and fading as the leaves become larger to an olive to dark-green. The foliage makes a beautiful appearance in the water garden pool. They are also used commonly in fish aquariums as a planted underwater center show piece.

614. What are the color of the flowers of the Primrose Creeper, *Ludwigia adscendens*?

The flowers of the Primrose Creeper are yellow. Interestingly the genus and species of the Primrose Creeper have changed over the years and this plant can be used as an example of the confusion that occurs over time with naming plants. Linneus named the plant *Jussiaea repens* in 1753 and denoted it *J. adscendens* in 1767. Japanese botanist Hara moved it to the genus *Ludwigia,* which would make this plant *Ludwigia repens.* But since the scientific name *Ludwigia repens* was already used by another plant, the previous Linneus species was used and thus the name has been corrected to *Ludwigia adscendens.*

615. Do the flowers of the Butterfly Lily have an aroma?

Yes. The flowers of the Butterfly Lily, *Hedychium coronarium,* makes beautiful flowers that are extremely fragrant. They produce an abundance of flowers in a growing season and can be used as cut flowers indoors. The aroma is very strong and will permeate rapidly throughout the air in large rooms.

616. Are there any aquatic plants that have leaves like the mimosa plant that close when touched?

Yes. The Water Sensitivity Plant, *Neptunia oleracea*, is an aquatic plant that closes the leaves when touched.

617. What causes the Water Sensitivity Plant to close when it is touched?

The leaves and sensitivity of the Water Sensitivity Plant is very similar to the well known sensitive plant *Mimosa pudica.* The closing and opening is called a **nastic movement** in plants. Nastic movements are often associated with the opening and closing of a flower, but this particular nastic movement differs by being immediate. Nastic movements are caused by a change in **turgor pressure** (water pressure) within the cells of the plant. As the hand touches the hairs on the leaves of the plant, the response is transferred into the base of the petiole where a mass of cells lose turgor pressure results in a relaxation and support of the leaves which then close. After touching the leaves, the plant will slowly open again once the turgor pressure is restored.

618. Must the leaves of the Water Sensitivity Plant be physically touched to close?

No. At night the leaves close by themselves without touch. In the day light the leaves again open. Thus, the plant not only reacts to touch but sunlight.

619. What are the white bulbous looking structures that the Water Sensitivity Plant makes along the water surface?

These are floatation devices the plant will use to spread across the water surface. They appear as round bulbous material that are full of air holes that make them excellent floatation devices. If the plant grows outside of the water garden, the bulbous material will not be produced and the plant will make hardened stems.

XII. Floating Aquatic Plants

CHARACTERISTICS

620. What are the "floating aquatic plants" that can be added to the water garden pool?

The floating aquatic plants are those plants that will simply "float" and live on the surface of the water.

621. Why should the water gardener add floating aquatic plants to the pool?

A wondrous beauty is added by introducing aquatic floating plants in any water garden pool. They float gently on the surface of the water and add a curiosity that cannot be seen in any other form of gardening. They need very little care. Some will flower and others will add a color dimension to a special location in the water garden.

622. Besides the beauty of the floating aquatic plants in a water garden pool, do the plants help with the water quality?

Yes. In addition to the beauty found with aquatic floating plants in the water garden, they help maintain the quality of the water. They assist in the control of algae. Fish and other animals in the water garden live in close harmony with the aquatic floating plants since they provide a natural environment.

623. How do the floating plants in the water garden pool get their nourishment?

The floating plants in the water garden derive their nourishment from the air and surrounding water. Different floating plants have a variety of methods to grow on the surface of the pond. The atmosphere can provide the necessary gases for **photosynthesis**, the process by which the plants manufacture food. Many have a root system that dangle into the water and can extract nourishment not only from the water but from any bottom soil that the roots may touch.

624. How do the floating plants control algae in the water garden pool?

The floating plants are good for controlling algae in the water garden pool. Not only do they shade the bottom of the pond preventing algae from reproducing or multiplying but they take vital nutrients out of the water that the algae use for food, specifically the **nitrates** and **phosphates**. Both the algae and floating plants will compete for the nitrates and phosphates in the water. Since the floating plants have a more advanced system than the algae, they will extract these nutrients faster and starve the algae.   The Floating Water Hyacinth, *Eichhnornia crassipes*, is one of the best known floating plants for controlling algae.

625. How do floating plants and fish get along in the water garden pool?

Fish love floating aquatic plants. Some floating aquatic plants, such as the duckweeds are an excellent food for fish. These provide fish with a good plant vegetable filled with nutrients. Many of the floating plants act as miniature filter factories. Fish waste products, such as the **toxic ammonia**, are broken down by bacteria living on the roots of the floating plants and made into a fertilizer which is consumed by the plants. The plants become fish food and the cycle, known as the **nitrogen cycle**, repeats itself. In addition, shelter from predators can be found in roots that dangle into the water by the floating aquatic plant.

177

626. What floating aquatic plants are used by fish to lay eggs on?

Most floating aquatic plants that have their roots dangling into the water will provide an excellent environment for the fish to lay eggs. These plants provide a good sheltered location from larger predators during egg hatching and development. In addition, many small microscopic animal and plant life (zooplankton and algae) that flourish within these dangling roots will be available for food. Excellent plants for this purpose would be the Floating Fern (*Ceratopteris pteriodoides*), Floating Water Hyacinth (*Eichhnoria crassipes*) or Shell Flower (*Pistia stratiotes*).

FLOATING AQUATIC PLANT SPECIES

627. When did the popular Floating Water Hyacinth, *Eichhornia crassipes* come to America?

The Water Hyacinth was first noticed by a Karl Von Martius, a renowned German botanist, in 1824 during a scientific research trip to Brazil, South America. The genus was defined by a German botanist C. S. Kunth (1788-1850) in 1842 and named after the Prussian Minister Eichhorn (1779-1850). The plant was introduced into the United States from Venezuela in 1884, when it was brought to the Cotton States Exposition in New Orleans, Louisiana by Japanese exhibitors. Within a short time, the plants spread in many water ways in the southern United States, with largest accumulation in Florida, Louisiana and Texas. Due to the fact that the plant floats on the surface of water, it can easily be spread by wind. With its tremendous growth rate, they quickly became a nuisance in boat navigation and restricted water movement. In the early 1900s control efforts began and have been addressed ever since.

628. How does the Floating Water Hyacinth (*Eichhornia crassipes*) spread across a water garden pond?

The Floating Water Hyacinth grows or spreads across a water garden pool by sending out runners from the main plant. These runners develop into a new plant. The new plants will grow into an adult plant and repeat the process of making runners which subsequently produce more plants. The Floating Water Hyacinth has a series of bulbous material (figure 73) that is filled with air chambers which are very buoyant in water and soon cover the surface of the water. The roots dangle below keeping the plant upright.

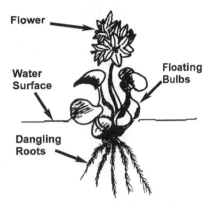

Figure 73. The Floating Water Hyacinth is a fascinating aquatic that simply floats upon the surface of the water.

629. If the Floating Water Hyacinth reproduces by a means of runners at the surface of the water garden pool, does it also produce seeds?

Yes. If after 48 hours the flower is not pollinated by insects, self-pollination takes place. During the next three weeks tiny black seeds will develop and drop into the water. It has been reported that the seeds can stay viable for fifteen years in the mud at the bottom of a pond.

630. Can the Floating Water Hyacinth be beneficial to man?

Yes. An abundance of research has been directed to the use of the Floating Water Hyacinth because of its rapid growth and physiological functions. Research has been done on the ability of the Floating Water Hyacinth to clean sewage in the treatment of water for drinking.

Since 1948 the Floating Water Hyacinth was studied in treatment of raw sewage or waste water management. The nitrogen fixing bacteria that live on the hanging roots provide the plant with nutrients to grow in profusion. It has been reported that the Floating Water Hyacinth, with the proper nutrients and weather conditions, can double its surface area in approximately six days and two plants are capable of covering an acre of water in less than eight months . It was found that dirty water in a pond full of hyacinths that flows 50 feet in 36

179

hours can clean the water sparkling clear. Most research regarding Floating Water Hyacinth waste water treatment is in the ability of the plant in removing nitrogens and phosphorus. Research is being conducted to convert Floating Water Hyacinths into fertilizer, as an energy source (methane generation), in the manufacture of paper or possible use as cattle feed. In addition, Floating Water Hyacinths have the ability to absorb organic pollutants, nitrogen, phosphorus, heavy metals (lead, mercury, cadmium, silver) pesticides, chemical wastes and other contaminates in our ecosystem. Research in this area can be very beneficial to our ecosystem.

A major hope is that the Floating Water Hyacinth can be used for food around the world. The plant can be processed into nutrients like protein, vitamin A, vitamin B-2 (riboflavin), vitamin E and vitamin B-12.

631. Besides the single species of Floating Water Hyacinth, are there any varieties?

Yes. There is a variety known as *Eichhnoria crassipes* variety *major*. This variety has rosy-lilac flowers and demonstrates a distinct spot of reddish coloration on each of the floating bulbs. In a crowded condition, this variety does not make strong and leggy stems and does not tolerate sustained cold temperatures as representative as the native species.

632. If the Floating Water Hyacinth is not blooming or growing well in the water garden pool, what can be done?

The Water Hyacinth thrives in water that contains an abundant amount of nitrogen and phosphorus. If the water is devoid of these nutrients then the plant will not perform well, as with many floating plants. Fish in the water garden can provide waste products in the form of ammonia which will subsequently be processed into the nitrates (providing the nitrogen) that can be used by the Floating Water Hyacinths. A container of soil with fertilizer can be placed into the water garden and by allowing the dangling roots of the Water Hyacinth to touch this soil will greatly enhance the growth.

633. Does the Shell Flower or Water Lettuce produce flowers?

Yes. The flowers of the Shell Flower or Water Lettuce (*Pistia stratoides*) are found inside the body of this velvet-green floating plant. They are small, approximately 1/2 inch tall, and can be seen enclosed in a leaflike whitish **spathe** (covering) without the aide of a microscope. A close look will show the unisexual flower with the **ovary** (female part) and two **stamens** (male part) growing in separate compartments. The flower is difficult to see since it blends in closely with the foliage. Therefore, the Shell Flower is chosen and admired for the attractive "lettuce-like" velvet-green foliage as it gently floats on the surface of the water garden pool and not for the inconspicuous flowers.

634. Since the Shell Flower is also called "Water Lettuce", can it be eaten like our table lettuce?

No. It has be reported that eating the Shell Flower or Water Lettuce (*Pistia stratiodes*) is poisonous. Similar to many plants in nature, unless a plant is known to be eatable, experimental consumption with unknown plants should be avoided.

635. Does the Shell Flower only reproduce by seeds?

No. The Shell Flower reproduces similar to the Floating Water Hyacinth by a means of stolons or runners (figure 74). During the summer months the Shell Flower has the ability to grow rapidly and cover the surface of a water garden pool. If overgrown, the surplus Shell Flowers can be manually removed and make a good addition to a compost pile.

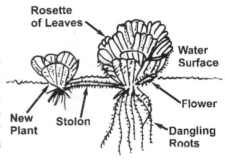

Figure 74. The Shell Flower reproduces asexually by producing a stolon and a new plant and sexually from a tiny flower located on the side of the plant.

636. What causes the velvet touch of the Shell Flower?

The pulpy leaves are covered with small hairs. These hairs not only give the leaves a velvet touch but create a silky luster appearance. The hairs keep water from moistening the surface of the leaves.

637. What is happening if the Shell Flower is turning white?

If the Shell Flower is turning white, the plant is dying. This will occur if the water is too cold for the Shell Flower. The water temperature should be at least 70 degrees Fahrenheit. This is a common problem if the Shell Flower is put out too early in the spring and the water is cold.

638. Does the Shell Flower require a great amount of sun light?

No, the Water Lettuce or Shell Flower (*Pistia stratiotes*) will flourish in shaded areas of the water garden. Due to the limited sunlight, the Shell Flower will grow somewhat smaller than in full sunlight.

639. What is happening if the roots of the Shell Flower are turning brown-black color?

This is normal. The newly developed roots of the Shell Flower are initially white. As they become older they typically will become brown-black in color.

640. Which floating aquatic plants can be considered a perennial or survive a winter in the water garden pool covered with ice?

The duckweeds (*Lemna* spp.) have the ability to survive harsh winters where ice is eminent to form on the ponds. Duckweeds are found throughout the world. The *Azolla* and *Salvinia* will not endure harsh winters. Their spores do not winter well and are killed in harsh winters. They both appear on all continents, but the greatest is in the tropics. In the United States *Azolla* species can be found mainly along the eastern and western coasts and somewhat inland in the southern states. They are commonly found in Mexico and South America. The Water Hyacinth (*Eichhornia*) and Water Lettuce or Shell Flower (*Pistia*) will definitely not survive a climate that has ice in the winters.

641. Does the duckweeds (*Lemna* spp.) produce a flower?

Yes, but very rarely. The duckweed's total leafless body or **thallus** is about 1/16 to about 1/8 of an inch in size and has small dangling roots. Located on this tiny body can rarely be found a very small structure which is the pistil and two stamens that are considered to be a flower. Thus, do not look for a colorful floral arrangement of petals since there are none. The plant mainly reproduces by division of the body mass.

642. If the small duckweeds (*Lemna* spp.) make flowers, is this then the smallest flowering plant?

No. The smallest flowering plants goes to an allied floating plant of the duckweeds called *Wolffia* spp. or commonly known as **Water Meal**. The term "water meal" signifies that it has been known as an excellent food source or "meal" for fish. There are about eight species, named for W.F. Wolff, 1788-

1806, who wrote on duckweeds. Water Meal is widely distributed in warm and tropical regions. The plant's **thallus** (main body) is less than 1/16 of an inch in length and has no roots or leaves. A handful of these plants rubbed between the fingers feels like small grains of sand. The flower is extremely rare and consists of one stamen or one pistil which is considered a flower.

643. Does the duckweed (*Lemna* spp.) have roots?

Yes. The duckweed of the genera *Lemna* spp. has a single root that dangles from the bottom of the thallus or body into the water. By scooping up a handful of duckweed, the single threadlike root can be seen on each of the duckweed.

FLOATING AQUATIC FERNS

644. Some of the aquatic floating plants have the word *"fern"* used to describe them, for example the *Floating Fern* or *Mosquito Fern*, why are they called "ferns"?

The **Floating Fern** and **Mosquito Fern** are classified botanically with the group of **ferns** because they are, in reality, true "**aquatic ferns**" and reproduce similar to land ferns by **spores** and not seeds. This group of ferns are very old geologically. Based upon fossil records, the ferns began on earth 350 million years ago during a period known to geologists as the Devonian era. This was 200 million years before the flowering or seed plants grew in the Jurassic era. In other words, there were no flowering or seed producing plants when the ferns dominated the earth.

As geologic history progressed the dominance of ferns lost out to the land seed producing plants. This was mainly due to the fact that the fern's spore method of reproduction depended upon an abundance of moisture or water. The land was becoming dryer which favored the seed producing plants.

645. What are the names of the aquatic ferns that are suitable for the water garden?

The true aquatic ferns that have the ability to reproduce by spores in the water garden are the Floating Fern (*Ceratopteris*), Salvinia and Azolla or

183

Mosquito Fern (*Azolla.*).   All of these are wonderful additions to the water garden.

646. Are there any aquatic floating plants that are known for "fixing" nitrogen as found in the well known land nitrogen fixing plant legumes such as the bean (*Phaseolus*) or clover (*Trifolium*)?

Yes. One of the most unusual aquatic plants is the aquatic ferns *Azolla* species which has a microscopic blue-green algae, *Anaebaenae azolla* growing with it. The blue-green algae, living in a small cavity found in the base of each leaf, has the ability to "fix" nitrogen or make it available for the *Azolla* as food in the form of nitrates. This relationship is known in the biological world as **symbiotic**. Symbiosis is used to indicate that the blue-green algae and the aquatic fern both benefit from this relationship and will live together in harmony. The Chinese have been well aware of this relationship and will grow *Azolla* in the rice fields which will provide a good supply of nitrates.

647. If aquatic ferns were the dominate plants over seed producing plants in our past geologic history, did any of the aquatic ferns become extinct?

Yes. The aquatic fern *Azolla* currently is made up of about six species. In fossil records there has been identified 25 species of *Azolla*. These are now extinct.

648. Why was *Azolla* known as the "Mosquito Fern"?

Early observations in the 1900s of the *Azolla* in Germany and Panama recognized that in natural conditions it grew rapidly and very close together. It soon covered the total water surface of a pond. By covering the surface of the water completely, the *Azolla* did not allow mosquito larvae to live. Mosquito larvae in the water need to "breath" air at the surface. Therefore, since the *Azolla* is considered an aquatic fern which reproduces by spores, the name "Mosquito Fern" was adopted.

649. What is happening when the *Azolla* is turning reddish-brown?

The *Azolla* will normally turn a reddish-brown in strong sunlight and towards the end of summer. Some of the *Azolla* will remain green as portions will turn a reddish color. This combination of colors adds a beautiful color pattern to the surface of the water in the garden pool.

650. Do any of the aquatic ferns have leaves that unroll like the commonly known land ferns?

Yes. The Floating Fern, *Ceratopteris pteridoides*, unrolls the leaves similar to the common land ferns. The daily observation of the leaves unrolling is a very attractive and unusual sight in the water garden pool. The other ferns such as *Azolla* and *Salvinia* do not unroll leaves similar to the common land fern but simply float on the surface of the water.

651. Does the *Salvinia* have roots?

No. A close look at the *Salvinia* will show three leaves on one node. Only two develop into the small floating leaf, the other is what will appear as a "rootlet" (figure 74) which is loaded with chloroplasts (chlorophyll). This third leaf has many tips and has the ability to develop the characteristic spores.

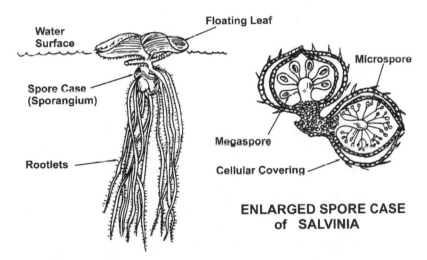

ENLARGED SPORE CASE of SALVINIA

Figure 75. Salvinia is an aquatic fern that makes spores in a spore case (sporangium). The enlarged drawing shows the two types of spores produced: megaspores (large spores) and microspores (small spores). Salvinia does not have true roots but a modified third leaf that functions similar to a root.

652. Do the *Salvinia* species produce flowers and seeds?

No. This aquatic floating plant is an aquatic fern. The plant produces spores in a structure known as a **sporocarp** and does not produce flowers.

653. What are the small growths found on the edges of the leaves of the Floating Fern, *Ceratopteris pteridoides***?**

Ceratopteris pteriodoides, the Floating Fern, is a true aquatic fern and has the ability to reproduce by spores or asexually (without a sperm and egg). The small growths along the margins of the leaf are buds or new plantlets and is typical of the floating fern. The leaves will form these buds normally within each leaf indentation. It is not abnormal to have 15 to 30 of these buds or plantlets on each leaf. Each bud has the ability to develop into another plant and it is fascinating to watch the growth of these new plants develop daily. Not only does this increase the number of plants in the water garden but the new growth takes on a contrasting green color which gives a beautiful overall appearance of the floating fern foliage. These plants add a special charm and appearance in the water garden pool.

654. Since the small buds on the Floating Fern develop into a new plant, does that mean that the entire plant with a root system is not necessary for propagation of the plant?

Yes. Small portions of the leaf that contain the buds from the Floating Fern, under the correct conditions, will grow into new plants. It is not necessary to have the entire plant with roots for a small plantlet to develop into a mature plant.

655. The Floating Fern is growing with unrolling of the broad green foliage as expected, however it is putting up different and unusual narrow leaves, what is happening?

The Floating Fern is **dimorphic**, that is, it has the ability to produce two different morphological leaf structures. One type is the broad flat leaf which makes new plantlets asexually. The other type is a narrow stem-looking leaf which contains the spore producing bodies of the plant known as **sporangia**. A good microscopic lens or dissecting scope can reveal the sporangia or structure that makes the spores. This can be easily seen by obtaining the narrow produced leaf and place the curled edge under a strong lens or dissecting scope. With a needle slowly peal away this edge. Under this curl will be found the sporangia which appear as small round green bodies. Both leaf types however will produce plantlets.

XIII. Oxygenating Plants
in the Water Garden Pool

* Characteristics * Selected Species * Planting and Care*

CHARACTERISTICS

656. What are the "oxygenating plants" that are found in the water garden pool?

These are the plants that grow basically under the surface of the water and are known for producing life sustaining "oxygen". They are also referred to as "submerged plants". Some well known oxygenators used in ornamental water gardens are **Ludwigia, Hygrophilia, Vallisineria, Cabomba, Anacharis** and **Water Milfoil**.

657. How do the oxygenating plants produce oxygen?

The oxygenating plants, as well as other plants, need the energy of light to make oxygen through a process known as **photosynthesis** which is indicated by a classical scientific formula:

$$6CO_2 + 12H_2O \text{ --light In the presence of chlorophyll--> } C_6H_{12}O_6 + 6O_2 + 6H_2O$$

The formula means that six molecules of carbon dioxide plus 12 molecules of water in the presence of light inside the **chlorophyll** (unit inside of the plant cell that contains the photosynthetic reaction) will give one molecule of glucose (sugar) and six molecules of oxygen and six molecules of water. Thus, in the presence of light the photosynthesis is operating and producing sugar for plant energy and oxygen for cellular respiration.

658. What happens to the plant at night when photosynthesis is not occurring by the sun?

At night, in the absence of light, photosynthesis will stop. No oxygen can be produced without the energy of the sun. **Respiration** is the process that cells use to metabolize or extract energy from sugar, protein or lipids. Respiration occurs both day and night and can be represented by the formula:

$$C_6H_{12}O_6 + 6O_2 \rightarrow 6H_2O + 6CO_2 + energy$$

This means that a molecule of glucose (sugar) and six molecules of oxygen produce six molecules of water and six molecules of carbon dioxide with energy for the plant to function. Thus, at night as well as during the day the normal respiration of the cells of the plant will produce carbon dioxide. Interestingly, the formula is the reverse of photosynthesis.

659. If plants produce carbon dioxide both day and night, does the plant use this carbon dioxide in the day for photosynthesis?

Yes. The carbon dioxide that is released into the water at night can be used by the oxygenators in the day in the process of respiration.

660. If an artificial light, such as a yard lamp, is on by the water garden pool will the plants still produce oxygen by photosynthesis?

Yes, depending upon the intensity of the light source. Photosynthesis needs light as energy and can be from the sun or an artificial source such as a light bulb. Photosynthesis would typically be reduced from an outside light bulb since the bulb can not produce the intensity of natural sunlight. Thus, very little oxygen is being produced in the water garden by artificial light.

661. Are the oxygenators the only plants that produces oxygen under the water?

No. Algae, which are plants, will also produce an abundant amount of oxygen by photosynthesis.

662. Do only the plants produce "photosynthesis" in the water garden?

No. There are two small photosynthetic groups of bacteria that can be considered "primitive plants". These are known as the **purple sulfur bacteria** and **green sulfur bacteria** which have the ability to use light as a source of energy similar to plants.

663. Where are the photosynthetic bacteria found in the water garden pool?

The photosynthetic bacteria normally live in the bottom mud of the aquatic water garden within any decaying plant material.

664. How do the photosynthetic bacteria compare to plant photosynthesis?

Instead of using the oxygen molecule in the water of the classical formula for photosynthesis for plants, the photosynthetic bacteria use sulfur. Thus, the photosynthesis of the sulfur bacteria can be represented as.

$$6CO_2 + 12H_2S + \text{light energy} \rightarrow C_6H_{12}O_6 + 12S + 6H_2O$$

This formula indicates that six molecules of carbon dioxide plus 12 molecules of hydrogen sulfide plus light energy will give a molecule of glucose (sugar) and 12 molecules of sulfur and six water molecules. Therefore, a special group of bacteria have the ability of photosynthesis or use the energy of light but do not add oxygen to the water garden pool which is characteristic of plants.

665. If the water garden pool has water lilies, does it still need oxygenators to add oxygen to the water?

Yes. The exchange of oxygen and carbon dioxide in plants occur mainly through a plant pore known as a **stomata**. Stomata are found between a pair of

189

cells on the plant leaf known as **guard cells.** The guard cells open and close making the stoma to allow the gases of photosynthesis, carbon dioxide and oxygen, to pass from inside the leaf to the outside and reverse. Contrary to many land plants the water lily has the stomata on the top of the floating leaf. Thus, the oxygen that is produced from a water lily enters the air directly and not into the water. Whereas, the submerged oxygenator adds the oxygen directly to the water.

666. Is the oxygen "pure" that is produced by the oxygenators?

Yes. If the bubbles that come directly from the oxygenators are collected and tested, they will be found to contain pure oxygen. Therefore, on a bright summer day, the oxygenators can be seen emitting bubbles of pure oxygen.

667. Can the water gardener actually "see" the oxygen coming from an oxygenator?

Yes, it is very easy to watch the bubbles of oxygen coming from an oxygenator plant. To observe the plant producing bubbles of oxygen, take a sprig of Anacharis and place into a glass of pond water. Set this glass with the Anacharis on a window shelf in a direct sunlight. Within minutes the small bubbles of pure oxygen can be seen coming off of the plant as photosynthesis is occurring.

668.   Can the water garden pool oxygenators be used in indoor fish aquariums?

Yes. The oxygenators used in water garden pools can be used in indoor fish aquariums.

SELECTED SPECIES
OF OXYGENATORS

669. Which aquatic plants are known to produce an abundance of oxygen in the water garden pool?

The aquatic plants Anacharis and Vallisineria will produce an abundance of oxygen. They are easy to grow and can be seen producing oxygen in strong sunlight.

670. Why is the oxygenator "Anacharis" sometimes called *Elodea*?

This common aquarium and water garden plant has been called both of the names Anacharis and *Elodea*. The history of these two names is classical in the problems of classification that resulted in the early 1800s as plants were being discovered, identified and named. *Anacharis* was the genus that L.C.M. Richard, a French botanist (1754-1821) identified in 1811 . Another French botanist, A. Michaux (1746-1802) described the same plant in 1803 and named and recorded it as *Elodea*. To add to more confusion Rafinesque named this plant *Philotria* in 1818. Individuals like J.E. Planchon, another well known French botanist (1823-1888) used the genus *Anacharis* in 1848 to name a new species following the genus given by Richard. Much of the literature contained both names by reputable botanists well after the turn of the century. Once the International Rules for Botanic Nomenclature was established, the rule to give the oldest name credit would establish the genus *Elodea* by Michaux in 1803. Planchon's *Anacharis* new species of 1848 was not formally changed to *Elodea* until 1920. However, the name Anacharis and *Elodea* are both commonly used today for the same plant.

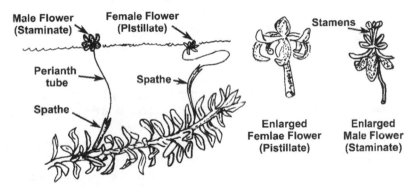

Figure 76. Anacharis or *Elodea* can make flowers, one a male producing pollen flower and the other a female flower which will make fertile seeds.

671. Does Anacharis produce flowers?

Yes. The tiny flowers of Anacharis have three sepals with usually three white petals. This flower is raised to the surface of the water by a greatly prolonged and slender tube arising from the underwater stem and float on the surface. It can produce both male and female flowers.

672. Is Anacharis a perennial?

Yes. It will survive winters were ice forms on the ponds by producing winter buds.

673. Is there only one species of Anacharis or *Elodea*?

No. There have been reported over 10 species of *Elodea* depending upon different classification systems. The different *Elodea* species basically look the same to the untrained eye. However, they differ fundamentally in appearance by the number of whorls of leaves on the stem, size of leaves and flowers.

674. What is the most common species of Anacharis in the trade?

The most commonly sold Anacharis is *Elodea canadensis*. It is extremely easy to grow and is an excellent oxygenator.

675. What oxygenator was known as "Babington's Curse"?

The name "Babington's Curse" is given to *Elodea canadensis*. During the latter 1840s an English professor of botany by the name of Babington was studying the mysteries of reproduction of an American submerged plant known as Anacharis. In 1851, a friend of Professor Babington asked for a specimen and innocently introduced it into the rivers of England. It spread uncontrollably and ran wild by becoming a botanic cancer in the life of the river population. It choked the native river plants out of existence, stopped fishing, swimming and rowing and an emergency was declared by the government. Fortunately, it later regressed miserably to a period of stagnation, and in fact, to a point of extinction for no apparent reason given at the time. However, the name "Babington's Curse" still is associated with *Elodea canadensis*. *Elodea* today can easily become a nuisance in an earth bottom pond and must be contained or controlled. However, for the water gardener using planting containers, it is an easy plant to grow and provides much needed oxygen.

676. What does the name of the oxygenator *Vallisneria* mean?

The species name *Vallisneria* was chosen by Linne in 1753 and was named after the Italian botanist Antonia Vallisneri (1661-1730) from Padua. Therefore the genus has no specific reference to any characteristic morphology or physiology of the plant.

677. How do the *Vallisneria* spp. reproduce or propagate?

The *Vallisneria* reproduce sexually by making flowers and vegetatively (figure 78) by producing runners. The male flower parts develop under the water and the female flower parts float on the surface of the water. The runners are made under the water and root quickly.

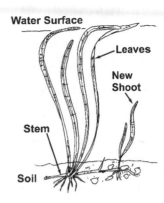

678. How do the flowers of the *Vallisneria* pollinate if the male flowers are submerged and the female flowers float on the water?

Pollination of the *Vallisneria* is fascinating and is known as "water pollination". The male flowers (staminate flowers) break off and float to the surface of the water where they will come in contact with the female flowers (pistillate flowers) which float on a long spiral stems.

Figure 77. Vallisneria is an excellent producer of oxygen and has attractive leaves that float gently on the surface of the water.

679. Why is *Vallisneria* sometimes referred to as "wild celery"?

The plant was called "wild celery" since it imparts a celery-like flavor to wild ducks that feed on it. It has also been called "ribbon grass" since it resembles a ribbon.

680. Is *Vallisneria* a good oxygenator?

Yes. *Vallisneria* is an excellent oxygenator and produces an abundant amount of oxygen for life in the water garden pool.

681. What does the genus of the oxygenator *Hygrophila* mean?

The genus is derived from the Greek word "hygros" which means wet or moist and the Greek word "philos" meaning *friend*.

682. Where are the *Hygrophila* found naturally in the world?

The *Hygrophila* are found in warm regions of the world, mainly in Africa and south east Asia.

683. Will the Moneywort survive under a winter of snow and ice?

Yes. It will survive the harsh winters of snow and ice and in the middle of a winter thaw can be seen with the small green leaves ready to emerge into growth in the spring .

684. Should the Moneywort, *Lysimachia Nummularia,* be planted under the water?

The Moneywort *Lysimachia Nummularia* can be planted either under the water as an oxygenator or can be placed at the surface of the water allowing the leaves to be exposed to the air.

685. Where would Moneywort be found growing in nature?

It is commonly found growing in very damp and wet places such as ditches and wet meadows in our northern latitudes in the United States. The finding of this plant in a wet meadow is an attractive sight with the dainty yellow flowers and deep green leaves as a background.

686. Does the Moneywort *Lysimachia Nummularia* prefer warm or cold water?

The Moneywort *Lysimachia Nummularia* prefers cold or cool water.

687. If the Moneywort purchased does not have roots, does that mean it will die?

No. It is typically propagated by cuttings without roots. By placing the stems into soil they will sprout roots within a short time.

688. What does the Water Milfoil's genus *Myriophyllum* mean?

The genus *Myriophyllum* was derived by Linne in 1753 which is derived from the Greek word "myrios" meaning innumerable and "phyllon" meaning leaves, or meaning "innumerable leaves". This name is aptly selected to describe the large number of feathery submerged leaves.

PLANTING AND CARE OF THE OXYGENATORS

689. If the oxygenators have a rubber band holding them together when purchased, should it be removed when planting?

Oxygenating Plant

Pea Gravel

Yes. The rubber band on a group of oxygenators should be removed before planting.

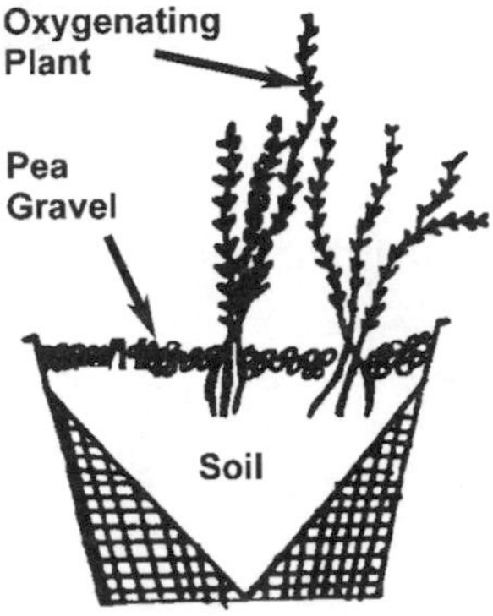

Soil

690. How are oxygenators planted?

Place the cut or rooted end of the oxygenators into the soil and compact gently (figure 76). Cover the soil with a layer of gravel and gently submerge the container with the oxygenators into the water garden.

Figure 78.

Oxygenators are planted similar to other aquatics.

691. Can more than one oxygenator be planted in a single container?

Yes. For example, a container 4 inches across can contain a single or two bunches of Anacharis.

692. Can the oxygenators be planted with the water lily?

Yes. Some prefer to hide the water lily container and plant a group of oxygenators in the same container as the water lily. It is best, however to place the oxygenators in their own planting container.

693. How deep should the oxygenators be submerged in the water garden?

Sunlight, the energy for photosynthesis, must reach the oxygenators to live. Therefore, the oxygenators should be submerged so that the tops are only a few inches from the surface of the water where they will receive plenty of sunlight.

694. What will happen if the oxygenators are placed too deep in the water garden pool?

If the oxygenating plants are too deep they will not receive enough sunlight which is necessary for life. If they remain at this depth, they will become mushy and brown and will eventually die.

695. Do oxygenators need to be fertilized?

Yes. The oxygenators are planted in soil with an aquatic fertilizer. Roots will soon develop which will require nutrients from the soil as well as the surrounding water.

XIV. Plant Diseases of Water Lilies

* Introduction * Aphids * Water Lily Leaf Beetle * Water Lily Beetle *
* Leaf Miners * Leaf Cutters * Fungus *

INTRODUCTION

696. What causes the diseases of water lilies?

The diseases of water lilies are similar to other diseases of land plants. The diseases of water lilies can be caused by insects, bacteria, fungus and viruses. The treatments vary with each type of disease causing agent, however prevention is better than trying to eradicate.

697. What is the best disease preventative measure of water lilies and aquatic plants?

The best way to prevent a diseased plant is to keep the plant healthy. The many diseases that can attack and kill a water lily are found naturally in our ecosystem awaiting for an opportunity to enter the plant. Once a plant is infected, the disease can spread rapidly if attempts are not made to control the causative agent. A healthy water lily is subjected to less stress and resists the

197

disease causing agents. A healthy water lily, as well as other aquatic plants, are maintained by using correct planting techniques, providing good growing conditions and adhering to a fertilization program by using a proven aquatic fertilizer.

WATER LILY APHIDS

698. What are the tiny little black "bugs" or insects on the pad of the water lily?

These are a common plant pest known as **aphids** (*Rhopalosiphum nymphaeae*). They can be very damaging to the leaves of the water lily causing disfigurement and eventually death. The aphids will attack a weakened or stressed aquatic plant and literally "suck" the plant juices or life from the plant. Damage by the aphids to the vegetation opens the door to other disease causing agents such as bacteria or fungi.

699. How do you get rid of the aphids on the pads of the water lily.

One of the best methods is to use a strong stream of water from a garden hose. The aphids will be flushed into the water and fish will consume them in a greedy manner. At first the aphids may attempt to return to the vegetation, however after a few rinsing periods the fish will quickly learn that this is a "feeding" method and love the aphids as a special treat.

700. Can chemicals or insecticides be used to kill aphids on the water lily leaves?

Yes, but it is not recommended. Any chemicals used around the pond should be used with extreme caution since the surrounding water may be contaminated with any treatments. The environmental life that lives around the pond, as well as in the pond, can be effected by most chemicals. Aphids can become a nuisance if not controlled at professional commercial aquatic establishments due to the close proximity and quantity of aquatic vegetation that are grown. The experienced commercial aquatic establishment may use different chemical remedies but they use extreme caution. It is best for the water gardener to adhere to flushing the aphids into the water and being consumed by fish.

701. If there are no fish in the pond, is it safe to use insecticides on aphids?

No. There are other "creatures" or animals that visit or live in the pond besides fish. There are tadpoles, microscopic plants and animals, valuable aquatic insects, crustaceans, etc. that can be effected by chemical treatments. The pond, whether it contains fish or not, is a miniature ecosystem teaming with life. This life works together in harmony to keep the water clear and often goes unnoticed by a novice. In attempting to kill aphids with insecticides in a water garden pool can be deadly to these unnoticed "creatures". Prevention is better than the cure in most cases. The growing of healthy aquatic plants will often keep the aphid population in control. It is still best to control the aphids by flushing with water and leaving the chemical control with insecticides to the years of experience and knowledge of the aquatic commercial establishments.

WATER LILY LEAF BEETLE

702. What is the name of the metallic green beetle that is seen on the water lily pads?

This is the **water lily leaf beetle** that the biologist classifies in the subfamily *Donaciinae*. They are dark-colored or metallic colored black, green or copper and have long antennae (figure 79). The eggs are usually laid on the underside of the water lily pads in rows. The beetle is found in nature.

703. How can you tell if the water lily leaf beetle has laid eggs?

By picking up the water lily pad and looking underneath will reveal the whitish crescent shaped eggs near a hole in the leaf

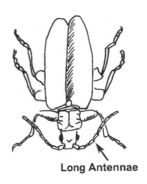

Long Antennae

Figure 79. The water lily leaf beetle *Donacia* can be recognized by a metallic coloration and the long characteristic antennae

cut by the adult. They are in perfect rows (figure 80).

704. Does the water lily leaf beetle cause damage to the water lily?

Yes. Not only does it cause destruction to the leaves of the water lily but the larva of the water lily leaf beetle feeds on the roots and tuber of the water lily. As the larva population increases the water lily plant can die.

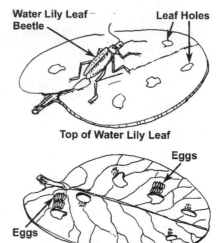

Top of Water Lily Leaf

Bottom of Water Lily Leaf

705. Can the larva of the water lily leaf beetle be seen?

Figure 80. The eggs can be seen on the bottom of the holes in the leaf in perfect rows.

Yes, especially when pulling up a hardy water lily and exposing the tuber and roots. It is a small, approximately one-quarter inch, white grub-like larva. The roots can also be infected with the small oval brown colored pupa or cocoons of this larva.

706. What happens to the water lily with an infestation of the water lily leaf beetle?

In severe infestations, the water lily pad will appear as if it were shot with a shotgun. There will be many round circular holes made by the adult female laying her eggs underneath the water lily pad.

707. What should be done to control the water lily leaf beetle?

The water lily leaf beetle is hard to control as with most insect pests in the water garden pool. The severely infected pads with holes should be removed and destroyed to kill the eggs. When dividing a hardy water lily tuber, any visible larva should be removed and be fed to fish or destroyed.

WATER LILY BEETLE

708. What causes the irregular grooves and brown lines that appear on the top of the pads of the water lilies?

This is caused by a dark brown beetle known as the **water lily beetle** (*Galerucella nymphaea*) and is one of the most destructive to the water lily. The yellowish-white eggs are laid on the upper surface of the water lily pad. The larva crawl around the pads of the water lily and eats off sections of the upper tissue. The larva are black with a yellow belly with three pair of legs. This beetle is found in nature. It is best controlled by removing and destroying the infected leaves that contain the eggs. Interestingly, a relative of this beetle, *Gallerucella calmariensis*, is being used successfully to control the invasive loosestrife in the United States and Canada.

WATER LILY LEAF MINERS

709. What causes the dark brown snake-like lines that are cutting through the surface of the water lily pad causing sections to turn brown?

There are many species of small flies, known as **midges**, that have a larvae (worm-like) stage that feed on the surface of the water lily leaf causing irregular snake-like lines as they "mine" or tunnel through the top layer of the leaf. One of the most common midges that tunnels through the top layer (epidermis) of the water lily pad is called the **water lily leaf miner**. These aquatic insects are small non biting flies that are often mistaken for mosquitoes (*Chironomous* spp.). Another similar larvae, of particular interest that causes snake-like lines over the surface of the water lily leaf is called the **false leaf mining midge** (*Cricotopus* spp.). Other species of flies have destructive larval stages that can burrow through the leaf and also have the ability to bore into the stem. Removal and destruction of the infected leaves with larvae is recommended. Control is best attained by the presence of fish which feed on the larval stages.

WATER LILY LEAF CUTTERS

710. What is occurring when the water lily pad has small oval shaped cuts and these oval cuts are found floating in the water garden pool?

This is caused by a the **water lily leaf cutters** (a cut worm, *Nymphala* spp.) which is the larva stage of moths. The larva stage will cut two small oval pieces of the water lily leaf (figure 81) and make a silky cocoon sticking the two pieces together. This cocoon and two pieces of leaves will float on the surface of the water. The leaf cutters not only effect the leaves of the hardy and tropical water lilies but many other aquatic plants that grow in the water garden.

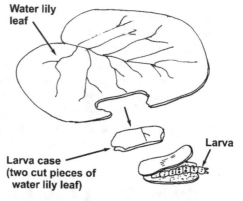

Figure 81. Water lily leaf cut worm is easily identified by the characteristic "cuts" of the leaf and the floating leaf case.

711. Where are the eggs laid by the water lily leaf cutter?

The whitish eggs are laid in groups of 10 to 50 on the underside of the water lily pads near the edges.

712. How can the water lily leaf cutter be controlled?

The water lily leaf cutter can be controlled by removing the larval floating "boats" of the two sandwiched oval shaped leaves and destroying. If the water lily leaf cutter has spread to any other water lilies the use of **Bacillus thuringiensis variety kurstaki or BTK** can be used to kill the larva.

713. Is *Bacillus thuringiensis* variety *kurstaki* or BTK a chemical?

No. The active agent is *Bacillus thuringiensis* variety *kurstaki* or BTK is a spore producing bacteria and not a chemical agent. It is considered a **biological insecticide**.

714. How does the bacteria BTK or *Bacillus thuringiensis* variety *kurstaki* kill the water lily leaf cutter larva?

The bacteria *Bacillus thuringiensis* causes a paralytic disease of insect caterpillars. This paralysis results from ingestion or eating of plant material that carry the spores or sporulating cells of this bacterium. As the bacteria sporulates it produces a pyramidal protein crystal along with making the spore. The protein of this crystal is toxic for insects after ingestion. It specifically dissolves in the alkaline gut of the caterpillar and causes a loosening of the (epithelial cells) lining of the gut wall. This results in a consequent diffusion of liquid from the gut into the blood and causes rapid paralysis and death of the caterpillar.

715. How is BTK applied to the water lilies?

The bacteria *Bacillus thuringiensis* variety *kurstaki* can be purchased commercially as a powdered mixture and made into a liquid solution by the addition of water. The BTK-water solution is then sprayed onto the water lily leaves. The water lily leaf cutter larva will continue to eat the treated leaf and within a few days the larva will be dead.

WATER LILY FUNGUS

716. Do fungus cause diseases in the water lilies?

Yes. As long ago as 1913, the United States Department of Agriculture recognized that fungus was a major problem with water lilies and began to study the course of this disease causing agent. The major commercial suppliers of water lilies were the target for study, such commercial growers as the company's of William Tricker and Henry Shaw as well as a few well known botanical gardens. Of the many fungal species, the specific species of *Helicosporium nymphaearum* was identified and collected from the aforementioned sights and studied for control.

717. How can a fungal infection of the water lily be recognized?

A fungal infection is often recognized as yellow spots on the surface of the water lily leaf and has been commonly referred to as **leaf spot of water lilies**. As the fungus causes damage the center of the yellow spot will turn black and decay to leave a hole.   The fungus can spread and move down into the stems of the water lily.

718. How does the fungus kill the water lily tissue?

The fungus is utilizing the water lily tissue or vegetation as food. As the fungus consumes the food, it is suspected that the fungus makes a substance or substances that go ahead of the infected fungal growth and kills the tissues. Thus, the fungus emits a substance that diffuses throughout the water lily leaf that kills the tissue as it invades.

719. How does the fungus spread to other water lilies?

The fungus will make spores that are resistant to adverse conditions. Once the water lily leaf dies and the food supply is exhausted, the fungi will make spores.   These spores can easily spread throughout the water or become airborne infecting another aquatic plant. The spores vegetate and become an active feeding fungus on another water lily causing destruction.

720. How can the specific fungal infection of water lilies be identified?

Since there are many types of fungus that can infect a water lily, specific identification must be made before treatment can be recommended.   This requires special laboratory equipment and can not be done by the average water gardener.   Commercial aquatic growers are aware that fungi can be very destructive and identification is mandatory so that the spread to customer ponds is avoided.

721. Can one "see" the fungus as it feeds on the water lily making holes in the leaves?

No, at least not the feeding or **vegetative stage**. The vegetative stage produces long microscopic filaments known as **mycelium**. These mycelium will extract food from the water lily leaf through digestion.   Under a microscope, bacteria and protozoa can also be seen in the effected area. These would be expected due to fact that they would be feeding on the dead tissue.

722. If a cotton-like substance appears in the holes of the water lily leaf, is this the fungus?

Yes. The fungus is now in the **reproductive stage** and is now making spores. This will look like the fungus seen on moldy bread which is also in the reproductive stage producing spores. If the infected water lily leaf remains in the water garden pool, the reproductive stage producing thousands of spores may begin to spread rapidly and contaminate other parts of the leaf or another leaf.

723. How does the fungus enter into the water lily pad?

It is thought that the fungus enters mainly through the **stomata** which are small openings on the top of the leaf that function in the exchange of air for photosynthesis. Experiments by taking the pathogenic fungi and infecting the bottom of the water lily leaf did not result in the infection as rapidly. Thus, it was concluded that the stomata plays an important role in the entry of the plant and not just from a torn or injured plant.

XV. Algae in the Water Garden Pool

* Characteristics * Control of Algae *

CHARACTERISTICS OF ALGAE

724. Is "algae" the green scum that is seen on ponds in the summer?

Yes. The masses of yellow, brown or green scum seen on the surface of the pond is most familiar to all of us as "pond scum". However, the term **algae** (singular, **alga**) is the correct biological term.

725. What is algae?

Algae are very primitive plants that do not have roots, stems and leaves. They are composed of a single cell or group of cells attached together to form colonies or filaments (figure 82).

726. Do the algae produce flowers?

No. The algae are very primitive plants that do not have specialized structures such as flowers. They are very successful in reproduction and do not need to rely upon flowers.

727. If algae do not make flowers, how do they reproduce?

The different species of algae reproduce by either simple division of the cells (asexual) without a sexual partner or they also have unusual methods to exchange the chromosomal genetic material (sexual). Either way, the algae has the ability to grow at a very rapid rate in ideal conditions without the production of flowers.

728. Do algae produce spores?

Yes. Many species produce **spores** to survive adverse conditions such as heat, cold or dryness. In general, the spores are round circular objects that are formed in the cells of the algae. Instead of making new cells for growth the algae will decide to make spores under certain circumstances.

729. Can the spores of the algae be seen in the water?

No. The spores, which are produced within the cells of the algae, are very small and can only be seen using a microscope (figure 82).

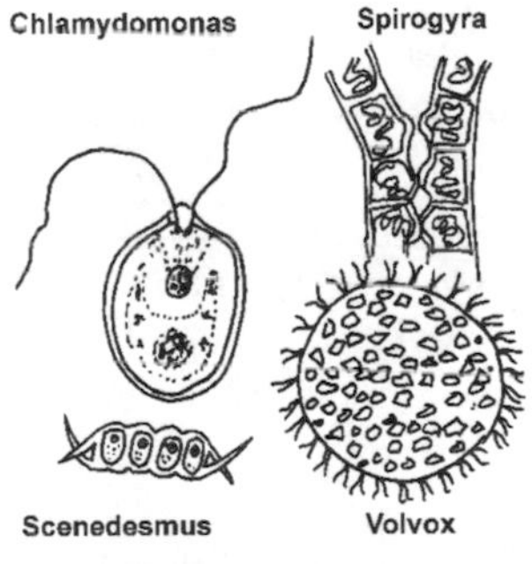

Chlamydomonas   Spirogyra

Scenedesmus   Volvox

Figure 82. Four drawings of different alga found in ponds that can only be seen with the aid of a microscope.

730. Is there only a single species of algae?

Absolutely not. There are estimates of over 30,000 species of algae in the world.

731. Are all types of algae destructive in the ponds?

No. Algae play a very important role in the ecology on Earth. They are the principal food producers in the ecosystem in the water. Directly or indirectly, most aquatic organisms depend upon algae for food and oxygen. However, some types of algae can become a problem if growth occurs too rapidly.

732. What causes algae to grow too rapidly in a water garden pool?

If an excess food source is supplied for algae in strong sunlight, the algae will flourish and grow rapidly in upper warm parts of the water garden pool.

733. What is the main food for algae in the water garden pool?

The main food of algae is **nitrates**. Under good growing conditions, such as warm water and abundant sunshine, algae will use these nitrates to grow at a rapid and sometimes uncontrollable rate.

734. What causes the nitrates to increase in the water garden pool that results in the heavy production of algae?

Fish produce waste products that eventually result in the compounds called **nitrates** that feed the algae. In a water garden pool that has too many fish without proper filtration or water balance, the nitrates will substantially increase. This is a very common cause of algae blooms in the water garden pool. Another common cause of increased nitrates in the water garden pool is the over fertilizing of the aquatic plants. The nitrates from the fertilizer can leach into the water and feed the algae.

735. What happens in the water garden pool when the algae grows too rapidly?

One of the main problems that occurs if algae grows too rapidly in a water garden pool is the depletion of dissolved oxygen. The increased numbers of algae demands more dissolved oxygen during their cellular respiration.

Another main problem of an increased algae growth is when they blanket or cover the surface of the water. This will prevent sunlight from reaching the submerged aquatic plants and they will begin to die. As the submerged plant dies, they will consume vital oxygen and the dissolved oxygen in the water becomes dangerously low or depleted. Other aquatic plants and animals will begin to die from this oxygen depletion.

736. If algae is a plant that can produce oxygen, how can an excess of algae deplete the oxygen in the water garden pool?

At night the lack of oxygen becomes deadly in water garden pools. Most living cells need oxygen to respire or "breathe", which includes both plants and animals. Since the sun is no longer available at night for plants to produce oxygen, the increased algae, other submerged plants, aquatic organisms and fish all compete for a limited supply of oxygen that was manufactured in the day. If a blanket of algae is formed on the surface of the water garden pool, it will prevent other submerged vegetation from producing oxygen by blocking the rays of the sun and further depletes the supply of dissolved oxygen. The algae, other submerged plants and animals will begin to die from lack of oxygen. The physical decaying process consumes more oxygen. The water garden pool will begin to stagnate unless the algae is brought under control and the return of the life sustaining dissolved oxygen is restored in the water garden pool.

737. Do ponds and lakes have algae problems?

Yes. One group of algae known as the **blue-green algae** (*Anabaena* or *Microcystis*) can become a problem when it grows too rapid under certain conditions in a pond or lake. The algae is named because of the blue-green color (derived from the chlorophyll color) of scum seen on the surface of the water. If this blue-green algae is growing in intense sunlight in water that is high with organic matter or polluted sources an **algal bloom** can occur.

738. Are blue-green algal blooms a very serious problem?

Yes. Some blue-green algal blooms can produce toxins that can kill birds and animals when they drink the water. At night the amount of dissolved oxygen is extremely low in the water. The algal blooms and other organisms will compete in these low oxygen levels and death will often ensue. The algal blooms will give the water an odor characteristic of stagnant pools.

739. Can the blue-green algae effect our drinking water?

Yes. The odor produced from blue-green algae can get into our water supplies in the summer. For example, the drinking water source for Cleveland, Ohio comes from a water pick up source five miles into Lake Erie. During hot summer days, the treated water supplied to Cleveland may have an unusual taste due to the by-products of algal blooms that occur in Lake Erie.

740. Can the blue-green algae become a problem in the water garden pool?

Yes. The blue-green algae can flourish under the same circumstances found in a lake or pond.

741. Where does the algae come from in the water garden pool?

Even a newly filled water garden pool with city water will produce algae in a short time. Since algae are microscopic they may be adhered to any aquatic plants brought into the water garden. Aquatic organisms such as frogs, tadpoles, snails, etc. can also bring algae into the pool. Birds will be able to carry the algae spores into the water garden pool from distant sources. Soil that is used for potting of aquatic plants can have algal spores.

742. If the water garden pool with an abundance of algae is drained during a winter in an area that produces ice and snow, will this algae be killed or return when filled in the spring?

A good chance the algae will return after the first filling in the spring. The algae has the ability to make resistant spores. Many algae spores can survive long, cold winters as well as summer droughts. Algae are very successful on Earth. They have dominated aquatic life on Earth since the Proterozoic era which began over one billion years ago. A single winter with snow and ice will not kill many algae that have developed the ability to produce spores over millions of years.

743. How can you tell the difference between the submerged aquatic plants (or oxygenators) and algae in the water garden pool?

Many water gardeners mistake the overgrowth of a submerged aquatic plant or an oxygenator with algae. If the aquatic plant has roots, stems or leaves, it is not an algae. By scooping up a sample of water can reveal whether or not it is an algae. If the scoop contains a dense matt of algae (made of microscopic cells in filaments or colonies) with no recognizable leaves, stems or roots, it is an algae. If the scoop is colored green with no identifiable "plant parts" it is definitely algae made up of millions of microscopic cellular algae.

CONTROL OF ALGAE IN THE WATER GARDEN POOL

744. How does the water gardener control the over growth of algae?

The water gardener uses many techniques to control the over growth of algae. The water gardener tries to balance the pool as in nature. This involves the adding of certain types of aquatic plants and animals that compete with or reduce the algae. Lastly, chemicals are available to temporarily reduce the

211

algae until the pool can balance itself in harmony with the aquatic plants and animals. These chemicals can indirectly kill the algae, such as colored dyes, or directly kill the algae, such as the chemical copper sulfate.

745. Is clear water without algae the desired goal of the water gardener?

No. Algae is necessary in the food chain in the water garden pool which also helps to maintain healthy water. Total eradication is not the goal with algae. Only the unsightly control of algae should be addressed. If the water garden pool water could talk, it sure would want to have the microscopic algae present.

746. How does the color dye that is added to the water garden pool control algae?

Colored dyes can be purchased to control algae in the water garden pool. They are added to the water garden pool and change the water a deep black-blue color. The dark color of the water blocks the rays of the sun or prevents photosynthesis from occurring within the algae. Without photosynthesis the algae will die.

747. Does the color dye used to control algae effect fish?

No, not directly. During treatment with the colored dye, the fish are not easily seen in the deeply blue colored water but are not directly harmed by the dye. However, the color dye will prevent any desired submerged aquatic vegetation, such as an Anacharis plant, from receiving sunlight to grow. The small microscopic organisms such as *Daphnia* which feed on the microscopic algae may be indirectly inhibited by the dye. These small microscopic organisms are vital in the food chain for fish, not to mention other microscopic organisms.

748. Can fish cause algae blooms in the water garden pool?

Yes, especially if there are too many fish in the water garden pool. The wastes of fish will be made into compounds known as **nitrates** by beneficial bacteria that will be supplied as plant food for algae. If there are too many nitrates in the pool, the algae will rapidly consume it and grow at an alarming rate. Thus, the water gardener must control the amount of fish in the water garden pool.

749. Do the aquatic submerged plants or oxygenators reduce algal blooms?

Yes. Aquatic submerged plants or oxygenators can help to keep the algae population down. These plants compete with the algae for minerals and nutrients in the water. The oxygenators are more successful in this competition and will reduce the algae.

750. Do the floating plants in the water garden pool help reduce algae?

Yes. The floating aquatic plants not only shade the sunlight from the algae but will starve the algae similar to the submerged aquatic vegetation by taking out vital plant nutrients (specifically the phosphates and nitrates). The most popular and well known floating plant that reduces algae is the Floating Water Hyacinth, *Eichhnoria crassipes*. Other aquatic floating plants such as Water Lettuce (*Pistia stratoides*) and the aquatic ferns will help reduce the algae population.

751. Do aquatic plants have their own defense against algae?

Yes. A group of chemicals known as **allelochemicals** are produced by specific aquatic plants that can be toxic not only by being eaten by an animal but to other plants, especially algae. For example, it has been reported that the Water Lettuce (*Pistia stratoides*) has many different chemicals that are produced and inhibits the growth of different types of algae. These chemicals, however, are not produced in sufficient quantities to individually control the algae in the water garden pool. Researchers are attempting to isolate the different allelochemicals from aquatic plants in hopes of making a safe chemical algicide. Some of these chemicals isolated have been found to be as effective as the potent and familiar algicide **copper sulfate**.

752. Can water lilies in the water garden pool help reduce the algae population?

Yes. The water lily pads will cover the surface of the water and prevent sunlight from reaching the algae. The algae will not be able to grow rapidly in this subdued area under the water lily pad. It is estimated that approximately

60 to 70 percent of the surface of the water lily pool should be covered to help reduce algal blooms.

753. Is it true that *Daphnia* will reduce algae in the water garden pool?

Yes. One of the most familiar organisms that love to eat the cellular algae is the crustacean *Daphnia*. These are well known to control algae since they consume the cellular algae in great numbers. A pea green soup algae is a special treat to any *Daphnia* which can be added directly to the water garden pool. In fact, a vital ingredient in commercial raising of *Daphnia* in the laboratory is to add pea-green soup algae to their food requirement.

754. Do the aquatic snails eat algae?

Yes. The **ramshorn snail** is well known to eat algae. The snails mainly consume the algae that grows on the rocks, plants and other submerged objects in the water garden pool.

755. Do mussels or clams help reduce algae?

Yes. The clam constantly filters water and will take in the cellular algae as a food source. Clams are excellent in reducing algae.

756. Should chemicals or algicides be added to kill algae in the water garden pool?

Algicides or chemicals to kill algae should only be used as a last resort. Too often the ecological balance of the water in the pool is upset by introducing any chemicals. The target of the chemical algicide may be a specific algae but other aquatic plants and animals may be effected either directly or indirectly. When the algae dies, the decay will consume dissolved oxygen and can be dangerous to fish who may need this oxygen.

757. How can a large lake or pond be treated for algae?

To treat a large lake or pond for algae problems the first step is to identify the specific type of algae. There are many chemicals available for the lake or pond. Since large lakes or ponds drain into the environment caution should be observed to make sure the treatment is not contaminating the draining treated water. Contacting the local authorities is recommended before use and strictly adhering to the manufacturer's directions. One of the most common treatments for algae is the use of formulations that contain the chemical **copper sulfate**.

758. When adding chemicals to the water garden pool how can you tell how much to add?

Commercial chemicals that can be added to the water garden pool are sold with a formula of the quantity to add to a particular number of gallons of water or, in some instances in lakes or large ponds, the surface acre area of water. Therefore, the water gardener will be required to know the amount of gallons of water in the pool.

759. How can the gallons of water in a water garden pool be computed?

The amount of gallons of water is computed by drawing a rectangle or square around the water garden pool. Multiply the length times the width times the depth times 7.5 will give the approximate gallons:

> **Length (feet) X Width (feet) X Depth (feet) X 7.5 = GALLONS**

For example, if the length is 12 feet and the width is 8 feet and the depth is 2 feet, then the approximate gallons is 1440 gallons of water:

> **12 x 8 x 2 x 7.5 = 1440 gallons of water**

760. What is the formula to estimate the amount of gallons of water in a round pool?

To compute the gallons of water in a round pool, multiply the depth times the diameter time the diameter times 0.8 times 7.5 equals approximate gallons:

Diameter (ft.) X Diameter (ft.) X Depth (ft.) X 0.8 X 7.5 = GALLONS

For example, if the diameter of the circular pool is 12 feet and has a depth of 2.5 feet, the circular pool would have 2160 gallons:

12 x 12 x 2.5 x 0.8 x 7.5 = 2160 GALLONS

XVI. Tub Water Gardens

*Introduction * Making a Tub Garden * Planting * Fish *

INTRODUCTION

761. What is a "tub" water garden?

A tub water garden is a special form of water gardening that can be admired in a small sized tub of water (figure 83).

762. Why are tub water gardens popular?

Figure 83. Tub gardens can be easily set anywhere in the yard.

The admiration of a water lily is a special sight and many people do not have the space for a water garden pool. The tub water garden can be placed on a balcony that receives direct sunlight or a special place on a deck or patio. And, some prefer to enjoy water gardening but do not want to have a large water garden pool.

763. Are tub water gardens used in the backyard?

Yes. The tub garden can be made by special geometric designs such as a trio which will add a unique garden feature in any yard.

MAKING A TUB GARDEN

764. What is used to make a tub water garden?

Virtually any small container that holds water can be made into a tub water garden. Commercially purchased plastic containers, about two to three foot across and 12 to 16 inches deep or old wine barrels cut in half are commonly selected for making tub gardens.

765. What material is used to make tub water gardens?

The tub water garden should be made of water retaining material that is nontoxic to plants and animals. Residual toxic chemical found in the material selected tub water garden material can leach into the water and must be avoided. Liners that are fish safe can be used.

766. Should wine barrels be lined before using as a tub water garden?

Yes. Wine barrels should be lined with a nontoxic lining material since they may bleed harmful chemicals into the water that may effect plants and fish. There are available preformed liners of plastic that fit directly into the barrels or PVC or rubber lining materials can be used.

767. Can the tubs for a water garden be sunk into the ground?

Yes. This is an attractive way of displaying a group of water garden tubs. Different color patterns of water lilies can be planted in each different tub. The temperature of the water is better maintained if the tub is sunk into the ground. A layer of stones can be put around the margin to give it an attractive look.

PLANTING A TUB GARDEN

768. Is the tub water garden filled with soil to plant the aquatics or should they be potted separately?

Either. It is recommended to pot the water lilies and aquatic plants and place them into the tub garden. Soil can be added and the aquatic plants planted directly into the soil (figure 85). Planting directly into a layer of bottom soil is not as desirable as individual potting since the replenishment of new soil is much more difficult and tends to grow more undesirable algae and other aquatic plants which may require routine weeding.

Figure 84. The sunken tub garden. 1. Rock Plants 2. Rocks 3. Giant Arrowhead 4. Water lily 5. Floating Water Hyacinth 6. Umbrella Palm 7. Shell Flower or Water Lettuce 8. Snail 9. Oxygenating Plant.

769. Can any type of water lilies be planted in tub water gardens?

No. Particular attention should be made to the characteristic size of the water lily before it is selected for a tub water garden. The ideal water lily is found in the group of water lilies known as **pygmy** water lilies. These are miniature water lilies that are extremely beautiful in the small tub garden.

770. What happens if the water lily selected for the tub water garden is not a pygmy water lily?

Most of the water lilies that are not pygmy water lilies will grow large water lily pads which rapidly cover the surface. As the plant grows, it will continually push the pads outside the rim of the tub garden and begin to send up aerial pads. The tub garden will become covered with foliage and the beauty of a miniature water garden will not be achieved.

771. How many water lilies can be planted in a tub water garden?

A good rule of thumb is to plant a single miniature or pygmy water lily for every two foot across the water garden tub. For example, if the tub water garden is approximately two feet wide, a single water lily should be planted. If the water lily tub garden is approximately two to four feet wide, two miniature water lilies can be added.

772. Can other aquatic plants be added with the water lily in the tub water garden?

Yes. The selection of oxygenators and marginal plants will add a wonderful beauty to the tub garden. Floating plants can also add a pleasing effect.

FISH AND OTHER LIVE ANIMALS IN THE TUB WATER GARDEN

773. Can fish be added to a tub water garden?

Yes. A covering of vegetation, such as water lilies, for any hot sunshiny summer days is recommended with fish in the tub gardens. Not only will the water lilies provide shade for the fish but a shelter from the rays of the sun.

774. Can the water in a tub garden pool get too hot for fish?

Yes. Cold water fish, such as goldfish and shubunkins, will seek the bottom of the tub if the weather becomes extremely hot. As the water is warmed the temperature will increase at the surface whereas the cooler water will remain at the bottom. Warm water does not hold as much oxygen as cold water. If the water becomes too hot, measured on the bottom (over 80 degrees Fahrenheit) the addition of fish is not recommended. In the northern part of the United States, increased water temperatures is not a problem, however in the southern parts of the country the water can reach such unbearable temperatures for fish and become a problem.

775. What should be done with the fish in the winter in a climate of freezing weather?

Since the tub gardens have a smaller amount of water than a water garden pool, it is subjected to freezing solid, especially if above ground. Therefore, the fish should be brought indoors and enjoyed in an aquarium (figure 85) and returned to the tub garden next spring. Note: The fish should not be released into a natural stream, pond or lake.

Figure 85. An indoor aquarium can be used to bring in fish for the winter.

776. Do the sunken tub gardens need to have the fish brought in for a winter with freezing temperatures?

Not necessarily. If keep over winter, the use of a pool heater would be recommended to keep a hole in the ice and allow the noxious gases to escape. In geographic areas were the water freezes the entire tub garden the fish should be brought inside.

777. Should snails and other scavengers be added to a tub water garden?

Yes. The tub water garden is a miniature water garden pool and also needs a delicate biological environment to exist. Aquatic plants, fish, snails, etc. are all a part of the beauty of having a tub garden.

778. Will frogs be attracted to a tub water garden?

Yes. The frog will surely make a home in a tub water garden. The small area is not a deterrent to a frog looking for a home.

221

XVII. Arranging the Aquatic Plants in the Pool

* Introduction * Medium Size Pool Planting * Small Size Pool Planting *
* Large Size Pool Planting * 1920s Pool Planting *

INTRODUCTION

779. Is there a set pattern to placing water lilies in the water garden pool?

No. The pattern of water lilies varies and is often the imagination and creation of the water gardener.

780. How many water lilies can be put into a water garden pool?

The hardy water and tropical day blooming water lilies generally spread to about 9 square feet of water surface (i.e. approximately 3 feet by 3 feet) in smaller pools and 16 square feet (i.e. 4 feet by 4 feet) in larger pools. The container size used to plant the water lilies will often produce different growth sizes of the water lilies, that is, the larger the container the larger will yield a larger water lily. There are exceptions to the spread across the pool that must be considered with the pygmy and night blooming tropical water lilies. The pygmy water lilies cover a smaller surface area of the pool and the tropical night blooming water lilies will cover a larger area.

781. Should the entire surface of the water garden pool be covered with water lilies?

Whether or not the surface should be covered with water lilies depends upon the final desired appearance. In the 1900s, the water garden pools were referred to as **reflecting pools**. This meant that the old time water gardeners made sure that an area of water was left open that "reflected" the blue sky with clouds and the images of the aquatic plants. Some water gardeners prefer to adorn the water garden with lush vegetation and many flowers which hide most of the surface of the water, while others prefer the "reflecting" qualities with limited vegetation.

782. How many potted lotus plants can be placed into the water garden pool?

The potted lotus does not have leaves that spread across the pool like the water lilies but is restricted to the size of the planting container. If the planting container is 15 inches across then the actual surface spread of a lotus plant on the water garden surface is 15 inches. Allowance should be given for the size of the aerial leaves which overlap slightly the container restriction of 15 inches. Usually only one or two lotus are planted with water lilies in a medium sized water garden pool (6 foot by 8 foot). However, it is not unusual to have more depending upon the desired appearance and the love of lotus.

783. How are the shallow water or marginal plants arranged in the water garden pool?

Consideration to the height and spread should be given to the shallow water or marginal plants. Many of the shallow water or marginal plants are restricted to the potted containers and do not spread across the pool, however some will wade across the surface of the pool, such as Bogbean (*Menyanthes trifoliata*), and cover a larger surface of the pool. The final height of the plant must also be taken in consideration when placing the plants in the water garden pool. For example, the Hardy Thalia (*Thalia dealbata*) can grow to five feet tall in the water garden while the Dwarf Papyrus (*Cyperus haspan* variety *viviparus*) grows to two feet tall.

ARRANGING PLANTS IN A MEDIUM SIZE WATER GARDEN POOL

784. What would a sample water garden pool look like that is planted in a medium sized pool of about eight feet across?

The following diagram shows a medium circular pool that is planted as indicated:

A. Four Water Lilies, any preference.

B. Shallow water plants for a "Centerpiece", such as shown Papyrus and Arrowhead.

C. Shallow water plants: Lower right are three Yellow iris and Radican. Upper right are two Taros and an Umbrella Palm. Upper left hand are two Taros and Umbrella Palm. Lower left hand are two Pickerel Rush and a Dwarf Sweet Flag.

Note: Not shown are the oxygenators such as Anacharis and others that would be under the surface of the water and the addition of graceful floating plants such as the Shell Flower that can be placed in the open surface areas.

Figure 86. A sample planting of a round 8 foot across water garden pool.

224

ARRANGING PLANTS IN
A SMALL SIZE WATER GARDEN POOL

785. What would a small sized water garden pool of about five or six feet across have planted?

The diagram (figure 87) shows a rectangular pool that is approximately six to seven feet long and four to five feet across and is planted as such:
   Note: Not shown are the oxygenators such as **Anacharis** and others that would be under the surface of the water and the addition of graceful floating plants such as the **Shell Flower** that can be placed in the open surface areas.

   A. Three Water Lilies, any preference.
   B. Shallow water plants for a "Centerpiece", such as the **Papyrus** and **Pickerel Rush**.
   C. Shallow water plants: Lower right hand corner is **Parrot Feather** and **Dwarf Papyrus**. Upper right corner is **Hardy Thalia, Forget-Me-Not** and **Primrose Creeper**. Upper left hand corner is a **Taro**. Lower left hand corner is a **Yellow Iris** or **Blue Iris** and a **Floating Heart**.

Figure 87. A sample planting of a water garden pool approximately 4-5 by 6-7 feet.

225

ARRANGING PLANTS IN A LARGE WATER GARDEN POOL

786. What would a large pool about 10 by 15 feet have planted?

A large water garden pool of about 10 by 15 feet (figure 88) could have the following arrangement of aquatic plants:

A through H. Eight selected **water lilies** of which many choices and color schemes can be used.

    I. Centerpiece shown consisting of a **Lotus** surrounded with a **Papyrus**.

    J. Corner with **Taro** and **Dwarf Papyrus**.

    K. Corner with **Flowering Rush** and **Pickerel Rush.**

    L. Corner with a **Floating Heart**, **Green Taro** and **Papyrus**.

    M. Corner with **Pickerel Rush**, **Parrot Feather** and **Giant Arrowhead**.

    Note: Not shown are the oxygenators that are placed below the surface of the water such as **Anacharis** or other types. Next to the water lily marked "G" is the **Floating Water Hyacinth** which can be substituted with any of the fine floating plants.

Figure 88. A rectangular water garden pool approximately 10 by 15 feet is displayed with aquatic plantings.

1920s WATER GARDEN POOL REFLECTION

787. What did the water gardens look like in the 1920s when water gardening was becoming extremely popular?

In the 1928 mail order catalog of William Tricker, Inc.® the following photograph in figure 89 was shown with identified aquatic plants. Note the long lasting concrete which was shaped into a very popular and exquisite design that has been seen in many historic water garden photographs. The water garden pool aquatic plants were labeled as follows:

1. **Lotus.** The lotus could easily be admired at the edge and would allow any admirer to smell the mysterious fragrance of the unusual flower.

2. **Umbrella Palm.** This plant added a balance of height and fullness to the lotus which was across the pool. A gentle breeze would make this foliage rustle ever so gently.

3. **Blue Beauty Water Lily.** This tropical water lily (Tricker hybrid) had five blooms at the time of the photograph, so typical of tropical water lilies.

4. **Gloriosa Water Lily.** This hardy water lily would show a glorious red color reflection in the water garden pool which could be seen from a distant.

5. **General Pershing Water Lily.** This tropical water lily has a pink blossom with beautiful water lily pads that are olive-green with small maroon dashes on them.

6. **Reflecting Water.** In many water gardens it is hard to omit a space to reflect the plants and sky. This mirror reflections are important since they can not be seen in any other type of water garden.

7. **Roses.** Roses can complement any water garden by showing the reflection into the water garden pool.

8. **Deciduous hedges.** These hedges or plantings enclose the area to make the water garden a focal place. Often these hedges follow or complement the contour of the water garden pool.

9. **Floating Water Plants.** These plants float on the surface to bring an interesting display and color pattern to any location of the water garden pool. These can be Shell Flower, Water Hyacinth, Floating Fern or Azolla.

Note: Not shown is the oxygenators which are placed under the water such as Anacharis, Cabomba or Vallisneria.

Figure 89. A water garden planting. Photograph pre-1928.

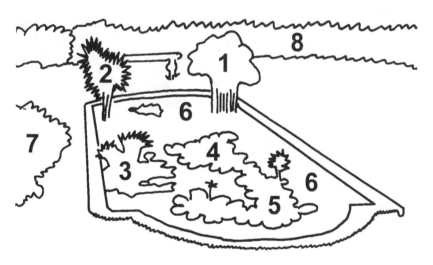

Figure 90. Outline of above photograph corresponding to plant key on previous page.

XVIII. Scavengers in the Water Garden Pool

* Introduction * Snails * Clams * Salamanders *

INTRODUCTION

788. What is a "scavenger"?

The term **scavenger** used by the biologist refers to any living thing that feeds on dead and decaying matter. Scavengers are part of the complex ecosystem of pond life which can be broken down into three components. First, there are the **producers** that are mainly the photosynthetic organisms such as algae and other aquatic plants which have the ability to produce their own food from radiant energy (light). Second, there are the **consumers** which are organisms that feed on the plants (primary consumers) and other organisms (secondary consumers) that feed on herbivores and each other. And lastly, the **decomposers** which is the final cleanup crew in the pond and function by breaking down dead and decaying items in the pond. The water gardener must introduce scavengers into the pool to maintain an ecological balance.

789. What organisms does the water gardener refer to as a scavenger?

For decades the term "scavengers" have been used by water gardeners in referring to the snails, tadpoles, clams and salamanders in the water garden pool. These scavengers help balance the ecosystem in the water garden pool and are not only necessary but add a beauty that can not be compared in any other form of gardening.

890. What should be done with the scavengers in the winter?

If the pool is not frozen solid in the winter, the scavengers will be able to survive on the bottom of the water garden pool in the winter. A pool heater should be used to keep a hole in any ice that forms. The hole in the ice will allow any noxious gases to escape that may build up under ice.

SNAILS

791. How does the biologist classify the snail?

The snail is grouped with the slugs, conches and abalones and belong to a group known as **mollusks** (a large group consisting of clams, snails and octopus) and called **gastropods** which literally means "stomach footed". Most kinds of gastropods have a one-piece shell referred to as a **univalve**.

792. Do the small lines or grooves on the shell of the snail mean anything?

These are lines of growth similar to the rings in the tree. As the snail grows so does the addition of these lines.

793. How can one tell the difference between a land snail and a water snail?

The land snail will occasionally be found by the water garden and can be confused with the true water snail. By examining the snail very close, the land snail will have four tentacles while the water snail will have only two.

794. How does the snail clean algae off the side of a rock?

The snail has a very important eating tool known as a **radula** which literally means "scraper". The radula is a flexible file by which the snail rasps off cells of algae off the stones. This radula is covered with small teeth and hooks which differ in the different species of snails.

795. Can the radula or rasp of the aquatic snail be seen working?

Yes. If the aquatic snail is placed in a glass aquarium the snail will move across the glass. In a glass aquarium the radula of the snail can be seen on the snail as it files or rasps the algae from the glass sides of the aquarium.

796. Do aquatic snails breathe by lungs or gills?

Depending upon the specific aquatic snail, they breathe by either lungs or gills.

797. Do aquatic snails lay eggs or give birth to live young?

Some snails will lay eggs and others give birth to living young (viviparous). The egg mass of the snails are jelly-like and can be found on the aquatic vegetation. It is very common to find these egg masses under the leaf of a water lily.

798. Do snails have "eyes"?

Yes. Aquatic snails characteristically have two eyes located at the top of the tentacles on the head.

799. What pond animals eat the snails?

When the snails are young or recently born the shells are soft and are easily consumed by both small and large fish. Frogs and wading birds are very fond of snails. Ducks can easily be seen eating the snails in a pond as they forage for food by submerging their heads below the water surface. Abandoned baby ducks that have been raised by hand have been found to be extremely fond of the pond snail and will consume them like candy to a child. At the aquatic nursery of William Tricker, Inc.® it is not unusual to find a group of ducks following a path of dislodged snails in a water lily pond made as the water lilies are harvested for sale.

800. How many snails should be added to the water garden pool?

It is recommended to add at least one snail for every one or two square feet of water. Thus, a water garden pool 10 feet by 15 feet (10 x 15 =150 square feet) should have at least 15 to 30 snails.

801. What are the names of the types of snails that are suitable for the water garden?

There are several aquatic snails that are excellent scavengers available for the water garden. These are the **Trapdoor, Ramshorn** (figure 91), **Melantho** and **Mystery snails**.

Figure 91. Ramshorn snail has a ram's horn appearance.

802. What type of snail should be added to the water garden pool?

It is highly recommended that a variety of snails (ramshorn, trapdoor, etc.) is added to each water garden pool. Each type of snail will have a different appetite and find a special ecological niche in the water garden pool. Not all water garden pools are the same, therefore the type of snail best at home in a water garden pool can only be determined by introducing a variety of snails.

803. How did the "Trapdoor Snail" get its name?

The Trapdoor Snail's (*Vivaparus malleatus*) common name is derived from a hinge-like shell material located on the bottom of the snail that can open and close like a "trapdoor" (figure 92). As this trapdoor opens the foot of the snail emerges and it can move about the pool. When the Trapdoor Snail is dislodged, disturbed or picked up, the trapdoor will close. The Trapdoor Snail is also referred to as the **Japanese Snail**.

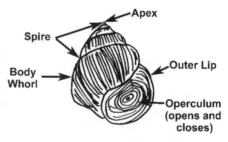

Figure 92. The operculum of the trapdoor snail opens and closes.

804. How large can a trapdoor snail grow?

The Trapdoor Snail will typically grow to the size of a walnut, often not larger than a few inches in diameter. This large shape can easily be seen in the water garden pool.

805. How does the snail get from one decayed water lily leaf to another?

Some of the snails will move along the bottom of the water while others may move across the surface of the water.

806. What type of snail can move across the surface of the water?

The melantho snail (*Lymnaea* spp.) (figure 93) can be seen moving upside down beneath the surface film of the water. In this position the two characteristic tentacles can be seen and slow movement of the body known as the **foot**.

Figure 93. Melantho Snail.

807. When are the snails most visible and active in the water garden pool?

The snails are most active early in the morning when the water is cool and can be seen actively climbing about the water garden vegetation. Many of the snails will go into the deeper depths of the water as the sun comes out and warms the water.

808. What is the largest of the aquatic snails?

The Mystery Snail (*Ampullaria* sp.) is considered one of the largest of the aquatic snails. It is the size of a large walnut and resembles a Trapdoor Snail without the trapdoor. It has a series of dark strips on the shell.

809. Where do the snails lay their eggs in the water garden pool?

Most of the snails will lay their jelly-like eggs under the water such as the underside of a water lily pad. Some aquatic snails will lay their eggs out of the water garden pool.

810. What aquatic snail lays eggs out of the water garden pool?

The Mystery Snail (*Ampullaria*) lays eggs out of the water. The snail will climb out of the water on a stem such as a cattail or iris and lay a cluster of about two inches of small white eggs.

CLAMS

811. How does the biologist classify the clam?

The clams are mollusks with two shells (**valves**) which are hinged and called **bivalves**. They are classified within a group known as **Pelecypoda** which means "hatchet-footed" referring to the shape the foot assumes during movement. After the foot is extended into the sand it is spread out to form a hatchet-shaped anchor.

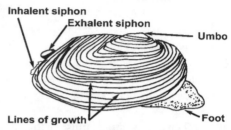

Figure 94. The clam has few visible parts as seen from the outside.

812. Do clams have a "eyes"?

No. The clams do not have any structures identified as "eyes" but do have sensory cells that are sensitive to light and contact located on the external siphons.

813. Do the lines on the shell of the clam mean anything?

Yes. The lines are similar but easier to see than on the snails and also, like snails, record growth. It is said that both hard times and easy times of the clam can be read by looking at these lines. The dark heavy lines signify slow growth and the spaces between the lines indicate rapid growth. Thus, the heavy lines indicate periods of cold, lack of food or something that kept it from growing. Whereas, the spaces indicate rapid growth typically reflecting an abundance of food and good growing conditions.

814. How many years can a clam live?

The record age for the clam is reported at 140 years and some species, such as the Ohio Washboard, over the years may become several inches in size and weigh several pounds.

234

815. What is the structure that looks like a tongue sticking out of the clam as it lies on the bottom of the water garden pool?

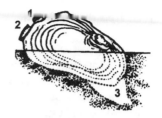

This structure which resembles a tongue is known as the **foot** (figure 95) of the clam. These "tongues" are the feet of the clams. The clam will slowly use this structure to move to any other location and anchor into the sand or mud.

Figure 95. 1. Exhalent siphon 2. Inhalant siphon 3. Foot into sand.

816. Are there male and female clams?

Yes, most of the clams are either male or female and only a few are considered **hermaphroditic** (both male and female). They can not be recognized externally but can only be sexed by observing the internal organs.

817. Can the clam "clean" the water?

Definitely. The clam constantly filters the water and can easily make turbid water crystal clear. It is a living biological filter.

818. How does the clam filter the water?

The clam, as well as other aquatic organisms, are known as **mucus feeders**. Small particles of organic matter stick to a thin layer of mucus on the gills as water passes over them from a water siphon tube (figure 94). Small hairs known as **cilia** carry the mucus up to the mouth where it is consumed. This mucus eating will bring up dead and decaying organic matter as well as numerous microscopic animals that settle to the bottom of the water garden pool.

819. Is the fresh water clam effected by pollution?

Yes. Pollution of our streams and rivers have depleted the supply of natural clams and many clam species have since gone extinct from their time of appearance during the dinosaur era. The sensitivity of the clam to pollution makes them a good indicator of the status of our waters and streams. Much of our runoff water contain insecticides, herbicides and fertilizers that stress and kill clams. Ecologist can "tell" the quality of water from occupied species.

820. Can the fresh water clam make pearls?

Yes. In fact, one of the great contributors to the severe reduction of clams in our history was the "Pearl Rush of 1857". The pearl rush began in 1857 when Tiffany of New York paid $2500 for a pearl from a fresh water clam. Since this was a lot of money during this time a "rush" for fresh water pearls began and rivers were literally depleted of clams.

821. Are fresh water clams becoming an endangered species?

Yes. If the "Pearl Rush of 1857" was not enough, a German immigrant by the name of Johann Boepple founded a factory in Muscatine, Iowa in 1891 that made mother-of-pearl buttons from fresh water clam shells. The success of this factory induced many others to follow and the harvesting of clams by the thousands continued. These two incidents greatly depleted the supply of clams in the early history of the United States. Recently, clams have become targeted at commercial collection and are being used at making pearl beads or nuclei to seed marine pearl oysters and has become a multimillion dollar industry. Many states are listing the fresh water clams as endangered, but the poachers are still in operation looking for a big profit.

822. What is the difference between a clam and a mussel?

Nothing. The term clam is used interchangeably with the word mussel. Another common name is naiades.

823. How many clams should be added to the water garden pool?

It is recommended to add at least a dozen clams to a medium sized pool, approximately 10 by 15 feet. Cloudy water should have more clams added to better help clear the water.

824. Can a salt water clam or oyster be used in the water garden in place of the fresh water clam?

No. The salt water clam or oyster needs the salinity of the ocean and will die in the fresh water of a water garden pool.

SALAMANDERS

825. Is the salamander an amphibian?

Yes. Salamanders belong to the class of animals known as *Amphibia* which means literally "having two lives", one of water and the other of land. The term *Amphibia* refers to the fact that although the amphibians have been able to develop some adaptations for life on land, they have never become completely free of water. Typically the amphibian must return to the water to lay eggs where the young are water bound and is characteristic of the salamander.

826. Since salamanders, toads and frogs are all amphibians, how does the biologist differ them?

Salamanders are amphibians with tails their entire life whereas the frogs and toads do not retain their tails in adulthood.

827. Is a newt and a salamander two different animals?

No. The terms "salamander" and "newts" are common names without scientific basis and both are referring to the tailed amphibian. The words appear to have evolved into meaning that the newt is the tailed amphibian found mainly as land-dwelling only to return to the water for reproduction, whereas the term salamander is used mainly to refer to any or all tailed amphibians. The word "newt" comes from the Anglo-Saxon word "efete" or "eft" a word used for both salamanders and lizards. In medieval English this word became "ewt" and finally "newt".

828. How does the salamander differ from a lizard?

The salamander has soft, moist skin without scales and has no claws on the toes. Lizards on the other hand have hard, dry skin with scales and claws on the toes.

829. How large do salamanders grow?

The different species of salamanders can range from a few inches to a few feet in length in the United States. Typically, the types of salamanders used in water gardens grow to only a few inches in length. Japan harbors a giant salamander that grow up to five feet in length and is the largest living amphibian.

830. Do salamanders have a voice like a frog?

No. The salamanders do not make a sound. It has been reported that some may make a "squeak" when a predator catches them.

831. What do the salamanders eat?

Salamanders will eat insects, especially aphids, worms and crustaceans such as the *Daphnia*.

832. Can the salamanders of the water garden pool be brought indoors to an aquarium in fall before winter?

Yes, but it is best to let the salamander begin a dormancy period and spend the winter in hibernation in the water garden pool. If the salamander is brought indoors, it will need care and food. The salamanders are subjected to a multitude of diseases in captivity and experience in handling is necessary. The biological cycle is interrupted by bringing salamanders indoors. For example the reproductive cycle is often inhibited, making a challenge to caring for the salamanders indoors.

833. Do salamander eggs hatch into a "tadpole" like a frog?

Yes, but it is called a **larva**. The larva of a salamander is very similar looking to a tadpole of a frog.

834. How can you tell the difference between the larva of a salamander and the tadpole of a frog?

They both will look like the classical tadpole, however the salamander will have large and bushy gills along the side of the head whereas the tadpole has none.

835. How many salamanders should be added to a water garden pool?

Salamanders do not require a great deal of space to become adapted to the area of the water garden pool. The more aquatic vegetation, submerged and marginal, the better environment for the salamander. This will provide a good home and attract the necessary insects that the salamander will consume. It is best to introduce a pair of salamanders at first. If they find a good home more salamanders may be introduced.

XIX. Frogs in the
Water Garden Pool

* Introduction * Identification * Characteristics * Life Cycle * Tadpoles *

INTRODUCTION

836. Why is the frog considered an "amphibian"?

The biological term **amphibia** means literally "having two lives" which was a term introduced by the Swedish biologist **Carolus Linnaeus** (1707-1778). The two lives referred to one life in the water and the other on land. The amphibians are able to survive on land, however they have never been completely free of living in or near water. They must all still use the water to lay their eggs and the young are water-bound for a short time. This is characteristic of the frogs which lays their eggs in water, develop into tadpoles and finally become a frog.

837. What animals of the water garden pool are known as amphibians?

There are over 4000 species of amphibians. This group consists of amphibians that are well known to most of us such as frogs, toads and salamanders. Each of these amphibians are desired in the water garden pool.

240

838. Why must all frogs live near or by the water?

There are many reasons that frogs have adapted to the life near or by the water. Frogs have skin that must stay moist and a life next to a body of water supplies this need. The reproduction of new frogs also depends upon water. They lay their eggs in the water which develop into tadpoles and grow into frogs. The water is protection from predators or intruders. A visit from any threatening predator or visitor, the frog will immediately leap into the water for protection.

839. Why is the toad considered "the gardeners friend"?

The toad is considered the "gardeners friend" because it will eat the many harmful insects in the garden.

840. Do toads make tadpoles like frogs?

Yes. A toad will lay their eggs in the water which will develop into tadpoles.

841. Will the gardener have more toads in the yard if there is a water garden nearby?

Yes. Toads require moisture and can be found in the garden often buried in the moist soil. However, water is necessary for reproduction by toads. The toad will lay eggs in the water garden pool and can supply a nearby garden with adults.

842. What other animals in the pond hibernate like the frog?

Turtles, frogs, snakes and salamanders are unable to regulate their body temperature like mammals and birds and hibernate in the winter similar to frogs.

FROG IDENTIFICATION

843. Is the loud peeping sound heard in the spring from crickets or frogs?

Frogs. These are common frogs (*Pseudacris crucifer* or previously classified as *Hyla crucifer*) which are found in the eastern and central United

States and are known for their continuous high pitched peeping sound at night in the early spring and are called **peepers**. They are very small frogs (figure 96), approximately one inch long, and can be identified with a pattern that looks like a dark "X" marked on their back. A very interesting fact about peepers is that the tadpole stage often leaves the water before the tail is entirely resorbed into the body. The spring peeper is considered a tree frog and after the breeding season in March, it will leave the confines of the pond and migrates throughout swamps and meadows.

Figure 96. The spring peeper, *Pseudacis crucifer*, is a very popular sound in the early spring. The frog can be identified by the "X" on the back.

844. Can the spring peeper be found or seen at night ?

Yes, all you need is a flashlight and a little curiosity. At night the full chorus of their high pitched peeping sound can lead one to them only to be seen with a flashlight. The small spring peepers should be looked for on water lily pads and clinging to emerged vegetation such as water irises. Once spotted, the flashlight will light up their white vocal sac. The light appears not to disturb the frog which will continue to call the high peeping sound. As long as there is no movement or startling noise the spring peeper will continue to sing their characteristic call as witnessed illuminated with the light of the flashlight.

845. What are the names of the common frogs found around ponds in the United States?

The common frogs found in the United States are the bullfrogs, leopard frogs and green frogs.

846. Why is the bullfrog called a "bullfrog"?

The North American bullfrog, *Rana catesbeiana*, is called a "bullfrog" because it makes a sound which resembles a distant bellowing bull. A pond full of bullfrogs can echo a loud chorus that can never be forgotten.

847. Does the northern bullfrogs like hot weather?

No. They prefer cooler weather. The frog does not have a device for cooling the body. In extreme hot weather the frog will often bury itself into the mud in the bottom of the pond where it is cooler. The condition of summer inactivity is known to the zoologist as **estivation.**

848. Why is the leopard frog called a "leopard frog"?

The name of the northern leopard frog, such as *Rana pipiens* and other associated species, is derived from the large dark spots surrounded by yellow or white rings that cover the grayish-green background of the skin which resemble a leopard. The belly is creamy white.

849. What color is the bullfrog?

The color of a bullfrog is green to nearly yellow, although some are greenish-brown. The belly of the bullfrog is grayish-white with numerous dark splotches. It is very similar to the green frog in color.

850. How can you tell the difference between a bullfrog and a green frog?

The bullfrog (*Rana catesbeiana*) can be differed from the green frog (*Rana clamitans*) by looking at the backs of the frogs. The green frog has two prominent ridges of skin down the back (dorsolateral folds) which are lacking in the bullfrog.

851. Can the different types of frogs be identified from their croaking?

Yes. The croaking or "calls" of the frogs are used by biologist to identify the different types of frogs without capturing them. The peeping sounds, the long sustained grumps, and other sounds are characteristic of each species of frogs.

852. Does the bullfrog sing in a chorus like the spring peepers?

No. The bullfrog does not sing in a chorus but the call is an isolated one.

CHARACTERISTICS OF FROGS

853. What do the frogs eat?

The main food of a frog is insects. The diet of a bullfrog consists of not only insects but worms, crayfish, small fish and other frogs. The spring peeper is very fond of gnats and ants.

854. Do the frogs use their front legs to catch insects?

No. Frogs use their specially adapted tongues to catch insects flying in the air. Their tongues are attached at the front of their mouth (figure 97) and are very sticky. When catching insects this tongue will extend over and outward to catch their prey. By being attached to the front of the mouth the tongue can reach further towards catching the prey. It is a spectacular sight to see a frog leap into the air and catch a dragonfly with one try.

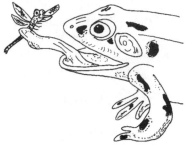

Figure 97. The frog has a tongue that is attached to the front of the mouth and is used to catch insects.

855. How does the frog swallow an insect?

A fascinating observation is when the frog captures and swallows an insect. The mouth is very large and the insect must be held in place before swallowing. After the insect is captured the large eyes of the frog will recess into the mouth and hold the insect from moving. After the frog swallows the insect the large eyes will reopen.

856. Do frogs have ears?

The frog has no external ears but have two circular structures on the side of the head just behind the eyes which it uses for hearing. This circular structure is an eardrum or called the **tympanic membrane** by which the frog hears.

857. Do frogs make other sounds than their familiar calls in the ponds?

Yes. If a frog is caught by a predator such as an otter or hawk, the frog will let out a most unexpected sound. It is a loud, prolonged, high-pitched scream that is similar to the cry of a human voice. Sometimes, if a child catches a large bullfrog, it may also give this loud shrill and escape from the frighten clutches of the child, leaving an unforgettable childhood experience.

858. Do the eyes of the frog have eyelids?

Yes. In fact, the frog has three eyelids. The first two eyelids of the frog consists of a lower eyelid and an upper eyelid which can close over the bulging eyes of the frog. A third eyelid is known as the **nictitating membrane** is a thin covering which serves to keep the eyeball of the frog moist when it is on land and adds to protect when the frog when swimming underwater.

859. Why are frogs slippery when trying to hold them?

The skin of the frog must stay moist. The skin has glands that secrets mucus which cause it to be slippery. Therefore, it is not only the smooth skin with water that is slippery but the mucus that is secreted.

860. Does the frog have webs on the front feet?

No. The front feet are not used in swimming. The main functions of the front feet are to hold the frog up when sitting, breaking the water surface when jumping and holding onto the back of the female frog when laying eggs.

861. Do frogs have teeth?

Yes, but only on the top or roof of the mouth. These are known as **vomerine teeth** which aid in holding their prey. The frog has no teeth on the lower jaw. In toads both sets of teeth are lacking.

862. Why can a lung or air breather such as frog stay under water so long?

Many a water gardener has spent a long time waiting for the surfacing of a frog they saw jump into the water garden pool only to give up. As the frog lays quietly on the bottom of the pond from danger the skin is able to absorb oxygen from the water. Therefore, the extended time by "breathing" under the water will often make the intruder give up and forget the frog.

863. Where does the frog go in the winter?

In the winter the frog will hibernate. It will go to the bottom of the pond and lie dormant. It will bury itself in the mud or lie next to a bunch of potting containers in the water garden pool.

864. How can the frog, which breathes air by lungs, survive a winter under the water?

The frog is considered **cold-blooded** as are fish and reptiles. This means that the temperature of the blood is influenced by the temperature of the surrounding water. Man, for example, is **warm-blooded** which maintains a constant body temperature of 98.6 degrees Fahrenheit. As the approaching winter temperature drops, the biological functions of the frog, such as the heart beat, will slow down with corresponding reduction of body temperature and the process of hibernation will begin. In this state the frog requires little oxygen which, when necessary, will be absorbed through the skin.

865. What happens if you touch a dormant frog?

If by accident you touch a frog that is dormant on the bottom of the pond, it will appear listless and move very slowly as if awakening from a deep sleep. The skin will be as cold as the surrounding water and the frog will be unable to escape as it would naturally do on a warm day in summer. This encounter can be made when draining a water garden to be cleaned in early spring when it is still cold. If this happens it is best not to disturb the dormant frog or death may ensue by bringing out of premature dormancy. Allow the frog to remain undisturbed.

866. Does a frog breathe oxygen only with lungs and through the external skin?

No, it can also breathe by the skin lining the mouth. Watching a frog carefully will show this trait. The frog has no diaphragm or ribs, therefore the characteristic breathing of humans is not seen. It is the up and down movement of the bottom of the mouth that allow the frog to breath by lungs or in the skin lining the mouth. The skin lining of the mouth of the frog is covered with many blood vessels. As the bottom of the closed mouth of the frog lowers air will be drawn in through the open nostrils and "breathing" now occurs in the lining of the blood vessels of the mouth. When the bottom of the closed mouth springs up air is expelled out through the open nostrils. When the lungs are used for

246

breathing the nostrils are closed with flaps of skin as the floor of the mouth rises. The muscles on the side of the frog contract and forces air into the lungs. The up and down motion of the bottom of the mouth can be seen as the mouth to lungs air is exchanged a few times with the nostrils closed. The lungs of the frog are small sacs and not made of the abundance of spongy tissue like ours. The frog therefore can, or must breathe either by the lungs, external skin or within the mouth.

LIFE CYCLE OF THE FROG

867. How long does it take for a frog egg to become an adult frog?

In many frogs the complete **metamorphosis** or change from egg to adult frog occurs within approximately 30 to 90 days. The bullfrog however will spend about two to three years as a tadpole before becoming a frog.

868. How can you tell the difference between a male and a female frog?

You can not externally tell the difference between a male and female frog by the reproductive organs (testes and ovaries) since they are internal in the frogs. In breeding season however, the **thumb** of the male is enlarged whereas the thumb of the female remains of normal size (figure 98).

Figure 98. During breeding season the male thumb of the frog is swollen.

869. When do the frogs lay their eggs?

Frogs lay their eggs in the spring usually beginning in May. The common Bullfrog breeds from May to July. The Leopard and Green Frog breeds throughout the month of April. Toads breed in May and June.

870. How are the eggs of the female frog fertilized by the male?

In the spring breeding season, the female and male frogs can be seen chasing each other and splashing throughout the pond. Once the male catches the female, the male will use his front legs and clasp female on her back. Once the male is on the back of the female, a term called **amplexus**, she releases thousands of eggs into the water and the sperm of the male is spread over the

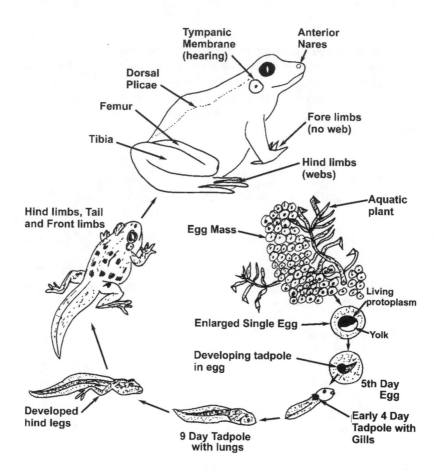

Figure 99. The frog life cycle depends upon the use of a pond to lay the eggs and develop the tadpole.

eggs. Fertilization will then occur. It has been estimated that the leopard frog (*Rana pipiens*) lays from 2,000 to 3,000 eggs and the bull frog (*Rana catesbiana*) has been known to lay as many as 20,000 eggs.

871. What do the eggs of the frogs look like?

The eggs which appear partly black and partly white spots (figure 99), about the size of a grain of sand, are produced in a long string of jelly-like substance that swells and binds the eggs together into a gelatinous mass. The white spots are the yolk material that will nourish the tadpole during development whereas the black spots are the actual living protoplasm that will develop into a tadpole. This gelatinous mass of frog eggs can be easily seen floating in the water garden pool. The yolk is heavier than the rest of the egg causing the eggs to float in the water dark side up. It is thought that by floating this way the black on top will absorb heat from the sun while the lighter half will blend in with the light from the sky and help to hide the eggs from potential predators that views the eggs from beneath in the water.

872. What is the difference between the eggs of a frog and the eggs of a toad in the water garden pool?

The eggs of both the frog and toad are very similar. Observation has been made to indicate that the eggs of frogs are commonly laid in jelly-like masses at the bottom of the water garden pool while the eggs of toads are laid in long strips of jelly in shallower water. The eggs of the Spring Peeper, however, are laid singly in a jelly-like substance and attached to a submerged plant or rock.

873. Since the female frog can lay thousands of eggs, does that mean thousands of adult frogs will be produced in the water garden pool?

Absolutely not. The frog must lay thousands of eggs since many of the eggs will not be fertilized and many of the developing tadpoles will never make it to adult status as a frog. There are many predators that will consume the tadpoles as food. The gelatinous covering is thought as a protection for the very young. As soon as the small tadpoles begin to swim they become a part of the food chain for many animals, such as ducks, fish, other frogs, aquatic insects, etc. Some eggs may also become toads or spring peepers which will leave the pond to become a vital part of nature. The production of many offspring by many animals in nature is part of the scheme of survival and is a natural selection that occurs with many animals that can not protect their young in development.

874. How long does it take for the frog egg to hatch?

Depending upon weather conditions and temperature, the eggs will develop into a tadpole in about eight to twenty days varying among species. A close observation within a few days after the frog lays the egg mass, which can be remarkable with a hand lens, of the newly laid eggs will reveal the movement of wiggling of the newly developing immature tadpoles before they become large and free of the gelatinous mass.

TADPOLES

875. Does the tadpole breathe by gills or have lungs?

The tadpoles first "breathe" by gills and has no lungs. As the tadpole matures, the lungs develop and replace the gills. Therefore, the tadpole has a stage with gills and later develops lungs.

876. Can the water gardener "tell" when the lungs of the tadpoles are functioning?

Yes. As soon as the back legs begin to develop in the tadpole the lungs are beginning to develop. The gills stop functioning and the tadpole will come to the surface of the water garden pool to gulp air. The entire change from tadpole to adult frog known as **metamorphosis** is extremely remarkable. Many changes occur and have been studied and marveled by scientists.

877. What do the tadpoles eat in the water garden pool?

The tadpoles will eat algae, mosquito larvae and other small microscopic animals (protozoans).

878. Do the tails of the tadpoles fall off as they become an adult frog?

No the tails of the tadpoles are resorbed into the body as they develop into a frog.

879. Do tadpoles winter in the water garden pool?

Yes. The tadpoles that did not mature into an adult frog will winter under a layer of ice.

880. Are there any other "organisms" such as the tadpole wintering under the ice?

Yes. Along with the tadpoles there are only a few cold blooded animals which are active in the very cold water under ice. These would be the fish, some insect larvae, burrowing worms and some crustaceans.

881. How many tadpoles should be added to the water garden pool?

It is recommended to add at least a dozen tadpoles to a medium sized pool, approximately 10 by 15 feet.

882. Is there a technique in adding the tadpoles to the water garden pool?

Yes. The plastic bag that contains the tadpoles should be floated in the water for about 15 minutes to equalize the temperatures. After this time the tadpoles can be released into the water garden pool.

XX. Water Quality with Fish

Acid Base pH

* Introduction to Water Quality * Introduction to pH * Testing pH *
*Nitrogen Cycle * Ammonia * Nitrates * Nitrates * Beneficial Bacteria *
* Sulfur Cycle *

INTRODUCTION TO WATER QUALITY

883. What are the important elements that a fish keeper should be concerned with in maintaining the quality of water for fish in the water garden pool?

The fish keeper should be concerned with maintaining the correct levels of **pH, ammonia, nitrates, nitrites** and **oxygen** in the water garden pool. In addition, the beneficial bacteria, that are the foundation of the water garden pool, must be established and maintained. There are a multitude of chemical reactions that correspond with the animal and plant life in the water garden pool. To maintain a healthy water garden pool is the goal of every water gardener, and it all starts with the quality of water.

INTRODUCTION TO pH

884. What does the symbol "pH" stand for?

The term **pH** was introduced by a Danish chemist Sorensen in 1909. The "p" stands for *Potenz* (German), *puissance* (French) or *power* (English). The "H" stands for the element **hydrogen** existing as an ion or charged particle. Thus, the symbol pH stands for the power or potential of the hydrogen ion concentration.

885. How is pH interpreted in the water garden pool?

The pH is indicated by a scale of numbers from 0 to 14 indicating whether a solution is **acid, neutral** or **alkaline**. The number 7 means the water is neutral, numbers less than 7 are acid and numbers greater than 7 are alkaline (figure 100).

Figure 100. Fish health is influenced by the pH of the water garden pool. Understanding the meaning of pH is important.

886. Is there a chemical formula for pH?

Yes. The chemist uses the expression pH in dealing with acid and alkaline solutions in the laboratory and has developed a formula to indicate the pH of a solution:

$$pH = - \text{logarithm } [H^+]$$

This formula is read by the chemist as *the pH equals the negative of the base ten logarithm of the molar concentration of hydrogen ion*. In other words, the chemist can mathematically compute the actual concentration of the hydrogen ions in a solution using a logarithm scale. This computation will give the actual pH of a solution.

887. What does the "base ten logarithm" mean in the pH formulation?

For the lay person, it is not necessary to understand logarithms but to understand the significance of logarithms when testing for pH. Mathematically, the **base 10 logarithm** of any number is the power to which the number 10 must be raised to equal that number. For example, the logarithm of 1000 is 3, that is, the number 10 must be raised to the third power (10^3) to be equal to 1000. When the chemist computes a pH using the formula, the difference between a pH of 7 and a pH of 6 is one pH change, however the single pH difference represents a 10 fold increase in hydrogen ions concentration or acidity. A pH change from pH 7 to a pH 9 is 100 times more acid. Thus, it is not necessary to compute with the pH formula using logarithms but to understand the magnitude and importance of pH numbers as they change, which are based upon logarithms.

888. Is "pH" used in areas besides water garden pools?

Definitely. In the hospital the pH of human blood is monitored, which is around pH 7.2, the pH of gastric juices is from 1.0 to 3.0 and saliva is from 6.5 to 7.5. In a routine urine test the pH is reported to the doctor and is commonly around 7.0 depending upon diet and physiological functions of the individual. In industry many solutions are measured by using pH. Many common household solutions have a specific pH: vinegar has a pH of about 3.0 and household ammonia has a pH of about 12.0. In other words, the solutions just cited can be interpreted as blood is slightly alkaline, gastric juices are strongly acidic, saliva is slightly acidic to slightly alkaline, vinegar is acidic and household ammonia is alkaline.

889. What is the pH of pure water?

From elementary science we learned that water is classically known in chemical formula as H_2O. It is from this symbolic representation of water that we can derive the pH of "pure water". Pure water would be defined as a solution of only water molecules. The symbol H_2O means that the water molecule is made of two molecules of **hydrogen** and one of **oxygen**. In solution the water molecule dissociates into one **hydrogen ion** (H^+) and one **hydroxide ion** (OH^-). The chemist refers to this as **autoprotolysis** or a self-ionization since the water molecule acts as both an acid and alkaline. The chemist shows this simple relationship where both the hydrogen and hydroxide ion is produced:

$$H_2O = H^+ + OH^-$$

The chemist also uses a "p" formula similar to the pH formula for determining the concentrations of hydroxide ions known as **pOH**. The pH and the pOH of a solution equals 14.

Therefore, since water dissociates into equal concentrations of hydrogen ions and hydroxide ions would mean that a pH and a pOH of seven would be representative of pure water, since 7 + 7 = 14. Thus, the pH of pure water is seven. (In addition, the chemist also must include a stipulation that this neutral pH exists at a temperature of 25 degrees Centigrade. As the temperature changes the autoprotolysis of water changes and changes the pH).

890. If pure water has a pH of 7, does this mean that clear pond water has a pH of 7?

Absolutely not. Pond water has a variety of chemicals and reactions that are constantly occurring and can effect the pH numbers. There is no pure water in nature. In fact, the chemist has a difficult time in attempting to make pure water. When the chemist makes pure water by **distillation** (evaporation and condensation of water), the water molecules immediately absorbs carbon dioxide from the atmosphere and makes the "pure water" become acid. This can be represented as:

$$CO_2 + H_2O <-> HCO_3^- + H^+$$

The chemist interprets the above formula as carbon dioxide plus water yields (both ways) bicarbonate and hydrogen ions (carbonic acid).

891. If city or public processed water is used to fill the water garden, would the water garden pool have a pH of seven?

No, not likely. Most city water is slightly alkaline and at times very alkaline. City water is not "pure water" and contains many other chemicals. In the United States it is not uncommon for people to purchase "bottled water" and not use the public "purified water" as well as using home devices to purify the city or public water further.

892. What pH should be maintained in a pond?

Fish have adapted to living at a specific pH in the pond, approximately a **pH of six to a pH of eight**. There are fish that have adapted to a pH outside of this range. Carp, for example, can live continually at a pH of four to a pH of nine. Normally, a pH for most fish outside the pH of six to pH of eight will cause stress and can lead to death from secondary causes.

893. Does pH effect other chemicals in the water?

Yes. Different pH's make many toxic chemicals more toxic and can be responsible for the fishes death. For example, a high pH can make heavy metals, such as the naturally present aluminum in the water, bind to the fish gills and cause suffocation. Other heavy metals such as copper in the water can also become more toxic to fish.

894. Can the pH effect the food chain in the water garden pool?

Yes. A high pH can kill algae that support small aquatic animals that are fed upon by fish. Thus, the food chain can be interrupted by a high pH.

895. Does rain water have a pH of 7?

No. Normal rain water is typically less than a pH of seven which makes it slightly acidic.

896. Why is normal rain water acidic?

Normally rain water is acidic due to the fact that the rain water contains small amounts of both weak and strong acids derived from adsorption of chemicals in the atmosphere. For example, carbon dioxide which is normally found in the atmosphere can react with water in making a solution known as **carbonic acid**. Carbonic acid will produce the excess hydrogen ions to make the rain slightly acidic. If many pollutants are found in the atmosphere and make the pH drop below six a condition known as **acid rain** results.

897. How is "acid rain" produced?

Acid precipitation or **acid rain** has received much attention in the United States. It is caused by burning fossil fuels, especially gasoline and high sulfur coal and oil. The sulfur dioxide and nitrogen oxides released into the atmosphere from burning react with water vapor to form sulfuric and nitric acids. The chemist can represent the release of the pollutant sulfur dioxide into the atmosphere as:

$$SO_2 + H_2O \rightarrow H_2CO_3 \text{ -oxidation-> } H_2SO_4$$

The chemist interprets the formula as sulfur dioxide (pollutant) plus water (rain drops) yield sulfurous acid and upon oxidation (addition of another oxygen) yields sulfuric acid.

898. How acid is the "acid rain" on the pH scale?

The acid rain provides the excess hydrogen ions in the water vapor to make the pH of the acid rain around 4.0. The United States have reported pH's lower than 2.0 which is lower than the pH of lemon juice! Acid rain has been recognized and documented in Europe since the 1950s. Beginning in 1950, the effects of acid rain have been identified in the Scandinavian countries and over the decades have shown the decease in life in the lakes as a result of acid rain. It has only been recent that the public has become aware of the problems of acid rain in the United States. Currently in the United States the Department of the Interior and Canada's Environment Canada monitor natural water conditions and produce a monthly report. The report indicates that most of the acid rain in American occurs in the eastern United States (figure 101). The pH is commonly found in the low pH 4 range.

Figure 101. The pH precipitation as recorded in the United States between July 25 through August 21, 1994 as shown in the monthly report by the United States Department of the Interior Geological Survey.

257

899. How does acid rain damage the plants and fish in ponds?

Acid rain damages plants by interfering with their ability to use nitrogen (nitrogen fixing) and extracts nutrients from leaves. The acid rain also can leach natural aluminum from the soil into our lakes and ponds which is toxic to fish.

900. Besides fish, what other aquatic animals are effected with acid rain?

Coupled with other environmental concerns and pH, aquatic life besides fish are being studied by scientists trying to understand and prevent future deaths and disruption of our ecosystem in ponds. These studies would include frogs, salamanders, snails, etc. The acid rain is found to be a complex network of problems on Earth. An interesting book, *Tracking the Vanishing Frogs* by Kathryn Phillips, published by St. Martins Press, New York, 1993 alerts the reader to our environmental problems.

901. What symptoms of the fish are caused by an excessively high or low pH in the water garden?

In an excessive high or low pH, the fish will be unable to maintain their normal body pH of fluids and unable to utilize oxygen. This will cause trauma to the skin and gills of the fish. The fish will become frenzied and may try to jump out of the water garden pool trying to escape this environment from irritation of their skin and gills.

902. How does the chemist test for pH?

The chemist has a variety of sophisticated instruments to determine pH and some of these instruments can be extremely expensive. These pH instruments are equipped with a variety of electrodes that are submersed into the water or test solution with an attached meter that electronically records the pH.

903. Who introduced the first pH water test kit that can be used by the amateur water gardener?

Mr. William G. O'Brien (1889-1928) a chemical engineer and vice-president and secretary of William Tricker, Inc.®, Independence, Ohio is credited with inventing and introducing the first aquatic **pH test kit** that is used throughout the entire world (figure 102).

904. Why did Mr. W. G. O'Brien invent the first pH test kit for the water garden pool?

After years of raising fish at William Tricker, Inc.®, Mr. W. G. O'Brien, a leading aquarist, concluded that pH and fish health were related. Being a chemical engineer, Mr. O'Brien used an electronic pH meter with electrodes and was not only able to study the effects of pH and fish health at William Tricker, Inc.®, but he came to the conclusion that knowing the specific pH number was significant. From his studies he saw the need for his customers recording pH measurements in water gardens as well as aquariums. It was not practical for the aquarist to purchase an expensive chemist pH meter. After publishing his findings and informing the world, with the

Figure 102. Mr. W.G. O'Brien is credited with the introduction of the first aquatic pH test kit in the world.

cooperation of the Lamotte Chemical Company of Philadelphia, Pennsylvania Mr. O'Brien developed and introduced the *first pH testing kit* for the amateur aquarist in 1927. It was called the **O'Brien Test Kit** and was introduced to the public in 1927 for $3.00 each.

905. Was the invention of the *O'Brien Test Kit* for pH rapidly accepted by the public?

No. Mr. W. G. O'Brien was a leading and well respected authority as an aquarist. He published many articles on fish and aquatic plants which gained him much notoriety in his field. Shortly after the introduction of Mr. W. G. O'Brien's pH test kit, he met with an accidental death in 1928. Criticism by skeptics appeared in the literature in response to his invention on pH testing. The notation of "pH" was extremely strange and hard to understand. Mr. W. G. O'Brien was a chemist, while most fish authorities of his time had no chemistry training. Even today, the concept of pH is often not completely understood by many water gardeners. Early criticism would entirely misinterpret pH. However, after the accidental death of Mr. W. G. O'Brien, many aquatic authorities throughout the world and William Tricker, Inc.® continued to support the importance of pH testing by the aquarist and water gardener which could easily be performed by the water with a pH test kit. In the years to follow, Mr. W. G. O'Brien's pH test kit became an universal and widely accepted practice around the world. History was made.

TESTING pH IN
THE WATER GARDEN POOL

906. How is the pH test kit performed at the edge of the water garden pool?

The pH test is a very easy test to perform at the edge of the water garden pool. The test kit consists of a small vial, a dropper bottle of an indicator dye and a color interpretation chart Figure 103).

To preform the test is simple. A small vial of water is taken from the water garden. A specific amount of drops of a special color indicator dye are added to the water in the vial and mixed. The color indicator dye has the property of changing color when the hydrogen ion concentrations or pH value changes. The color indicator dye selected is known as **bromthymol blue**, which is originally a deep blue color. After mixing the bromthymol blue with the water in the vial, the solution will become yellow at a pH below 6.0, blue at a pH above 7.6 and varying shades of green (mixture of blue and yellow) between pH 6.0 and 7.6. The resulting color solution can be compared to a **color chart** that shows the different colors of bromthymol blue at different pH's. Thus, a blue color is definitely above a pH of 7.6 or alkaline and a yellow color is definitely below 6.0 or acid. The color chart will discriminate the specific pH of green shaded colors which are a mixtures of yellow and blue colors.

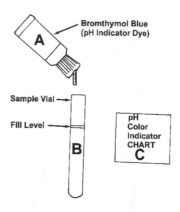

Figure 103. pH testing is simple: A pH color indicator (A) is added by drops to a sample vial (B) and is compared to a color chart (C). The color will correspond to a pH number.

907. Did the original pH test kit introduced by Mr. W.G. O'Brien work the same as today?

Yes. Interestingly, the pH kit of Mr. O'Brien's invention of 1927 used the same method today and the same color indicator (bromthymol blue) he selected. It should be noted that there are many color indicators or dyes that Mr.

O'Brien could have selected to indicate the pH changes. For example, he could have chosen a dye **phenolphthalein** which changes from colorless to pink within a pH 8.2 to 10.0, **bromcresol green** which changes color from yellow to blue within a pH 3.8 to 5.4 or **methyl red** with a color change from red to yellow within a pH from 4.8 to 6.0. Mr. O'Brien selected bromthymol blue because of the change of color within what he considered an important range for fish health, a pH 6.0 to 7.6 range. Since bromthymol blue has such a narrow range above and below neutrality, it is obviously a good choice to indicate sensitive, slight changes from neutrality into either acidity or alkalinity. It would be the interpretation of this color indicator that Mr. O'Brien felt would reveal problems that need to be addressed in the water garden or aquarium and history was made.

908. Is it better to use more drops of the blue color indicator, making the test color solution darker and better to read, when using the pH test kit?

Absolutely not. The chemist refers to this as **indicator error**. The color indicator, bromthymol blue, is made with a specific concentration. The color indicator reacts with a specific amount of test solution or pond water. The formula prescribed by the manufacturer for the amount of drops of color indicator and quantity of pool water must be followed exactly or an erroneous result will occur.

909. If a water garden pool is checked for pH, what would cause changes of pH at a later date?

Many natural processes occur in the water garden that continually attempt to change the pH. For example, fish and other animals as well as the aquatic plants in the pond or water garden give off carbon dioxide in normal respiration. Carbon dioxide will combine with water and make a weak acid known as carbonic acid, which provides more hydrogen ions in the water garden pool. Fish wastes, as well as other animals and decaying plant life, will make ammonia which will cause an excess of hydroxyl ions. These hydroxyl ions make the water more alkaline. In intense sunlight during the day, the aquatic plants utilize carbon dioxide in photosynthesis and this process will reduce the carbon dioxide in the water and cause the water to lose hydrogen ions, again changing the pH.

910. Can an experimental test be done to see the changing of the pH test colors?

Yes. An interesting experiment can be done to observe the changing of pH in water and identifying the different pH color changes. Add a few drops of the dye bromthymol blue (found in the pH test kit) to a small glass of city water and mix. The solution should be green to blue, indicating a neutral to alkaline solution. City water is typically alkaline. With a straw blow bubbles of air into the water and dye mixture. Continue to blow through the straw until the water solution turns yellow. The water solution has become acidic. This is because the air you are blowing contains carbon dioxide and reacts with the water to form a weak carbonic acid. The carbonic acid will provide excess hydrogen ions to turn the bromthymol blue yellow.

911. If many changes are occurring in the water garden that can effect the pH, why are there not constant rapid changes to pH?

Ponds and a water gardens will naturally resist a drastic change in pH, even when hydrogen ions are added to change the pH. The chemist term for a solution to resist change in a hydrogen ion concentration is called a **buffer solution**. There are a multitude of chemicals that are found in the pond that act as buffers, keeping the pH from constant changing values. If there are no buffers in the pond water or the buffers have been exhausted minor additions of hydrogen ions will be reflected by a significant change in pH. This is what can occur in lakes and streams with acid rain. If the buffers are used up or absent the water cannot maintain a specific pH and the acid rain can become deadly in a short amount of time.

912. Can the aquatic plants in the water garden pool change the pH?

Yes. A large number of aquatic plants in the water garden pool may make the water extremely alkaline after exposures to long periods of sunlight. Carbon dioxide that is dissolved in the water makes a weak acid known as **carbonic acid**. During a very sunny day, the plants use large amounts of carbon dioxide in photosynthesis and reduce the carbonic acid (decreasing the hydrogen ions) thereby raising the pH. Algal blooms are notorious in causing a high pH.

913. If the pH of the water garden pool is not within the recommended safe limits of a pH six to eight range, what could be the reason?

If the pH is outside the safe range, pH six to eight, the reason for such an abnormal pH should be identified and corrected. Is there an imbalance of fish? Is there too much decaying, uneaten fish food? Is a filter necessary? Is there contaminated runoff water that just entered the water garden? Is there any dead fish or other animals? Were any new rocks added that may contain limestone? What type of soil was used to plant the aquatics? It is important that a **base line pH** for each pond should be established and checked weekly, since the severeity of any pH change is coupled with the established base line pH . The water gardener should know the typical or base line pH of their pond.

914. If an abnormal pH is recorded and the cause can not be identified, what can be done?

If all measures to identify the source of an abnormal pH have been exhausted, then the final choice of commercial chemicals can be added which will correct the pH, either increase of decrease the values.

915. What is the most common problem with pH in the water garden pool, a high pH or a low pH?

An extremely common problem with the pH is the drifting above eight or an increase in the pH. If the water tested is highly alkaline (an increase in pH), then the addition of hydrogen ions or an acid is required to lower the pH. Mr. W. G. O'Brien, inventor of the pH test kit, had a bottle of hydrochloric acid (a very strong acid) in his original pH test kit. His published findings suggested that the pH of pond water should be maintained slightly acidic to rid sores on fish. Also, high alkaline conditions are commonly found causing other problems in water garden pools, such as with plants. Therefore, he had a bottle of hydrochloric acid in his pH test kit which could be added to water that tested alkaline. Hydrochloric acid has since been replaced by weaker and safer acids for lowering the commonly found high pH. These chemicals can be purchased specifically for this need.

916. How often should chemicals be used to change the pH in the water garden pool?

The changing of the pH by chemicals should be a temporary remedy. The pH should not be adjusted more than 0.1 to 0.2 pH units per day. Correcting the cause of extreme pH results is more important. Buffers are present in the water garden which resist a pH change. When adding chemicals to adjust the pH and the buffer is used up, the pH will change rapidly. If adding chemicals over a few days does not remedy the situation, consultation with a commercial source is recommended.

NITROGEN CYCLE
IN THE WATER GARDEN POOL

917. What chemical compounds that effect the health of fish should be monitored in the water garden pool?

An excess of nitrogen compounds found in the water garden pool can effect the health of the fish and should be monitored. These are **ammonia, nitrates** and **nitrites** which all have the element **nitrogen** in their chemical makeup.

918. Do the nitrogen compounds found in the water provide any benefits?

The nitrogen compounds (i.e. ammonia, nitrates and nitrites) in the water garden pool contain the element **nitrogen** which is a very important and essential ingredient for life. The aquatic plants need the nitrogen that is found in these compounds to survive. Nitrogen is the major constituent of **amino acids** (the building blocks of protein), **nucleic acids** (DNA and RNA) and many other important molecules. The atmosphere contains approximately 79% gaseous nitrogen (N_2), yet it cannot be used by most plants and animals as a gas. Nitrogen must be "fixed" into specific compounds before it can be utilized by living things in the water garden pool.

919. How does the element nitrogen get "fixed" so that the plant can use it for food?

The biological term **nitrogen cycle** (figure 104) has been given to the process that makes the element nitrogen into nitrogen compounds available for plant food. The name is derived from the element "nitrogen" as it is "cycled" into different chemical compounds.

920. What happens if the nitrogen cycle is upset or disrupted in the water garden pool?

If the nitrogen cycle is upset or disrupted, the nitrogen compounds can accumulate in the water at toxic levels and cause diseases in fish which may lead to death or directly kill fish.

264

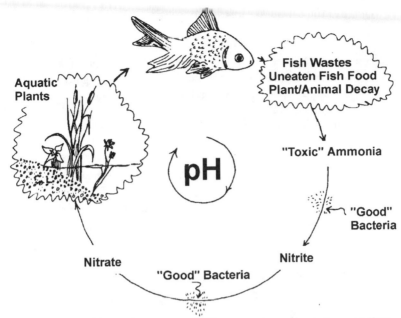

Figure 104. The "nitrogen cycle" is a very important process that occurs in all water garden pools. The cycle begins with the fish at the top and cycles through different stages.

921. What are the names of the nitrogen compounds that are produced in the nitrogen cycle?

The first nitrogen compound formed is **ammonia** (NH_3 or NH_4^+), followed by **nitrites** (NO_2^-), and finally **nitrates** (NO_3^-). All of these compounds have the element nitrogen in them as seen by the "N" in each formula. The plants can not use the nitrogen until it is in the nitrate form.

AMMONIA

922. What is the most toxic nitrogenous compound to animals produced by the nitrogen cycle in the water garden pool?

Ammonia is by far the most toxic and dangerous nitrogen compound to animals. A very small amount of ammonia can begin to cause problems in fish.

923. What are the common causes of increasing "ammonia" in the water garden?

Ammonia is produced by the excretion of fish, uneaten fish food and decaying plants and animals. Thus, the more fish in the water garden, the more ammonia. Excess fish food fed to fish and not eaten will increase the ammonia levels as it decays. And finally, dead or decaying plants should be removed from the water garden since their decay will increase the ammonia levels.

924. Does the pH of the water effect the ammonia toxicity?

Yes. Ammonia exists in two forms depending upon the pH or temperature of the water, **regular ammonia** (NH_4^+, ammonium ion) and **toxic ammonia** (NH_3). An increase in regular ammonia is not good for the fish, however toxic ammonia can be deadly to fish. At a pH of eight, 5% of the ammonia is toxic and at a pH of nine, 30% of the ammonia is toxic. Thus, as the pH increases so does the toxicity of the existing ammonia.

925. Does the temperature of the water effect the ammonia toxicity?

Yes. As the temperature of the water increases, the ammonia becomes more toxic. Water holds more toxic ammonia at higher temperatures than at lower temperatures. For example, at a pH of seven over 30% of the ammonia is toxic around 60 degrees Fahrenheit, over 45% at 70 degrees Fahrenheit, about 70% over 80 degrees Fahrenheit and 95% at about 90 degrees Fahrenheit.

926. What are the symptoms of the fish if an excess of ammonia is in the water?

Ammonia increases can destroy the protective mucus membranes and gills of fish and cause internal bleeding. The fish will show rapid and irregular swimming and gasping for air at the surface. This observation can be mistaken as a lack of oxygen in the water, but is related to the destructive or inability of red blood cells to carry oxygen caused by the presence of increased ammonia. If the ammonia levels increase, the fish cannot breathe due to lack or ability to carry the life sustaining oxygen, not the lack of oxygen in the water.

927. How is an ammonia test done on the water garden pool?

Like the pH test, there is an ammonia test kit that works on the basis of a color change. A small vial of sample water is taken from the water garden. A few drops of ammonia test solution is added and mixed. The color produced is compared to a color chart which indicates the parts per million (ppm) ammonia. The range commonly offered by ammonia test kits is from 0 ppm to approximately 7 ppm. The ammonia testing should be performed on a regular basis.

928. How are the ammonia test kit results interpreted?

At a 0.5 to 1.0 parts per million (ppm) of ammonia the fish will begin to show signs of stress, clamped fins and begin to die. Bacterial infections, a secondary reaction, can begin to spread and kill the fish. As the ppm of ammonia rises so do the fish kills, which correspondingly create more ammonia upon decay.

929. If there are two forms of ammonia, which one does the ammonia test kit measure?

Most ammonia test kits available measure the total combination of **toxic ammonia** (NH_3) and **regular ammonia** (NH_4^+). This is not truly indicative to the toxicity of the ammonia. The temperature and pH of the water is also important. As the temperature and pH increases, the toxicity of the ammonia increases.

NITRITES

930. What naturally breaks down or gets rid of the ammonia in the water garden?

Nature provides a specific bacteria, of the genus *Nitrosomonas*, to oxidize or break down the ammonia into another nitrogen compound called **nitrite** in the presence of oxygen. This is the normal process that this specific bacteria uses for energy. Since these bacteria require oxygen they are known as **aerobic bacteria**. The chemical equation, known as **nitrification**, is represented as:

$$2NH_3 + 3O_2 \longleftrightarrow 2HNO_2 + energy\ liberated$$

The formula is read as two molecules of ammonia plus three molecules of oxygen yield two molecules of nitrite and this provides energy for the bacteria. Thus, for the ammonia to be made into the nitrite, the requirement of oxygen is necessary and this is the function of the bacteria called *Nitrosomomas*.

931. How does excess nitrite in the water garden effect the fish?

Nitrite is not as toxic as ammonia but can still effect the health of the fish. Excess nitrites effect the red blood cells of the fish. The nitrite can destroy the red blood cells and cause the existing red blood cells not to be able to carry the life sustaining oxygen. The fish will become very slow and settle on the bottom of the water garden.

932. What naturally breaks down or gets rid of the nitrites in the water garden?

Nature provides another specific bacteria, of the genus *Nitrobacter*, to oxidize or break down the nitrites into another nitrogen compound called **nitrate** in the presence of oxygen. Since these bacteria need oxygen they are referred to as "aerobic bacteria". The chemical equation, known as **nitrification**, is written as:

$$2HNO_2 + O_2 <-> 2HNO_3 + \text{energy generated}$$

This is read as two molecules of nitrite plus oxygen yields two molecules of nitrate and energy is produced for the bacteria. Thus, for energy to be produced for the bacteria oxygen is necessary.

NITRATES

933. What happens to the nitrates produced in the water garden pool?

Of the nitrogen compounds produced in the nitrogen cycle, the nitrates are the least toxic to fish. The aquatic plants in the water garden utilize the nitrates growing in the water garden. Aquatic floating plants such as the Floating Water Hyacinth, Duckweed, etc. will grow rapidly in an excess of nitrates. The cycle is complete when the animal life, including the fish, consume the aquatic plants (duckweed is a good food for fish) and the nitrogen waste product ammonia is produced and enters the never ending nitrogen cycle.

BENEFICIAL BACTERIA

934. How can the ammonia and nitrites be constantly reduced in the water garden pool?

A **biological filter system**, which can be purchased, is designed to reduce or "filter" the ammonia in the water garden pool "biologically". The design and operation of a biological filter system is simple. It is designed with a filter medium, such as rocks, plastic fibers, etc. and a method of flowing the water over this medium. The filter medium, with adequate surface area, is where the "good" bacteria, *Nitrosomonas* and *Nitrobacter*, whose job it is to break down the ammonia into non toxic elements, will live and grow. An aquatic pump is used to constantly circulate the water with the toxic nitrogenous elements that will be fed to the bacteria living on the filter medium. Thus, a "biological filter system" is a living filter that contains beneficial bacteria.

935. Where does the bacteria, *Nitrosomonas* and *Nitrobacter*, that works in the biological filter come from?

Bacteria are commonly referred to as ubiquitous or found virtually everywhere in nature and the two bacteria, *Nitrosomas* and *Nitrobacter*, in the water garden pool are no exceptions. They are found on the fish, plants, snails, tadpoles, rocks, soil, etc. that enter the water garden. Nature also will bring them in by wind, rain, ducks, etc. Within a few weeks a biological filter will be found to have a multitude of these bacteria and will be functioning at full strength in a month.

936. Are the bacteria *Nitrosomas* and *Nitrobacter* dangerous to our health?

No, not normally. These two bacteria are considered soil bacteria by the bacteriologist. As with many bacteria however, they can become opportunistic pathogens. They can become potential disease causing agents under rare circumstances in certain types of clinical conditions.

937. If there is reduced oxygen in the water garden pool, what will happen to the nitrogen fixing bacteria?

If there is reduced oxygen in the water garden pool, the group of soil bacteria that thrive in depleted oxygen, known as **anaerobic bacteria**, will begin to dominate. These bacteria do not need oxygen to survive and derive their energy from another source. **Denitrification** will begin and the nitrogen fixing bacteria will cease to function. The denitrificating bacteria will reduce nitrates to nitrites, nitrogen or ammonia. Large quantities of unfermented organic matter stimulate the denitrification process. Bacteria that denitrify organic matter are: *Pseudomonas, Flavobacterium* and *Thiobacillus.*

938. Overfeeding of fish can result in excess food decaying on the bottom of the water garden. Will this fish food decay into ammonia if the water garden pool has a good source of oxygen supply?

Yes. The decay or putrefaction of the excess fish food is caused by a number of bacteria in the presence of oxygen, or **aerobic bacteria**. Bacteria such as *Bacillus mycoides* and *Proteus vulgaris* and some fungi can completely decompose protein in the fish food into ammonia in the presence of oxygen. On the other hand, there are other bacteria, such as *Clostridium* spp. that can **anaerobically** (without oxygen) decompose proteins.

939. Do the nitrogen fixing bacteria function under the ice in winter?

Yes. The nitrogen fixing bacteria are known by bacteriologist as **mesophiles** and are able to grow at a "middle range" temperature (Greek "meso" = middle or medium and "philic" = prefer) which represents a temperature range from slightly above freezing or 33 degrees Fahrenheit to about 100 degrees Fahrenheit. Therefore, the nitrogen fixing bacteria will still function under the ice in extreme cold water since the unfrozen water below the ice is above 32 degrees Fahrenheit.

940. At what pH does the nitrogen fixing bacteria function best?

The nitrogen fixing bacteria grow best at a neutral pH, around pH 7. *Nitrobacter* is somewhat less tolerant of a lower temperature and high pH which can lead to a slight accumulations of nitrites. In very acid bogs or acidic lakes (less than pH 5) the nitrogen fixing bacteria will proceed slower.

SULFUR CYCLE

941. Are there any other cycles similar to the nitrogen cycle that occurs in the water garden?

Yes, there is another biological cycle that occurs in the soil and mud similar to the nitrogen cycle in the water garden pool but uses the element **sulfur**. This cycle has been named the **sulfur cycle**. Sulfur cannot be directly used by plants and animals and must be made into compounds known as **sulfates** which contain sulfur and oxygen. Like nitrogen, sulfur is essential in compounds in the biological cells of plants and animals (such as the amino acids cystine, cysteine and methionine) and "cycles" mainly with the aide of **sulfur bacteria**. Sulfur is commonly added to agricultural soils as gypsum or as ammonium sulfate. In the sulfur cycle the organic compounds such as proteins are released by anaerobic decomposition (putrefaction) by bacteria to hydrogen sulfide (H_2S) gas. Hydrogen sulfide gives a classical offensive "rotten egg" odor as experienced by the smell of a handful of black muck from the bottom of a pond. The release of hydrogen sulfide is analogous to ammonia (NH_3) in the nitrogen cycle.

942. What organisms are responsible for the sulfur cycle in the water garden pool?

There are two groups of photosynthetic bacteria commonly referred to as **sulfur bacteria** (*Chromatiaceae*, the **purple sulfur bacteria** and the *Chlorobiaceae*, the **green sulfur bacteria**) can oxidize hydrogen sulfide to elemental sulfur and others oxidize elemental sulfur to sulfuric acid. In addition, other classes of bacteria, *Thiobacillus spp.*, thrive in the mud or soil in the bottom of the water garden. Interestingly, some of these bacteria utilize minerals in their diet rather than carbon diets of proteins, carbohydrates and lipids used by man. And more surprisingly, they excrete corrosive hydrochloric acid as a waste product. Very low pH ranges have been tolerated by these bacteria and have been recorded to live in pH of 1.0 and grows readily at a pH of 3.0. The chemical reaction is indicated as:

$$2S + 2H_2O + 3O_2 \rightarrow 2H_2SO_4$$

The reaction is read as two molecules of sulfur plus two molecules of water plus three molecules of oxygen yields two molecules of sulfuric acid. Note that this occurs only in the presence of oxygen.

943. Does the sulfuric acid produced by the sulfur bacteria have any beneficial effect?

Yes. The sulfur bacteria produce sulfuric acid which acts on insoluble soil compounds such as calcium carbonate, magnesium carbonate, calcium silicate, tricalcium phosphate, making them soluble and thus available to plants. Again nature has a plan for most events that occur in the scheme of life.

944. What happens in the water garden pool if the sulfur cycle is interrupted?

A lack of oxygen can upset the sulfur cycle. Under anaerobic conditions (lack of oxygen) a bacteria such as the genus *Desulfovibrio* will begin to reduce sulfates to **hydrogen sulfide** (H_2S). The classical "rotten egg" odor will be evident. Hydrogen sulfide is toxic to many plants and animals and is nearly as poisonous as hydrogen cyanide.

XXI. FISH in the Water Garden

* Introduction * Goldfish * Koi * Fish Care * Fish Food*

INTRODUCTION

945. Why are fish added to a water garden pool?

Fish add a special beauty to the water garden pool. They combine color, movement and a grace that cannot be seen with any other type of gardening. Many water gardeners treat their fish like pets. The water gardener soon discovers that each fish has their own personality and within a short time will be given their own name. In addition, they will add a balance to the ecology of the water garden pool.

946. Are fish necessary in the water garden pool?

No. Fish do not need to be added to a water garden pool.

947. What would be a major reason to add fish to a water garden?

Fish love to eat mosquitoes and thus become an excellent biological control of these insects. A water garden with fish is never plagued with mosquitoes.

948. Do fish sleep?

It is a common observation that fish rest on the bottom of the water garden pool. Since fish have no eyelids, it is hard to determine whether a blank stare is sleep or not. There are some behaviors of fish that appear as if the fish are "sleeping". These are identified by the fish resting on their side on the bottom of the pond the same time each night and in the day returning to activity. But again, with no eyelids, it can only be assumed that the fish is sleeping.

949. Do fish have blood like humans?

Yes. It is truly amazing to look at a stained sample of the blood of a fish under a microscope and see such cellular similarities to our own blood.

950. What does the blood of a fish compared to a human look like under a microscope?

Under the microscope, a stained smear of blood from the fish will reveal the same cellular elements found in humans. The **red blood cells** which carry oxygen in the plasma of fish is very similar in size and content to the red blood cells of humans. However, the shape of the red blood cell is oval in the fish whereas round in the human. The human red blood cell have no **nucleus** (the center structure of most cells that control the cell's functions) whereas the fish red blood cell have a nucleus. Having an oval shaped red blood cell with a nucleus is similar to reptiles such as frogs. Another type of cell found similar to a human in the blood smear is the **white blood cell**, which is known to fight infections (bacteria, virus, parasites, etc.). There are a variety of morphological types of white blood cells in fish and these are virtually identical in size and appearance to humans.

951. Do fish make antibodies like humans?

Yes. Fish produce two special types of white blood cells used for immunity. These special cells are known as **T-lymphocytes** and **B-lymphocytes** which produce antibodies in a complex series of reactions. Interestingly, these fish T-lymphocytes and B-lymphocytes are similar in appearance and function to the

T-lymphocytes and B-lymphocytes of humans which produce similar complex antibodies in our immune system.

952. Does fish blood clot like humans?

Yes. In the blood of humans there is a special cell fragment known as a **thrombocyte** (platelet) and other **plasma factors** (other chemical molecules that are involved in forming the clot). When a cut occurs the thrombocyte activates the plasma factors and produces a blood clot to stop bleeding. Fish blood also have thrombocytes and the plasma factors in their blood which functions with clotting as in humans.

953. Can fish hear?

This is an age old question. Who has not talked to their fish when feeding as if they were listening? Fish do not have the ear structures (cochlea) of humans and thus the early fish specialists concluded they could not hear. However, there is a structure known as the **lateral line** that goes across the fishes body. It is believed that this is made of a sensory organ similar to the inner ear of humans. Thus, it can be assumed that fish "hear" or interpret sound by the lateral line.

GOLDFISH

954 What is the best type of fish to put into a water garden for the novice?

The common **goldfish** is one of the best fishes to put into the water garden pool for the novice. It is a brilliant color, extremely hardy, eats most any food and is easily tamed. They also are very compatible with other types of fish and they will easily survive winter in a water garden pool.

955. Are goldfish "Carp"?

Yes. Goldfish are found in the Carp family (Cyprinidae) in the scientific epithet *Carassius auratus.*

956. Is there only one type of goldfish?

No. There are many subspecies of goldfish. Many of them were developed by the Japanese over 1000 years ago and have produced some very strange and grotesque fish. In the trade, many of these strange fish are known as "fancy goldfish" and have adopted such names as **Lionheads, Orandas, Celestials, Pearl Scales, Ranchu's, Bubble-eyes** etc. Some of the popular varieties of fancy goldfish that are used in the water garden are **Veiltail, Shubunkin** and **Calico Goldfishes.**

957. How long do goldfish live?

In nature, goldfish are known to live over 30 years.

958. Why is the common goldfish called "common"?

The designation of "common" refers to the "typical morphological" looking goldfish (figure 105). The common goldfish has a body that is rather long and flattened on the sides. The head is short and wide without scales. It has a fin on its back (**dorsal fin**), a tail fin (**caudal fin**) and a small single fin near its tail (**anal fin**). In addition, the common goldfish has a pair of fins nearest the head (**pectoral fins**) and on the bottom nearer to the head (**ventral fins**).

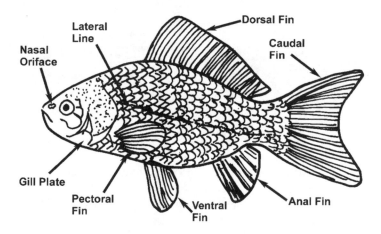

Common Goldfish

Figure 105. The common goldfish has "typical" structures found in most fish.

959. What are the purposes of the different fins on the fish?

In the water garden pool the observation of the fish may be a new and exciting experience to many. The fins are mainly used in their swimming attributes. The **ventral fins** are mainly used for stopping or as a brake and backing up. The **dorsal** and **anal fins** are used to balance the body of the fish. The propulsion of the fish forward is done by the strong **caudal fin**. The **pectoral fins** can seen moving water near the gills.

960. Are the common goldfish native to America?

No. They are native to China and have spread to Japan, Europe and finally America. The goldfish is commonly found in old Chinese paintings and appears to be held in high esteem. Several ancient and distinguished families among the Chinese carried the goldfish as a component part of the family coat of arms or as an ornament on their armor. The famous aquarist Hugo Mulertt has claimed that the goldfish arrived in Europe from China anywhere from 1611 to 1728. And he says that the goldfish *"variety introduced was the poorest and cheapest the Chinese had"*.

961. Who introduced the "comet" goldfish to the world?

The well known **comet goldfish** is an American introduction. The aquarist named Hugo Mulertt (figure 106) claims to have produced the comet goldfish by crossing the common goldfish in the summer of 1881. He says that on the day of his naming this fish, a long tail comet was illuminating the heavens. Thus, he said he named it "comet" due to the fishes large tail and elongated structure being the prominent feature in appearance.

962. Besides introducing the comet goldfish to the world in 1881, who was Hugo Mulertt?

Hugo Mulertt is a well known individual to the aquarium hobby and is known as the *"father of aquarium hobby in America"*. He was born in Delitzsch (near Leipzig)

Figure 106. Hugo Mulertt is best known as the "Father of Aquarium Hobby" in America. Photograph from *The Goldfish and its Culture* by Hugo Mulertt, 1910.

Germany and immigrated to the United States in the 1860s. He had an intense interest in goldfish and aquatic plants and in 1869 he began a business in Cincinnati, Ohio. His business sold goldfish, aquarium sand, aquarium cement, tropical fish, tadpoles, snails, fish food and multitude of aquatic plants. He published a book titled *The Goldfish and Its Culture*, published in 1883 with later editions. He introduced many new aquatic plants. In 1878 he was involved in publishing an aquarium magazine that led to a well known magazine at the turn of the century called *The Aquarium*. It is in this same magazine in 1927 that Mr. W.G. O'Brien, aquarist of William Tricker, Inc.®, Independence, Ohio published his pH findings and introduced the first pH aquatic test kit to the world.

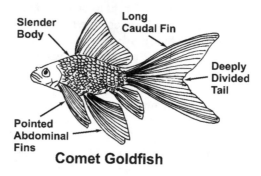

Slender Body
Long Caudal Fin
Deeply Divided Tail
Pointed Abdominal Fins
Comet Goldfish

Figure 107. The comet goldfish is a very attractive fish with beautiful fins.

963. How does the common goldfish differ from the comet goldfish?

Since Hugo Mulertt's discovered the well known comet of today, it is most fitting to have the comet (figure 107) described in his own words from 1883: "***THE COMET***: *Body slender, longer than in the common goldfish; butt three times as long as deep; fins very large and flexible; abdominal fins pointed; tail deeply divided and as long as the body; color of the body and eyes very variable. Any color or lustre met with in the other types may be seen in a comet. A noble type!*" Thus, the comet has a longer tail and is very free flowing which adds beauty and grace to the fish.

964. What do the fish called "Shubunkins" look like?

This is a common goldfish that is transparently scaled and highly mottled. They are found with a multitude of colors of blue, dark red, brown, yellow and black. They are also known as **Calico Shubunkins** (figure 108) in the trade. The shubunkin always has a straight single tail fin (caudal) which allows it to move quickly in the water garden pool. They are a very attractive fish in any water garden pool with their beautiful long tail and multitude of decorative colors.

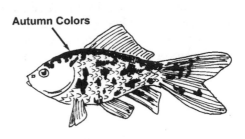

Autumn Colors

Figure 108. The shubunkins have many wonderful autumn colorations.

965. What do the fish called "Fantails" look like?

The fantails (figure 109) are common goldfish with double tailed anal and caudal fins. They are slower moving than the comets and shubunkins.

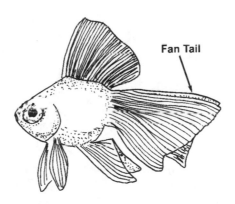

Fan Tail

Figure 109. The fantails have a beautiful fan tail.

966. What are the "Black Moors"?

These are velvety black goldfish (figure 110) that have projecting eyes suggestive of a telescope barrel. They make a very unusual appearance on the fish. The telescope-like eyes vary quite considerably in shape and direction. The intensely black color of these fish makes them a wonderful contrast to other colors of fish and vegetation in the water garden pool.

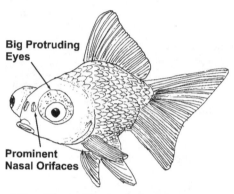

Figure 110. Black Moors have very large protruding eyes and add a contrasting black color with goldfish.

967. Do goldfish breed all year?

No. The main breeding season is from January until August.

968. Can the sex of the goldfish be identified?

Yes. During the main breeding season the male fish (buck) will have small **tubercles** (pinhead bumps) appearing on his gill plates (figure 111) and sometimes on the first ray of the pectoral fins. The female fish (roe) is usually shorter and fuller in body especially if carrying spawn.

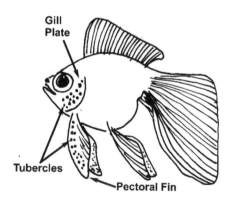

Figure 111. Tubercles on the gill plates and pectoral fins can be seen on the male fish during breeding season.

969. Do the male goldfish always have the tubercles on the gills?

No. Only during the mating season do these small bumps or tubercles appear on the gill plates. Therefore, it is virtually impossible to tell the difference between a male and female goldfish when they are not in the breeding season.

970. How can you tell if the goldfish are breeding in the water garden pool?

Early in the year the males will begin to swim after and chase the females. They will splash around in the water as if at an amusement water park. Quite often there will be more than one male chasing a female which can appear as a great deal of action in the pool.

971. Where does the female goldfish lay their eggs in the water garden?

The female will lay eggs on aquatic vegetation such as the floating types such as Water Hyacinth or Water Lettuce. As the female deposits the eggs the male swims over and deposits sperm. The eggs, about 1/16 of an inch and a pale amber in color, will then adhere to the aquatic vegetation.

972. How many goldfish eggs are deposited by the female?

During a single spawning, the female will lay 10 to 20 eggs at a time in repeated operations. A single spawning of the female can produce 500 to 1000 eggs.

973. If the goldfish can deposit over 500 eggs, does that mean the water garden pool will have hundreds of goldfish soon?

No. The reason many animals produce a great number of offspring is that survival to adulthood is rather difficult with many perils of nature. There are many reasons that the eggs of the female may never develop into fish that live to adulthood. Many of the eggs may not have been fertilized by the sperm of the male, some eggs can become infected with a fungus or bacteria and other eggs may be eaten by predators such as other fish. To increase stock of fish, many fish breeders will commonly remove the parents so they do not eat the eggs.

974. How long does it take for the goldfish egg to hatch?

Depending upon temperature, the hatching will occur from four to 14 days after the eggs are laid and fertilized.

975. What does the newly hatched goldfish look like in the water garden pool?

It is very difficult to see the newly hatched goldfish in the water garden pool. The newly hatched fry are very small, less than a 1/16 of an inch, and appear as a clear thread-like creatures which do not resemble the adult fish. They have large black dots that are eyes at one end attached to a center yolk sac. If seen, they will be swimming in a jerky manner.

976. How can one observe the small fry hatched from goldfish eggs?

After spawning has occurred in the water garden pool, the removal of any floating vegetation with eggs to an indoor aquarium can be done. Hatching goldfish eggs in an aquarium is very fascinating and can be observed closely. The small fry will attach themselves to the side of the glass aquarium. When attached to the glass, they can be observed as a marvel of nature and watched to progress into the recognizable fish.

977. Can a goldfish obtain oxygen directly from the atmosphere or must it only obtain the dissolved oxygen in the water?

Normally the goldfish will obtain dissolved oxygen in the water as it passes through the mouth and then across the gills where it is absorbed into the bloodstream. However, the goldfish can come to the surface and gasp atmospheric air to increase the oxygen supply. This can be seen if dissolved oxygen is low in the water and the fish are under stress to get more oxygen. If this occurs the fish must be supplied with more oxygen (i.e. waterfall, air pump, etc.). This should not be confused with feeding at the surface of the water.

KOI

978. What are the fish known as "Koi"?

Koi are extremely colorful fish that are carp (*Cyprinus carpio*). The Japanese are credited with breeding these colorful fish and named them **nishikigoi**. The nishikigoi are believed to be derived from the common or wild carp which has no color. The Japanese name for **carp** is "goi" or "koi" (pronounced as "coy") which means "love". Since the Japanese are credited with the breeding of these colorful fish the short name of "koi" has been retained. It has been estimated that the Japanese bred koi as far back as 500 A.D. Today there are thousands of colors and patterns of koi. Some of these select color patterns have demanded a huge sum of money.

979. How expensive have koi been sold?

Some koi can cost over a thousand of United States dollars. Sales of over tens of thousands of dollars have been reported for many select koi and sales of over a million dollars have been recently reported for rare varieties.

980. Why are some koi so expensive?

Koi are desired like special breeds of dogs. They have beautiful bodies with scales and fins. Values of koi are determined by the size, location and intensities of colored patterns on the fish. The fish have specific names assigned to the thousands of color patterns in an attempt to classify them into groups. It is these specific patterns of colors and intensities that the names of the koi are derived. The Japanese have koi shows which judge and classify the varieties of koi. From these shows many expensive koi have been reported.

981. How are the names of the koi derived from the color patterns?

Since the names are derived from Japanese words an understanding of the Japanese language would be helpful in interpreting the names given to the colors and patterns of koi. The prized koi shows will group the patterns and colors of koi into a dozen or more major categories with subcategories for judging. For example, the **single colored** koi of platinum, white or gold is known as known as "**Metallic Ohgon**". The **two colored** highly prized white koi with red markings is known as "**Kohaku**" and **three colored** with a mostly black body with markings of red and white is known as "**Showa-Sanshoku**". With the many **multicolored** koi and many patterns of colors the names go on.

982. How big can koi grow?

It is not uncommon for a koi to grow over 30 inches. These are known as **Jumbo Koi.**

983. How can a novice tell the difference between a koi and the goldfish varieties?

To an untrained eye, the goldfish varieties and koi can be confused when seen in great numbers at a commercial establishment. An immediate identification is the fact that the koi, being carp, have long **barbels** (figure 112) or whiskers by their mouth. The barbels are sensory organs for taste and touch designed for foraging for food on the bottom of the pond. The goldfish varieties do not have barbels.

Barbels

Figure 112. Koi have characteristic barbels.

984. Are koi the only fish that have barbels or whiskers?

No. There are many other fishes that have barbels. Barbels are found on the well known scaleless **catfishes** (Siluroids) which are bottom feeders. There is a large group of tropical fish with barbels found on many of the fish collectively known in the trade as the "Barbs" and are found in the genus *Barbus*. Most aquarium lovers are very familiar with this group.

985. What is the life span of a koi?

It is estimated that the life span of a koi is about 50 to 80 years. However, it is testified by some Japanese families to have koi over hundreds of years old.

986. Are the male or female koi different in color patterns and intensity?

No. The koi have been selectively breed and both the male and female have outstanding color patterns.

987. Once the koi is a few inches in size, is the color pattern and intensities established?

No. A koi of only a few inches can greatly change color patterns and intensities as it matures. It is this reason that makes purchasing koi exciting. As the fish grow, the colors and intensities may transform into a highly desired fish by experts.

CARE OF THE FISH

988. Are the newly purchased fish added directly to the water garden pool?

No. The plastic bag that contained the newly purchased fish should be floated in the water garden pool for at least 15 minutes (figure 113). Fish can not tolerate a rapid change in water temperature and can be killed. Floating the plastic bag containing the fish in the water will equalize the temperature of the water inside the bag with the water in the pool. After the 15 minutes the fish can be gently released into the water garden pool.

Figure 113. It is very important to float the newly purchased fish in the water garden pool for at least 15 minutes before releasing.

989. What is a floating "pool heater" that is used with the water garden?

The floating pool heater is an electrical device that floats on the water surface and keeps an area in the surface from freezing by a heating element.

990. Do floating pool heaters heat the entire pool?

No. The floating pool heater will only heat the immediate surrounding area of water. It will only keep a small portion of water from freezing.

991. Why is a floating pool heater necessary?

Noxious gases such as **methane** are formed under the ice from the decay of organic debris deposited in the summer. This can cause the water to foul and animal life, especially fish, are effected and can be killed.

992. Does a floating pool heater continuously heat the water all winter?

No. The floating pool heater has a thermostat that will turn on when the temperature drops below a certain temperature and ice will form. Thus, during the winter on warmer days, the floating pool heater is not operating.

993. Since natural ponds do not have pool heaters, are they in danger of killing fish in the winter?

Yes, this can result from an atypical severe cold winter that has an extended period of ice coverage. The large body of water in a natural pond is conditioned to handle the typical freezing and thawing that occurs during a normal winter. It is the abnormally severe cold winter of weeks of sub zero weather that can have adverse effects on a large natural pond and cause "fish kills".

994. What are the signs of a raccoon visiting the water garden?

Raccoons live near water and love water. The slight sound of water will attract a raccoon. Tears and scratches in the water lily pads are a result of the battle to pull the water lily to the side of the water garden by a raccoon. They will overturn pots of soil that contain the aquatic plant in hopes of finding food. The water garden will soon look as if a small tornado went through it. Often, mud foot prints of a raccoon can be seen around the water garden and the case is solved.

995. Do the raccoons eat the entire fish they catch from the water garden?

No. The raccoons typically eat portions of the heads of the fish and discard the bodies. Therefore, the finding of fish without heads lying on the ground by the water garden pool is a tell tale sign of a visit by a hungry raccoon.

996. How can raccoons be kept out of the water garden?

Trapping of the raccoon can be done. However, as soon as one is trapped and removed another moves in. A special electrical fence for pests of this sort can be purchased that is very effective to put around the water garden. It is similar to a horse fence, in that it will provide a mild but memorable shock to the intruder. Once the raccoon learns to stay away from the water garden the fence can be removed. If the raccoon returns it will be necessary to repeat the process.

997. Can raccoons swim?

Definitely, they are excellent swimmers. It is not abnormal for a naturalist to report seeing a mother raccoon and her young paddling across a pond. Thus, the water garden pool is open game for a hungry raccoon.

FISH FOOD

998. What type of fish food should be fed to fish in the water garden pool?

Since fish are in an small body of water in the water garden the fish should be fed a variety of fish food (figure 114). This should include not only dry prepared commercial fish foods but live foods such as Duckweed and *Daphnia*. Duckweed is a natural plant that can be considered a vegetable by the fish.

Figure 114. Fish should be fed a variety of fish foods.

999. How often should fish be fed dry commercial fish food?

One of the hardest things to do is not overfeed the fish with dry commercial fish food. It is best to sprinkle (figure 115) a small amount of fish food in the water. Wait for the fish to eat it. If they eat the food, sprinkle another small amount on the surface of the pool. If, in five minutes the food remains, do not feed any more. Fish love to dart around and appear as if they are hungry. One of the most common problems with the "loving" water gardener is overfeeding the constant hunger that is perceived.

287

1000. What happens to the excess fish food that is not consumed by the fish?

Excess fish food that accumulates on the bottom of the water garden pool can become a problem. It will begin to decay and promote the growth of undesirable bacteria and fungus. This bacteria or fungus can become opportunistic pathogens (disease producers) to the fish. In addition, the chemical breakdown of the decaying fish food will produce unwanted excess ammonia that can become toxic to fish.

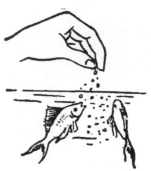

Figure 115. Learn the feeding habits of your fish. Do not over feed.

1001. Should sinking or floating fish food be used?

The use of floating fish foods are good to teach the fish to come to the surface of the water to feed. Therefore, the owner can easily view the colorful and attractive fish during the feeding times. However, if raccoons are a nuisance by the water garden pond, the use of floating food is not recommended. Raccoons are very intelligent animals and are creative fishermen. They are known to come to a water garden, swish their paws into the water, which is interpreted by the fish as floating fish food striking the surface of the water which attracts the fish, only to face a hungry raccoon.

1002. Should goldfish be fed all winter?

No. The goldfish will stop eating when the water temperature is below 50 degrees Fahrenheit. Thus, if fish food is added to the water garden pool below 50 degrees Fahrenheit it will only be left on the bottom to foul.

1003. What is *"Daphnia"*?

When the fish hobbyist desires the BEST live fish food, *Daphnia* tops the list! *Daphnia* spp. are small crustaceans about the size of a pin head that are consumed by fish in a greedy manner. They are commonly called "water fleas" or "ditch fleas" due to the fact that they have a hopping and jumping about in the water, not because they bite. Their familiar movement consisting of short jerky movements makes them very attractive to fish. The biologist classification of the animal kingdom is divided into phylum, class, order, genus and species. The *Daphnia* spp. are in the phylum **Arthropoda** (spiders, insects, crabs, etc.), class **crustacea** (crabs, shrimps, sow-bugs, barnacles, etc.) and order **cladocera** of which the *Daphnia* spp. are identified along with other genera.

1004. What do the *Daphnia* eat in the water garden pool?

The *Daphnia* eat small microscopic bacteria and other organic substances found in the pond mud. In addition they also love to consume single celled algae and can be used to control these algae.

1005. What does *Daphnia* look like under a microscope?

Under a microscope the *Daphnia* will look as if they just got off a spaceship from Mars. Microscopically (figure 116) a live *Daphnia* can be seen to have a single compound eye, which is usually in active motion. Normally there are two rather long branch arms or **antennae** used for swimming which is characteristic of the order Cladocera. There are also five or six pair of limbs or **appendages** attached to the **thorax** or body. It has a transparent **carapace** (shell) that allows the sight of the **heart** beating approximately 150 times a minute and motion of the blood cells can be seen. The *Daphnia* has been used in biology classes in schools to show the effect of certain temperature changes, drugs, hormones, etc. on the beating heart that can be seen through a microscope.

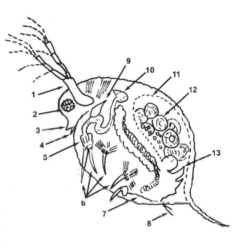

Figure 116. Daphnia. 1. Antenna 2. Eye 3. Rostrum or Beak 4. Antennule 5. Shell Gland 6. Legs 7. Post Abdomen with Anal Spines and Terminal Claw 8. Abdominal Setae 9. Mandible 10. Heart 11. Brood Case 12. Eggs 13. Abdominal Processes.

1006. How does *Daphnia* reproduce?

In the spring the *Daphnia* will begin to multiply rapidly into thousands and make a wondrous sight in a pond known as **Daphnia blooms**. The females are known as **parthenogenetic**. This means that in the spring the females can produce eggs without a male counterpart or simply **asexually**. These eggs are produced and stored in the body of the female *Daphnia* under the carapace known as a **brood pouch**. Later in the season or under adverse conditions, males will begin to develop and mate with the females producing a **resting egg** (ephippia) for the next bloom of *Daphnia*. These resting eggs are extremely viable in that they can survive the passage through the digestive tracts of fish, birds and other mammals. They can also survive several years as a resting egg to survive a drying of a pond, severe winter, predation, lack of food, etc. Purchased *Daphnia* contain both live *Daphnia* with eggs giving birth to young and the ephippia or resting eggs.

1007. How is *Daphnia* purchased?

They can be purchased as freeze dried or live. Some fish foods contain the freeze dried forms.

1008. If Daphnia is such a good fish food why is it hard to obtain from commercial sources?

Live *Daphnia* was once considered the best fish food available by fish experts and highly desired in the 1920s and 1930s. *Daphnia* was often collected in standing water and ponds found in our meadows and backyard farms. All that one needed was a *Daphnia* collecting net and a bucket. Today, much of our ecology and life styles have changed and the *Daphnia* is not found in abundance in nature and must be purchased from commercial sources.

1009. When is the best time to purchase *Daphnia*?

Daphnia blooms are naturally found in the spring and fall in our outside ponds. This cycle is easily reproduced by commercial suppliers in large quantities. This supply of *Daphnia* are loaded with many eggs that can "seed" the water garden. It has been estimated that in 60 days a single female *Daphnia* can produce over 12 billion offspring.

1010. After the live *Daphnia* are put into the water garden are they visible?

Not very well. In a water garden pool, due to the large amount of water and difficult visibility, the extremely small transparent *Daphnia* are difficult to follow and see. Since these are natural foods the fish will easily find and consume the *Daphnia*. In an aquarium they can be seen easily swimming with the characteristic jerking movement and the fish consuming them.

1011. Are there any other crustaceans besides *Daphnia* that are known as good food for fish?

Yes. A small sample of seasoned pond water as viewed with a microscope has many thousands of animal and plant life of which many are crustaceans relative to the *Daphnia*. In fact, a fertile specimen of pond water will look as if the sight is from a space invasion movie or a sample of pond water on another planet. The sight of these tiny creatures is often a first time experience for anyone. One of the most common crustaceans besides *Daphnia* is another water flea known as *Cyclops* (figure 117), reflecting the single median eye located in the middle of its "forehead". Another is a popular *Cypris* or **hard-shell** *Daphnia* which look like small round seeds with a hard covering. All of these creatures are important in the aquatic food chain and are consumed and enjoyed by fish.

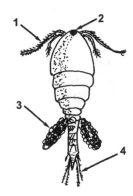

Figure 117. Cyclops. 1. Antenna 2. Single Eye 3. Egg Sacks 4. Tail Fork (Furca)

1012. May mosquito larvae be used to feed fish?

Yes. Most standing water without fish will breed mosquito larvae. Water gardens with fish will never be plagued with mosquito larvae. To breed mosquito larvae for fish is simple. Just place a bucket of water outside and within a few weeks the mosquito larvae will begin to form. Pour this solution of mosquito larvae into the water garden and the fish will consume them.

1013. How often should live fish food be fed to fish?

Live fish food should be given to fish as often as possible. This food is natures best. The advantage of feeding live fish food over dry commercial food is that overfeeding is not a problem and the nutritious value is beyond compare.

XXII. Diseases of Fish

* Introduction * Bacteria * Fungus * Algae * Protozoan *
*Preventative Measures *

INTRODUCTION

1014. How can you "tell" what a healthy fish looks like?

Before one can recognize a diseased fish, one first must be able to identify a healthy fish. Examine the fish carefully looking for perfect fins, absence of white spots on the skin, sunken eyes and smooth slender bodies. A healthy fish will spread its tail fin and has its dorsal fin erect or standing up except under stress or emotional disturbance. The eye will normally be projecting slightly beyond the line of the head in a healthy fish.

1015. What fish diseases can be found in the water garden?

It is very disheartening for the novice water gardener to discover how many diseases of fish can be found in a water garden. There are more than likely as many diseases of fish as that of man. However, if we were to dwell upon the all diseases of mankind, we would quickly wonder how we managed to survive at all. There are many textbooks and research studies dealing with the multitude of diseases that are found in fish. However, it is rewarding to hear that many water gardeners derive a great amount of enjoyment from their fish without the pains of dealing with fish diseases.

1016. What are the causes of diseases associated with fish?

Basically the same group of disease causing agents that plague mankind attack fish. These are caused by such agents as **protozoa, fungi, bacteria viruses, tapeworms, roundworms, flukes, algae, crustaceans, etc.**

1017. How are fish diseases treated in the water garden pool?

Fish diseases are best prevented by maintaining quality water conditions. However, diseases may eventually attack the fish and should be addressed. The treatment methods used vary among the fish hobbyist and can get very involved. The simplest method is to treat the entire pond, if possible, with specific chemicals that kill the parasites. This method depends on the size of the pond. Other treatment methods involve the removal of the diseased fish into a **isolation tank** for treatment.

1018. Are the diseases that kill fish contagious to man?

Not necessarily. Most of the specific disease causing agents are specific to the fish and are not contagious to man. As with most human health concerns, in rare instances, a fish bacteria or fungus may effect an individual that is debilitated. Caution should always be used in handling sick fish.

BACTERIAL DISEASES

1019. What are "bacteria"?

Bacteria represent a large group of microscopic single celled organisms in terms of both variety and numbers. There are over 1700 species of bacteria and are truly ubiquitous. The duties of the bacteria are too numerous to mention. Many times we think of bacteria as "bad" or disease producing, but they are an important part of our ecosystem and life processes. For example, bacteria live in our intestine helping with digestion (bacteria provide the vitally needed vitamin K in the large intestine) and help to break down toxic chemicals that would destroy life in our ponds. Many bacteriologist agree that if all the bacteria were to die, life on Earth would cease to exist.

1020. Can bacteria move or swim through the water garden pool?

Yes. Some species are equipped with a **flagella** which is a thread-like whip that extends from the cell and can propel the bacterial through the water. Flagella can be found singly or many surrounding the cell. Under a microscope, with proper stains, the bacterial flagella appear as minute threads.

1021. What do the bacteria "eat"?

Some bacteria are **saprophytes**, which means that they live on dead and decaying organic matter. Others are **parasitic** or invade the bodies of plants and animals and take nourishment directly from living tissue (the organism, plant or animal, is called a **host**). A relatively small number of bacteria are **autotrophic**, which means that they can manufacture their own food by photosynthesis.

1022. How do the bacteria "breathe" under the water?

The single celled bacteria do not have lungs or gills. Respiration or "breathing" is a simple process of the necessary elements for life diffusing directly from the water into the cell. Therefore, if the bacteria requires oxygen, it simply diffuses or passes directly through the bacterial cell from the water.

1023. Do all bacteria need oxygen to survive under the water in the water garden pool?

No. Not all bacteria need oxygen to live under the water. The bacteriologist has special names given to bacteria oxygen requirements. The bacterial species that require oxygen are called **obligate aerobes** and the bacteria that can not grow in the presence of oxygen and are called **obligate anaerobes**. There are some bacteria that can live as an aerobe or anaerobe and these are called **facultative anaerobes**. Thus, different types of bacteria have a variety of oxygen demands. These demands can easily survive the variety of conditions found in the water garden pool. The bacteria that demands oxygen, or the obligate aerobe, is the most desired in the water garden pool.

1024. How do the bacteria reproduce or multiply in the water garden pool?

Bacteria can reproduce **asexually** by a simple division of the cell known as **binary fission**. When conditions are good the bacteria can multiply at an amazing rate. Some bacteria can divide and grow to adult status and divide again within 15 to 20 minutes! This is why a bacterial disease, whether in a fish or human, must be immediately addressed. Bacteria can also reproduce **sexually** (bacteria are represented by a male-type and female-type of bacteria, where a exchange of genetic material is involved).

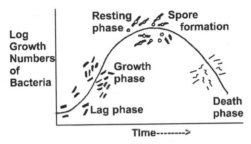

Figure 118. Bacteria can reproduce rapidly. The bacteriologist identifies specific growth stages that the bacteria will pass through known as "phases".

1025. If the water garden pool is drained and dried in the sun or left empty during a freezing winter, does the bacteria die?

Not necessarily. Many bacteria are able to withstand adverse conditions. Many bacteria have the ability to develop a special structure known as an **endospore**. These endospores or "spores" are resistant to adverse environmental conditions of heat, cold, drying and other conditions. Bacterial spores have been found in deep layers of ice in the Antarctic and have apparently been trapped there for thousands of years. When placed in a warmer climate they began to grow into bacterial cells.

1026. Do all disease producing bacteria produce endospores?

No, and thank goodness for that. Many disease producing bacteria that causes fish diseases do not produce endospores and can be controlled with classical treatments. As a side note, a well known bacteria that produces endospores is the feared tetanus that is caused by the bacteria *Clostridium*.

1027. If you need a microscope to "see" bacteria, then how can you tell if a pathogenic or disease producing bacteria is on the fish?

You cannot "see" the bacteria on the fish. The observation of the fishes appearance and reaction to the bacteria is relative to identifying a bacterial disease. It is similar to the doctor looking into your soar throat and seeing redness and swollen glands and assuming it to be caused by a bacteria known as *Streptococcus* or Strep. To actually name or identify the specific genus of a bacteria that causes a disease requires special laboratory equipment and testing.

1028. How could the bacteriologist identify a specific pathological or disease causing species of bacteria on the fish?

The process that the bacteriologist uses to identify a specific pathological species of bacteria is similar to the familiar throat culture taken at the doctors office. The bacteriologist will take a sample of the suspected bacterial infection, for example a reddened sore on the fish, by using a sterile cotton swab. This cotton swab is placed into or on a media that favors the growth of the particular pathogenic bacteria. Since the bacteria grow rapidly, within 24 hours the bacteria will grow into a colony on or in the media and exhibit known growth patterns. The test media may also have color indicators to better identify the bacteria by metabolism. Other specific chemical tests can be performed. Within a short time the bacteriologist will be able to identify the specific species of bacteria and make a diagnosis as to whether or not it is the causative agent of the disease.

1029. What are the signs of a bacterial infection of fish?

Classical signs of bacterial infections in fish are body lesions, ulcers or sores and reddening at the base of the fins which appear frayed. Normally the fish will lose appetite and stop eating.

1030. What causes fin rot in fish?

Fin rot is caused by bacteria, specifically identified as *Aeromonas* spp. or *Pseudomonas* spp. which are commonly found in the environment. The first sign is when the fins appear slightly turbid and as the bacteria grow, the fins become reddened. It may spread to the skin and cause chunks of skin to flake off. Fungus can become a secondary infection as the bacteria spread.

1031. What should be done to treat a bacterial infection of fish?

They are many external commercial chemical formulations used to treat bacterial infections of fish. **Acriflavine** (trypaflavin) is a good remedy that can be added directly into the water. It is a yellow dye that dissolves easily in water. Not only is it effective against bacterial infections but also against other fish parasites such as the skin and gill diseases caused by protozoa and other trematodes.

1032. Is there any simple way for the water gardener to give antibiotics to the fish for a bacterial infection?

Yes, through the oral route in fish foods. Fish foods can be purchased that has antibiotics and are commonly known as "medicated fish foods". Antibiotics used in the fish industry are similar to the ones used to treat our bacterial diseases: erythromycin, oxytetracycline, kanamycin, sulfadiazine, etc.

1033. What are the reddish boil-like lesions seen on the fish?

These can be caused by the fish disease called **furunculosis**. Furunculosis was first reported in the early 1890s and caused by a bacteria of the species *Aeromonas*. Typically the disease shows in the reddish-like lesions on the skin of the fish but also can show redness on the fins and around the mouth. It is systemic in that the bacteria will spread through the internal organs of the fish.

1034. What medicated fish food is recommended to treat the fish disease known as furunculosis?

An antibiotic that has been used successfully for furunculosis is **oxytetracycline** or also known as **terramycin**. Other drugs have also be reported as successful treatments.

1035. Where does the bacteria *Aeromonas* come from that is found in the water garden pool?

The bacterial genus *Aeromonas* are found in nature in water and soil. The bacteria are motile, which means it can swim though the water to find a host. When the fish are stressed or their immunity is reduced, the bacteria now has the opportunity to cause a disease. The bacteria can be ingested from the water or find an open sore to infect and spread internally. The bacteria not only infects fish but other aquatic animals such as frogs.

FUNGUS DISEASES

1036. What is a fungus?

Fungi (plural for fungus, a word derived from Latin for *mushroom*) are plants without chlorophyll and are a group made up of over 75,000 species. Fungi never develop roots, stems or leaves. Since they have no chlorophyll and can not manufacture their own food, the fungi must be able to extract their food supply from another source. Many are **saprophytes**, a term used to indicate that they feed on dead and decaying organic matter, such as the common toadstools found in the woods living on the trunk of a dead tree. Fungi can be either single celled or multicellular. The fungi that are well known to us are yeasts, molds, mildews, rusts, smuts and mushrooms. Other fungi are parasites living on animals or plants.

1037. How do fungi reproduce?

Fungi can reproduce sexually (male and female strains) or asexually (vegetatively) producing very resistant spores similar to the bacteria. They do not make seeds like plants and thus have no flowers.

1038. Why are spores produced by fungi?

Spores are produced by the fungi as a form of resistance and survival. The spores are resistant to heat, cold, drying, disinfectants and immune mechanisms of the fish. If a pond is empty of water, the fungal spores can lie dormant in the mud or dry soil. As soon as the water returns and an organic source (food) is available, the spores will begin to grow and the life of the fungus begins again.

1039. How does a fungus spread from one fish to another?

Spores produced by fungi are the means of transportation from one location to another. A fish that is infected with a fungus can produce thousands of spores. These spores are easily transferred in the water to another fish. The fungus on a dead fish in a water garden pool will continue to produce many spores and spread to other fish. It is for this very reason that a dead fish should be removed from a water garden immediately.

1040. What does a fungus that lives in the water garden pool look like?

Many of us have seen a piece of fish food that has been setting on the bottom of the water garden pool. Within a day a fungus will begin to grow. The common group of fungus in the water garden pool is called the **water molds** and is classified as the *Saprolegniales.* The fungus will begin to grow a fine filament, known as **hyphae**, through the piece of fish food. The fish food will become a tangled mass of fungus **mycelium** (many hyphae). The fish food will now appear like a small ball of cotton as the fungi uses its hyphae to secret enzymes to digest and consume the fish food. After the fungi has digested the fish food, it will produce spores and remain in a dormant stage until another piece of fish food or other organic source is supplied to repeat the growing process of hyphae.

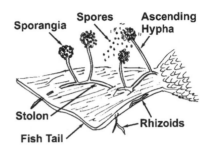

Figure 119. Enlarged to show detail is a fungi infecting a fish tail. The fungi will derive nutrients from the fish tail as it grows through the tissue. The spores produced in "sporangla" wlll spread ln the water to other parts of the fish or to another fish.

1041. How does fungi infect the fish?

Fish naturally have a protective mucus covering the skin of fish. Damage to this covering may introduce a fungal infection. Any rough handling of fish, such as during netting, can damage the mucus covering and give the fungus a chance for invasion. Fungus can also infect a fish after bacteria have begun to cause lesions in the skin of the fish. Since the fungus is the second infection, it is commonly referred to as a secondary infection.

1042. What does the fish look like that has a fungus infection?

The presence of a fluffy, cotton-like white to gray-brown on the skin, gills, fins or eyes of fishes can represent a fungal infection.

299

1043. What should be done if the fish has a fungal infection?

Since fungus is often a secondary infection to bacteria, the fish should be treated for both. Special natural **salt** treatments for fish are effective with fungus infections. Table salt should not be used since it may contain harmful chemicals and lack the important elements found in natural salts. Commercial sources for natural salt in treating fish should be used.

ALGAE DISEASES

1044. Can algae cause fish disease?

Yes. A well known aquarium disease of fish is caused by an algae is known as **velvet disease**. This causative unusual group of algae, known as **dinoflagellates**, have flagella (for motion) and are common in the ocean. They have been involved in the notorious "red tide" that kills by releasing toxins and killing millions of fish in the Gulf of Mexico. A fresh water species, *Oodinium* spp., can effect fish in the water garden pool but is most common with tropical fish. The dinoflagellates appear as tiny spots on the skin and gills of the fish, not under the skin as in disease Ich. It is sometimes referred to as **gold spot disease** since the spots of infection appear golden or yellow. Acriflavine (Typaflavin) can be used as a treatment or other commercial remedies are available.

PROTOZOAN DISEASES

1045. What are the white spots that look like salt on the skin of the fish?

This is caused by a microscopic protozoan and is one of the most common fish diseases found in aquariums and water garden pools. It is known as **White Spot Disease** or **Ich**. The name " **Ich**" is derived from the only represented species *Ichthyphthirius multifiliis*. Ich effects all types of fish throughout the world.

1046. Does Ich attack only a specific type of fish?

No, unfortunately Ich effects almost all freshwater fish. Thus the koi, goldfish, etc. are all targets of this protozoan.

1047. What is a "protozoan"?

During the early biological classifications the biologist placed all living things into the two phylums (large groups), plants or animals. The single celled organisms were difficult to classify and thus a new phylum was created called the **protozoa,** which means literally "first animals". There are estimated anywhere from 15,000 to 100,000 protozoans.

1048. Is Ich a relatively new disease of fish?

No. It was identified and named in 1876 by an individual named Fouquet. Ever since it has plagued man in trying to eradicate it. This has led to a great understanding of the life cycle of this protozoan and many remedies.

1049. Why is Ich so common in fish?

There are many ways a successful parasite such as Ich finds the path to a water garden. It can be introduced by adding infected or contaminated fish, plants, other animals (frogs, ducks, etc.) to the water garden pool. Once in the water garden pool, it can spread rapidly.

1050. Does stress in fish cause Ich to spread in the water garden pool?

Yes. One of the most common problems of fish disease in the water garden pool is from the result of "stress". Stress in fish may be caused by rough handling with a net which can also damage the skin of the fish, transportation in the plastic bag to the water garden pool or poor water quality, such as a condition of high ammonia and nitrate levels. These conditions create an environment for the Ich to invade the skin of the fish.

1051. How does the fish react to being infected with Ich?

The fish will typically be seen rubbing the Ich parasites on the skin along rocks or aquatic plants. They also will not want to feed.

Ich
Cycle

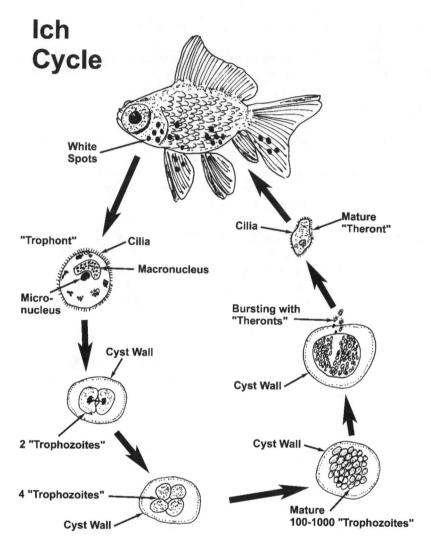

Figure 120. Ich is one of the most·common diseases of fish. The cycle of the protozoan that causes Ich has been studied and known in detail for many years.

1052. What is the life cycle of Ich?

Ich is caused by a **ciliated protozoan** (a single celled animal) that can swim in the water by a hair-like structures located all around the cell called **cilia** and is known as the **trophont**. In this stage it has a **macronucleus** and a

302

micronucleus which will function in cellular division. The trophont develops into a **cyst** which can attach to a substrate such as an aquatic plant or falls to the bottom of the water garden pool. Inside the cyst the cellular material begins to divide into two cells of **trophozoites** followed by four cells of trophozoites until there are 100 to 1000 trophozoites which will become mature ciliated **tomites**. The ciliated tomites release from the cyst and are known as **theronts** which can swim in the water. Within 48 hours the theronts must reinfest the same fish or infect another fish or die.

1053. Is the Ich parasite located on the surface of the skin of the fish?

No. The white spots will appear to be on the surface of the skin of the fish but the protozoan actually burrows under the skin of the fish (between the epidermis and the subcutaneous tissue). It is here that the parasite feeds on tissue fluid and cellular fragments. Attempts to remove these parasites or white spots by hand should not be done, since it may damage the fishes skin further.

1054. What remedies are used to treat Ich in the water garden pool?

A popular treatment for Ich is a solution of a chemical known as **malachite green** (triphenylmethane). This makes a blue-green solution that can be added directly to the water. Other chemicals have been used successfully are formalin, methylene blue, potassium permanganate and sodium chloride.

1055. Does the treatment for Ich kill the parasite on the fish?

No. Treatments will kill the ciliated Ich protozoan (theronts or mature trophont) that swims in the water only. The cysts and the parasites under the skin of the infected fish are not effected by the treatments. This is why the treatment must be continued to kill the newly emerged ciliated protozoan from the cysts. Usually the entire cycle of Ich takes place in warm weather in three or four days. Thus to kill the ciliated protozoans that cause Ich, the treatment must be over at least three to four days.

1056. Where does the Ich come from on the fish in the water garden pool?

Ich can be introduced from adding contaminated fish to the water garden pool or aquatic plants. Nature also can introduce Ich. Birds, ducks, frogs, salamanders or any animals that migrate from one pond to another can introduce the Ich parasite.

DISEASE PREVENTION

1057. Should newly purchased fish be added directly to the water garden pool?

No, not if the pond already has fish. A **quarantine period** should established before introducing new fish to a pool that already contains fish. Two things may occur. First, the water may already have the Ich parasite. The newly introduced fish may be stressed from transportation and is strongly subject to becoming infected with Ich. Second, the newly introduced fish may be carrying Ich. The Ich can spread to the existing healthy fish. Therefore a quarantine period of at least two weeks with a preventative treatment for the common disease Ich is a good recommendation. Suspected plants of Ich should also be quarantined.

1058. Is there any general tonic or routine remedy that should be used with fish in the water garden pool to prevent disease?

Yes. The addition of remedies that contain natural **salt** treatments is recommended periodically in the water garden pool. Fish pond salt is important in maintaining the natural balance of certain chemicals known as **electrolytes** (i.e. potassium, sodium, chloride, calcium and magnesium) in the body fluids of the fish. The fish have special cells in their gills known as **chloride cells** that function to maintain this delicate balance of electrolytes. The electrolytes are important for the uptake of oxygen and release of carbon dioxide and ammonia in the gills of the fish.

1059. Should salt treatments be used for stress in fish that results from transportation?

Yes. Normally the transportation of fish will result in stress where the gill function is disturbed sometimes referred to as **osmotic shock**. The electrolytes are lost through the gills and need to be replenished. For any stress, the use of a fish salt treatment is recommended.

1060. Can "table salt" be used for the "salt treatment" with fish?

No. Table salt contains the compound sodium chloride whereas the natural salt supplied for fish treatments has the necessary electrolytes for pond fish such as calcium chloride, magnesium chloride, sodium chloride, calcium sulfate, potassium chloride and magnesium sulfate. In addition, table salt has anticaking chemicals which may be harmful to the fish.

XXIII. Aquatic Insects in the Water Garden

* Introduction * Dragonfly * Damselfly * Water Strider * Mosquito *

INTRODUCTION

1061. Why should the water gardener be familiar with the aquatic insects and other small creatures that are in or around the pond?

In any form of gardening, insects and other small creatures that visit the flowers or live in close proximity are quickly learned as being a friend or foe. This same philosophy is adopted by the water gardener. The water gardener will come face to face with a new battery of these "creatures". Some of these creatures will be recalled from childhood memories when we had time to ponder or spend hours of endless summer days by a natural pond in the woods. Only correct identification and learning their lives can result in whether or not these "creatures" are in conflict with the water gardener. And, finally, our curiosity is aroused and we often wonder who or what this tiny little "creature" is doing in our water garden pool?

1062. How can you "tell" the difference between an "insect" and a spider or other similar creatures in or around the water garden?

Entomologists, biologists who specialize in insects, have developed a method to identify or classify the different types of insects which excludes spiders and other similar creatures. By using this method of classification, the water gardener can also recognize or identify a true "insect". Biologist classify the insects in a large group known as the **Arthropods** (phylum *Arthropoda*). This large group is further divided into "classes" that subdivide crabs, centipedes, spiders, scorpions and insects to mention a few. The insects, class **Insecta**, are characterized by having three body regions (head, thorax and abdomen), one pair of antennae, nearly always three pairs of legs and usually one or two pairs of wings. A quick way of recognizing the difference between a spider and an insect is observing the number of legs on each. The insect has the characteristic three pair of legs whereas the spider has four pairs of legs or eight legs.

1063. What is meant by an "aquatic insect"?

These would be the insects that use a body of water such as a lake, pond or water garden pool in their life cycle. Some of the well known aquatic insects are the mayflies, stoneflies, dragonflies, damselflies, water bugs, caddis flies, many types of moths and beetles to name but a few.

1064. What is meant by a "life cycle" of an aquatic insect?

A "life cycle" is a term used by biologist to indicate the "life" or living stages most life forms go through or "cycle" from birth to adult to perpetuate the species. Most insects undergo several distinct stages in their life cycle during their development from egg to adult which is known as **metamorphosis**. The stages of an insect are labeled by the entomologist in complete metamorphosis as **egg, larva, pupa** and **adult**. These stages are each distinctly different morphologically. It is during some of these stages that are found in gardens and are known as "pests".

1065. What is the most destructive stage of the insect recognized by the gardener?

The most recognized destructive stage of the insect is the larval stage. The larval stage begins when the **egg** hatches into a **larva**. The larva is the motile feeding stage where it is not abnormal for the insect larva to eat several times its weight a day in plant foliage. These are known to the gardener as caterpillars, grubs, nymphs, etc.

1066. Can the water gardener tell what the larva of an insect will look like as an adult?

Yes. The larva stage of insects have been identified by different common names which are familiar to most gardeners, such as caterpillar, moth, maggot, etc. These common names are usually indicative of the final metamorphosed adult stage. For example, if the larva is called a **caterpillar** it will become an adult moth or butterfly, a **grub** will become a beetle, bee or wasp, a **maggot** will become a fly, a **wiggler** will become a mosquito and a **nymph** will become a dragonfly or damselfly.

DRAGONFLY and DAMSELFLY

1067. Which spelling is correct , DRAGONFLY or DRAGON FLY?

This is a classical problem of using common names, since no scientific rules have been established. However, these common names have developed a particular pattern of spelling and is used by most biologists. When the "fly" of an insect's name is written separately, such as black fly, blow fly or horse fly the insect is in the biological classification of what is known as **true flies** or *Diptera* (whereas "*Di*" means two and "*tera*" means wings). True flies have only one pair of wings (with a pair of small hind "wings" reduced to small knobs used primarily for balance). When the fly is written together with the descriptive word such as "mayfly", "damselfly", "butterfly", the insect is in a classification other than true flies. Since the dragonfly has two pair of wings, it is not a true fly and is therefore correctly written "dragonfly".

1068. What does the adult dragonfly eat around the water garden pool?

The adult dragonfly eats mosquitoes and other insects such as aphids. The dragonfly can be seen capturing insects in flight over the water garden pool or has been observed capturing insects on its perch by the water garden pool.

1069. How does the adult dragonfly lay its eggs?

Watching the dragonfly lay eggs is a fascinating sight. The female dragonfly can be seen flying or "skimming" over the surface of the water garden pool and dipping her tail into the water depositing her eggs. It is from this observation that the pond dragonfly gets it name as "skimmers". Some of the common names of dragonfly skimmers are the **belted skimmer, green-eyed skimmer, ten-spot skimmer** and the **common skimmer.**

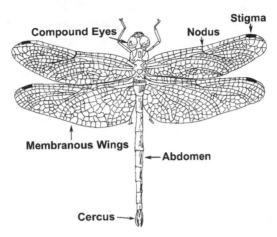

Figure 121. The dragonfly is shown with the nodus or joint characteristic of the wings of dragonflies and damselflies. All dragonflies are aquatic.

1070. Do the wings of the different types of dragonflies have characteristic markings?

Yes, the four membranous wings of the dragonfly have characteristic markings. These characteristic markings on the wings are used by the entomologist as the primary separation of different species. The hind wings are as large or larger than the fore wings. Each wing has, near the middle of the front margin, a joint-like structure called the **nodus**. Some wings have a characteristic marking or pigment at the tip of the wing called the **stigma**. Some wings have white, black and brown blotches on the clear membranous wings, whereas others are absent of such markings. One of the best known pond loving species is the **Ten-spot Skimmer**. It has three blackish-brown blotches on each wing. Between the blotches, on the male, is a spot of white. This dragonfly is commonly found "skimming" the water of many ponds.

1071. Can the adult dragonfly or damselfly sting or bite the water gardener?

No. In fact, within an aquatic commercial greenhouse they become so friendly to workers that they will perch upon a shoulder or welcomed finger only to be admired in a beauty that is unexplainable.

1072. What is the difference between an adult damselfly and a dragonfly?

The biologist classifies them in the same order, **Odonata** which indicates that they both have similar characteristics. The damselfly and dragonfly both have four many veined and membranous wings, large compound eyes, small and bristle-like antennae, and other similar characteristics, such as the nodus in the wing. The water gardener however, can easily recognize the difference by the size of each. The body of the dragonfly is larger than the damselfly. The damselfly has a smaller, slender body. The dragonfly all spread their wings horizontally when at rest. In this position it is easy to see each of their four wings. The damselfly, on the other hand, folds their wings together over the back and parallel to the body when at rest.

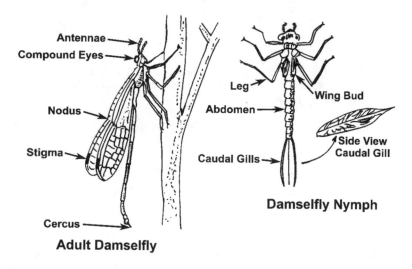

Figure 122. The adult damselfly closes their wings when at rest while the dragonfly keeps their wings open. The damselfly nymph has three caudal gills used for "breathing" while living under the water.

1073. How does the immature dragonfly larva or nymph "breathe" under the water?

The immature dragonfly or nymph breathes by gills under the water.

1074. What is the difference between the nymph or aquatic stage of the damselfly and dragonfly?

The damselfly has three leaf-like structures at the end of the abdomen which are gills. The dragonfly, on the other hand, does not have these three structures (figure 122).

1075. How big can the adult dragonfly grow?

The body of the dragonfly varies from 3/4 of an inch to about 3.5 inches long. The wings can measure 5 inches across, which is commonly found in the largest and most powerful of the dragonflies known as **Darners**, represented by one of the largest *Epiae'schna heros*. This dragonfly is dark brown with indistinct greenish markings on the body (thorax and abdomen). They were frequently called **Devil's Darning-Needles** because they were once believed to be able to sew up the eyes, ears or mouths of bad little boys and girls.

1076. Were the dragonflies found in geologic history?

Yes, and they were quite spectacular in size. The largest dragonfly known from fossils over 250 million years ago and had a wing spread of 27 inches.

1077. How long does the dragonfly or damselfly live as an adult flying insect once it leaves the water?

Since the adult flying stage is mainly for reproduction, the life spans are relatively short outside of the aquatic stage. The average life span of the adult damselfly is about three or four weeks. The life span of the dragonfly is about six to eight weeks.

1078. How fast can the dragonfly fly?

It is estimated that the dragonfly can fly 20 to 25 miles per hour. This is fast enough to capture most insects and escape flying birds.

1079. Can a dragonfly hover?

Yes. The dragonfly is an excellent flier. It can rise and change direction like a helicopter. This ability is excellent in capturing insects and escaping the flight of a bird.

1080. How does the frog capture the fast flying dragonfly?

The frog, like any good hunter, knows the habits of one of his favorite meals, the dragonfly. In the spring the dragonfly is busy laying eggs by dipping her tail into the water by skimming the surface of the water. The frog, with his skin as the excellent camouflage outfit, will set motionless and wait for the unknowing dragonfly to come close. The frog can either be on shore, on a water lily pad, hidden in a patch of irises or quietly floating in the water with only their big frog eyes showing and breathing through their nostrils. Once the dragonfly makes a flight pass or lays eggs within the frogs reach, the frog will go into action. A leap across the water surface or extension of the head to release the sticky tongue will often, but not always, result in the capture of the dragonfly. Many water gardeners may suspect "just another frog is jumping into the pond", however a close watchful eye will detect nature in progress.

AQUATIC BUGS

1081. Do the aquatic bugs "breathe" by gills in the water garden pool?

No. The aquatic bugs in the water garden pool all breathe or respirate by obtaining air at the surface of the water. Many have the ability to carry an air bubble under the wing or surface of the body to stay submerged a long time, but they have no gills.

1082. What is the name of a small black beetle that is seen constantly going up and down in the water?

There are many aquatic beetles found in the pool but a common one is the **diving beetle**, *Dytiscus* spp. which has a characteristic rapid oar-like stroke of its hind legs. The beetle is about one to one and a half inches long. It is a true beetle belonging into the order of classification **Coleoptera**. The true beetles typically have hard forewings that fit closely over the body like a shell. The name "Coleoptera" means "sheathed-winged".

1083. Can the aquatic diving beetle leave the water and fly?

Yes. At night it is known to leave the water and fly towards light.

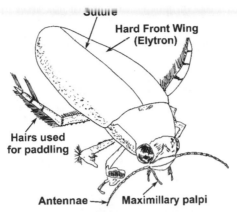

Figure 123. The diving beetle *Dytiscus* showing the bristles on the legs used in swimming.

1084. What does the diving beetle feed on?

The diving beetle is very predaceous. The larva and adult stage both feed on a variety of small animals, including small fish. The larvae are called **water tigers** due to the fact that they can attack a prey and suck out its body fluids.

1085. What is the name of the bug that appears to be swimming upside down in the water garden pool?

This is the **backswimmer** (represented by three genera *Notonecta, Buenoa* and *Plea*) and are also very predaceous like the diving beetle and so named because they swim upside down. It is not a beetle but is classified as a true bug, order **Hemiptera**. Differing from the true beetles is the fact that their wings are only half thickened and overlap at the edges. The backs of these insects are keeled and shaped like the bottom of a boat. They love to float on the surface of the water. When disturbed, the backswimmer dives under the water taking a bubble of air under their wings and uses this to breathe. The bubble not only carries oxygen but will continue to absorb oxygen from the water while submerged. This unusual adaptation allows the backswimmer to stay under water for several hours. They should not be touched since they have the ability to bite.

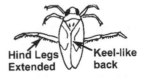

Figure 124. The backswimmer always swims on their backs and has a back shaped like the bottom of a boat.

313

WATER STRIDER

1086. What is the name of the "spider" that is skating over the surface of the water garden pool?

This is the well known **water strider** (*Gerris* spp.) which has long legs that glide or skate over the surface of the water. It is a true bug and not a spider. Many children have grown up to misunderstand the pronunciation as "water spider" only to be corrected later in life to find out it is not a spider but an insect with six legs known as a "water strider".

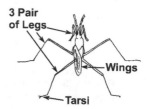

Figure 125. Water striders are often confused with spiders. Note the six legs characteristic of insects and not eight legs which is characteristic of spiders.

1087. What does the water striders eat?

The water striders feed on insects that fall or touch upon the surface of the water. An emerging mosquito from its pupa stage is a sure meal for a water strider. The front legs are short and used to capture food. The fact that the water strider is attracted to light is suggestive of how it is able to recognize a potential insect that come in contact with the surface of the water. When an insect touches the surface of the water, a ripple of water will reflect light and attracts the strider to a meal.

1088. How does the water strider stay on top of the water?

The water strider actually is on top of the water surface film. The legs of the insect do not get wet but are held above by water surface tension. If the legs (tarsi) of the water strider becomes wet, it will sink and must crawl to some vegetation to climb onto and dry. It is not recommended for children to catch a water strider in a jar of water since the water will splash around and sink the insect only to die. Be careful, if one is caught, since the water strider can puncture the skin with their sharp beak.

MOSQUITOES

1089. What is the life cycle of the mosquito?

Mosquitoes are insects that have four stages in their life cycle. The first stage is the **egg** which is laid by the female in the water. The second stage is the **larvae** (plural is written as "larvae" and single as "larva") which main function is eating and is the common "**wiggler**" seen in the water. The third stage is the **pupae** (or single is **pupa**) which usually does not feed in the insect world but in the case of mosquitoes does remain active in the water. They are also known as "**tumblers**" which have the ability to breathe at the surface of the water. And the fourth stage is the **adults** which flies and breeds.

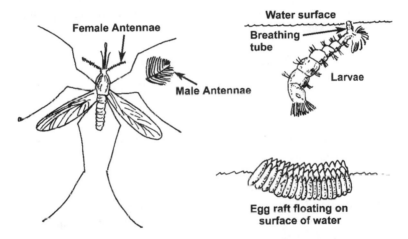

Figure 126. The female mosquito can be differed from the male mosquito by the appearance of the antennae. The larva of the mosquito "breathes" by coming to the surface of the water. The eggs of the mosquito float on the surface of the water.

1090. How long does it take for the mosquito to complete the life cycle from egg to adult?

The mosquito may pass from egg to adult in two weeks or less during hot weather, or they may remain in larva for months and molt three or four times before turning into a pupa. The eggs of mosquito can be laid early in the

315

morning and hatch into a larvae by two o'clock on the same afternoon. Usually it takes about a week for the mosquito larvae to turn into a pupae, and in this case the pupae, though it does not eat, remains active, furnishing excellent food for fishes in both larval and pupal states.

1091. What do the wrigglers or larvae of the mosquito eat in the water garden pool?

The mosquito larva will eat algae and other organic debris. Some species are known to eat other mosquito larvae.

1092. Do the mosquito larvae breathe by gills in the water garden pool?

No. The mosquito larvae must come to the surface of the water to take in oxygen. This is why the mosquito can easily breed in stagnant water without dissolved oxygen. It is this up and down movement of wriggling to come to the surface for oxygen that attract fish.

1093. Is it true that only the female mosquito bites?

Yes. Only the female mosquito is equipped with mouth parts to take a "blood meal" or bite.

1094. Can you tell the difference of the sex of the mosquito without being bite by a female mosquito?

Yes. The main difference between the male and female mosquitoes are in the form of their antennae (figure 126). Look closely at a mosquito, and if the antennae have a very plumose appearance it is a male. The females have only short hairs for antennae.

1095. If you do not have fish, how can you keep mosquitoes from breeding in the water garden pool?

Fish will biologically control the mosquito population of water garden pools. They love mosquito larvae as a natural food. If fish can not be added to the water garden pool, another biological source is available. A species variety of bacteria was discovered that has the ability to kill the larvae of mosquitoes. This bacteria is known as *Bacillus thuringiensis* variety *Israelensis* or **BTI**. A commercial preparation of BTI can be purchased. It is purchased in a dried form and added directly to the water garden pool and will kill the larval stages of the mosquito.

1096. Does the BTI harm other living creatures in the pond such as *Daphnia*?

The test studies for BTI sccm inclusive of many environmental animals but caution must always be used as with any products. In 1996 William Tricker, Inc.®, Independence, Ohio tested the commercially prepared BTI formulation with *Daphnia* and mosquito larvae. The results showed that the *Daphnia* was not harmed and the mosquito larvae were killed.

1097. Can the familiar cut worm or caterpillar killing bacteria be used instead of BTI to kill mosquito larva since it is the same genus and species?

No. The cut worm or caterpillar killing bacteria is a different variety and is not specific to mosquito larvae. The familiar caterpillar killing bacteria sold under trade names such as Dipel® is *Bacillus thuringiensis* variety *berliner-kurstaki*, called **BT**, whereas the BTI is *Bacillus thuringiensis* variety *Israelensis*.

1098. Should the electric insect light traps be used to control mosquitoes?

No. Research has shown that the electric insect traps are not effective in targeting or killing the mosquito (Culicidae). In a 1996 research publication by two entomologist (scientists who study insects), T. Frick and D. Tallamy, from the University of Delaware reported in *Entomological News* that of the 13,789 insects killed by the electric insect traps, only 31 were biting insects. Of the 31 biting insects, only 18 were female mosquitoes. Therefore, the electric insect light traps were indicated as killing **non-target insects** or insects that are not capable of biting us.

1099. What are the names of the non-target insects that the electric insect light traps were reported in killing?

Of the thousands of non-target insects that the insect light traps are killing in the previous mentioned report some are very familiar to the gardener. The **ladybug** or ladybird beetle (Coccinellidae) is one of these non-target insects killed. The ladybug is a most beneficial insect that feeds on aphids, scale insects and many other injurious species of insects. The non biting **lightningbugs** or fireflies (Lampyridae), which is a familiar sign of summer with the "tail light" blinking in the night, is also attracted to electric insect light traps and killed.

317

1100. Do the electric insect light traps kill insects that use the water garden pool in their life cycle?

Yes. In the previous study mentioned, there were many insects that use the water in their life cycle were killed by the electric insect light traps. These would include insects that live a larval stage in the water and emerge out of the water as a flying insect to breed. The non biting **crane fly** (Tipulidae) is one of these unfortunate insects. This insect looks like a large or giant mosquito, about an inch long, but is a fly. The larva of the crane fly lives in the water and feeds on decaying plants. Another group of aquatic dependent insects is the **mayflies** (Ephemeroptera) which lays her eggs in the water and the larva produced becomes a vital food for fish. Fishermen often model artificial flies after these insects. The mayfly, as it enters the adult flying stage from the water, not only does not bite but does not even have mouth parts to feed. A totally defenseless insect, whose main purpose is to reproduce, can be killed by the electric insect traps that may have been purchased to kill mosquitoes.

1101. Are there any natural predators of the adult flying mosquitoes?

Yes. The bat and birds (i.e. Purple Martins) are known for eating insects which include the flying adult mosquitoes. Since bats are active at night, they become a excellent adversary for the night active mosquitoes. In addition, dragonflies are also responsible for capturing mosquitoes.

Index

A

Acid Rain 256
Acorus
   Calamus 154
   gramineus 155
   gramineus Variegatus 155
Acriflavine 297, 300
Aerobic Bacteria 267
Aeromonas species 296, 297
Afterglow, Nymphaea 70, 89
Albert Greenberg, Nymphaea 89
Algae
   alleochemicals 213
   cause for overgrowth 208
   control
      chemicals 213, 214
      colored dyes 212
      copper sulfate 215
      Daphnia 214
      floating plants 213
      mussels or clams 214
      oxygenators 213
      snails 214
      surface, water plants 213
   controlling 211
   definition 206
   reproduction 207
   species 207
   spores 207
Algal Bloom 209
Alice Tricker, Nymphaea *87*
Alisma species 151
Allelochemicals 213
American Beauty, Nymphaea *88*
American Lotus 138
Ammonia
   fish symptoms 266
   pH, effects of 266
   regular ammonia 266
   temperature, effects of 266
   testing 266
   toxic ammonia 266
   toxicity 265
Amphibia 237
Amphibian 240
Ampullaria species 233
Anabaena 209

Anacharis
   Babington's Curse 192
   flowers 191
   species 192
   vs. Elodea 190
Anaebaenae azolla 184

Angiosperms 38
Antares, Nymphaea 97
Aphids 198
   chemical treatments 198
   hosing off 198
Aponogeton distachyus 165
Aquatic Bugs
   backswimmer 313
   diving beetle 312
   respiration 312
   water strider 314
Aquatic Ferns 183
Aquatic Insects
   definition 307
   destructive stages of 307
   identification of stages 308
   life cycle 307
Aristotle 52
Arranging Plants in Pool 222
Arrow Arum 164
Arrowhead 148
Arthropoda 288, 307
Asiatic Lotus 141
Attraction, Nymphaea 101, 107
August Koch, Nymphaea 82, 89, 91
Aurora, Nymphaea 100, 101, 109
Autoprotolysis 254
Azolla 183
   mosquito fern 184
   reddish-brown color 104
   species 184
   symbiotic relationship 184

B

B-Lymphocytes 274
Babington's Curse 192
Bacillus thuringiensis variety *Israelensis* 316
Bacillus thuringiensis variety *kurstaki* 202
Bacteria
   Bacillus mycoides 270
   characteristics
      feeding 294
      movement 294
      reproduction 294
      respiration 294
      winter preparation 295
   Clostridium 295
   Desulfovibrio 272
   Flavobacterium 270
   green sulfur bacteria 189, 271
   Nitrobacter 268, 269
   Nitrosomonas 267, 269

319

O

P

List of Figures

Tricker's
1101 Water Gardening Questions and Answers

331